£6

D0493043

The Field Marshal's Revenge

The Breakdown of a Special Relationship

And if there is a moral to be drawn . . . it is this. Brilliant military commanders do not come cheap. You have to pay the price. In this case in our soured relations with our principal ally. Nor do faithful allies come on the cheap. You have to pay the price. In this case, in the bigger dominating the smaller. And this, it may be said, was the political price which we are still paying off today.

Sir Carol Mather SAS,
one of Montgomery's former 'eyes and ears'

THE FIELD MARSHAL'S REVENGE

THE BREAKDOWN
OF A SPECIAL RELATIONSHIP

by

Charles Whiting

SPELLMOUNT
Staplehurst

British Library Cataloguing in Publication Data:
A catalogue record for this book is available
from the British Library

Copyright © Charles Whiting 2004

ISBN 1-86227-232-8

First published in the UK in 2004
by
Spellmount Limited
The Village Centre
Staplehurst
Kent TN12 0BJ

Tel: 01580 893730
Fax: 01580 893731
E-mail: enquiries@spellmount.com
Website: www.spellmount.com

1 3 5 7 9 8 6 4 2

The right of Charles Whiting to be identified
as the author of this work has been asserted by him
in accordance with the Copyright, Designs
and Patents Act 1988

All rights reserved. No part of this publication may be
reproduced, stored in a retrieval system or transmitted in
any form or by any means, electronic, mechanical,
photocopying, recording or otherwise,
without prior permission in writing from
Spellmount Limited, Publishers.

Typeset in Palatino by MATS, Southend-on-Sea, Essex
Printed in Great Britain by
TJ International Ltd, Padstow, Cornwall

Contents

Acknowledgements

I should like to thank in the USA: two 'good ole boys' who did the fighting, Tom Dickinson and Hy Schoor, veterans of the US 70th Infantry Division, and Mr Don Carmichael for his knowledge of Roosevelt; in the UK: my son Julian Whiting; my two fellow authors Carl Shiletto and Eric Taylor, survivors of North Africa, Sicily and Italy with the Infantry; the two veterans of the 13th Battalion of the Parachute Rgt, Major Jack Watson and Maj-General Sir Peter Downward KCVO, CB, DSO, DFC; Sir Carol Mather, SAS; in Belgium: Dr Paul Maquet and the Tourist Board of the Wallonie; and Mrs Gil Tidmus for her moral support.

Introduction

*A brave fighting man under fire, and with that tenacity in battle
which stamps a first class soldier; all these qualities have been shown
in a marked degree during the present battle . . . I salute the brave
fighting man of America; I never want to fight alongside better
soldiers . . . I have tried to feel I am almost an American soldier
myself so that I might take no unsuitable action
to offend them in any way,*
Field Marshal Montgomery, 7 January 1945
at the Zonhoven Press Conference towards
the end of the Battle of the Bulge

In 1921, three years after the end of WW1, the United States prepared to
fight Britain, her wartime ally. In Congress, where the British Empire was
described as a 'red pox spreading across the Pacific', there were calls for
America to 'seize maritime control of the world'. A US admiral warned:
'We are nearer to war today than ever before.' As war fever mounted in
Washington, a best-selling book declared: 'We were Britain's colony once.
She will be *our* colony before she is done'.

In due course that particular crisis between the two great English-
speaking democracies passed. But right through the 20s and 30s, the
intense dislike of things British continued among broad sections of the US
public. This dislike, even hatred, sprang from several sources. There were,
for instance, the Irish and German Americans with long memories. These
were used by public-office seekers who were only too eager to twist the
moth-eaten British lion's tail. Then there was a general distaste for
imperialism (though the USA had a tidy little empire of its own by now),
which most Americans associated with their one-time 18th century
colonial masters, the British.

Another factor was the legacy of WWl, into which many educated
Americans believed the USA had been tricked by smooth-talking English

diplomats, who wore monocles and fancy striped pants. But by the mid-1930s this American anglophobia was fueled ever more by Colonel Lindbergh and other 'American Firsters'. They were not going to allow America to become involved in another war in Europe in order, as they believed, to save the British Empire.

It was against this background that in 1940 Winston Churchill, the Prime Minister of a country which now stood alone against the might of Nazi Germany, attempted to develop the first 'special relationship' with the USA. Desperately he wooed the US President, Roosevelt, not only to convince him to send war supplies and food to the hard-pressed island, but also to join in the fight on Britain's side against Hitler.

By 1941 the still neutral Roosevelt had dreamed up 'Lease-Lend' aid to Britain. Many Americans didn't like the idea – they saw it, correctly, as leading to the US's involvement in a shooting war. But as one popular author of the time, Margaret Haley, explained it: 'It was like a stupid, but exquisitely beautiful wife. Whenever you have made up your mind to send her to a home for morons, she turns her heart-stopping profile and you are unstrung and victimized again.' Someone else used a less beautiful simile to describe Lease-Lend and the exchange of US destroyers for American bases in the Bahamas. He wrote it was 'like a dog gone back to its vomit!'

The attack on Pearl Harbor finally brought America into the war and suddenly Britain was no longer alone. It had been hard work, even including a little pimping by Churchill. The PM was overjoyed. But he little realised until it was too late that he had created a monster that one day would help to devour and destroy the British Empire, which he would fight for the next four years to save. For FDR, of whom it was said that he played with his cards held so close to his chest that the ink rubbed off on his shirt, had other plans for this new 'special relationship'. But Roosevelt being Roosevelt, an enigma even to his own family, didn't tell Churchill that.

He wanted an end to empires, in particular the British Empire, and throughout the war he worked directly and indirectly to achieve that aim. For FDR, a politician to his fingertips, whose main concern, it often seemed, was winning elections and not the war, represented the old American view of the British and the British Empire. As he said himself just after Pearl Harbor: 'This distrust, this dislike, even hatred of Britain – it's in the American tradition.' He seemed to be right, too. For in a survey carried out in June 1942, six months after the 'special relationship' commenced, it was found that 'sixty percent of Americans regard the British as "oppressors"'.

In the end, after the Japanese surrender, the new President, Harry Truman, the tough little ex-haberdasher from Missouri, needed the British partner no longer. He started to call in the Lease-Lend debts, although

Britain was in hock to the tune of 26 billion pounds, ten percent of its entire wartime output and twice what it could borrow from its colonies. It didn't worry the average American. As another politician from Missouri snorted: 'As long as they have the crown jewels and wear ermine, I am not going to vote one dollar and take food out of American mouths.' It was the beginning of the end of the British Empire.

However, Churchill held on to his dream of the 'special relationship' right to the end of the war. Some Britons who worked very closely with these 'cousins from over the sea', especially if they were military, didn't. Field Marshal Bernard Law Montgomery, vain and opinionated himself, had been critical of the Americans right from the start. He didn't think much of their generals, their strategies, and the way they led their men. Even when he began to realise that Britain had become the military junior partner in the coalition, Montgomery was not prepared to play the part. He simply wouldn't take orders from Eisenhower when he thought the 'Supreme Commander' wrong. Even when Churchill, fearful for the success of his 'special relationship', put on the pressure, Montgomery still persisted in being the lone critic of the Americans. He and Eisenhower might well be 'Monty' and 'Ike' in the media, but in reality they were enemies fighting for command.

In December 1944, when the Americans were caught off guard by the German attack in the Ardennes in what has become known as 'America's Gettysburg of the 20th Century', Montgomery's chance came. He took command of most of the Americans in the area of the battle and led them to success. It was a great victory and another British general, knowing Churchill's attitude and Britain's new position in the Anglo–American coalition, would have conceded the victory to the US command. Not Montgomery. It was almost as if he wished to rub the Americans' noses in the failure of their strategy during the eleven-month campaign in Europe.

He proceeded to do so in an unprecedented press interview at the end of the 'Battle of the Bulge'. Churchill stepped in speedily. Montgomery was forced to concede that perhaps he had made a slight mistake. But in his heart of hearts he knew he hadn't. He had taken his revenge for the humiliations that he and his country had suffered at the hands of the world's new superpower. But in the post-war years to come, America, her military and then her politicians, would pay Britain back for that final desperate act of the 'cocky little limey fart', as Patton called Montgomery. The Field Marshal's revenge would come to naught.

Soon after the war had ended, Dean Acheson, the anglophile US statesman who had been very sympathetic to Britain's position during WW2, stated that Britain had lost an empire, but still had not found a new role. That was as true half a century ago as it is today. At the beginning of the 21st century, Britain still hovers between Europe and a new 'special relationship' with the United States. What is to be her role?

Back in 1940, when Churchill made his conscious decision to bring neutral America into the war one way or another, he believed, as we have seen, that he had created 'a special relationship' with the USA. He hadn't. Roosevelt had a different agenda from Churchill's – and it didn't include preserving the British Empire. Indeed, latterday revisionist historians maintain that by continuing the war against Germany with America's aid, Churchill himself directly helped to bring about the end of 'all that red on the map' and reduce Britain to the status of an impoverished, third-rate power. Be that as it may, those young men who fought for 'King and Country' believed they were fighting to preserve a certain British heritage, even if it came in the form of their regiment and their comrades. Just like those 'good ol' boys' who crossed the Atlantic from the USA to fight in a war that was none of their asking, the British survivors are proud too of what they did then when they were young.

These days they are stiff, bent and creaky. Many support themselves on sticks. But when they visit the scenes of their violent youth, the silent white ranks of stone which are the graves of their long dead comrades, they seem for a moment to straighten up. Perhaps it is a trick of the light, a sentimental delusion, but age slips from their wrinkled faces and they are those young soldiers once more – Monty's men, who fought in a battle that no one remembers. But only for a moment. Then they clutch their sticks more firmly and hobble off, their polished medals clinking and reflecting in the sun, to their waiting buses to return home – and to death. Forgotten men . . .

1940

Secure from actual warfare, we have loved
To swell the war-whoop, passionate for war
Coleridge

CHAPTER I

We shall drag the US in

On Monday 10 June 1940 the President's special train was speeding through the foothills of Virginia. The President, known to everyone in the United States since he had been elected back in 1933 as 'FDR', was preoccupied. His aides and Secret Service guards noted that he kept altering the speech he was to make to the graduating class of the University of Virginia. It wasn't an important occasion and they wondered why he was making such a fuss. However, they supposed in this election year, all speeches were important.

For the opponents of his re-election for yet another term were massing against him. Back in 1933, Roosevelt had won on his 'New Deal' ticket: the promise he would end the Depression and get America back to work. Now, it appeared to a large section of the electorate that 'FDR' was hellbent on leading America to a new disaster – into the war which was raging in Europe.

His opponents, ranging from college students to senior US senators, firmly believed that if FDR was re-elected, America would be in the war on the side of the western Allies, France and Britain, before the end of the first year of his new term in office.

In Washington, students, many from Ivy League colleges, were calling for 'scholarships not battleships'. On other campuses, they chanted: 'No, we will not go! We'll wager, we'll wager this ain't our show. Remember we're not so keen as the boys in seventeen.' Some senators, and not only those who advocated 'America First' or believed in isolationism, refused to vote money for the President's proposed re-armament programme.

Even the British, whom the President seemingly wanted to aid, appeared to be against him. Writing to the British minister in Washington, Lord Lothian, Lord Chatfield sneered: 'They [the Americans under Roosevelt] will fight the battle for freedom and democracy to the last Briton.' The newly deposed British Premier Neville Chamberlain went even further. He declared that 'President Roosevelt is ready to play a dirty trick on the world and risk the destruction of the Western democracies in order to secure the re-election of democratic candidates in the United States'. Indeed at the top level in London, Winston Churchill, the recently

3

appointed successor to Chamberlain, appeared to be the only one who sincerely believed that FDR really wanted to bring America into the war on Britain's side.

But the pugnacious head of an almost defeated Britain really didn't know what was going on in FDR's head. In retrospect, it appears that no one who had dealings with him, even his own family, did. Once he told his friend and Secretary of the Treasury, Henry Morgenthau in a surprising moment of confidence: 'You know, Harry, I'm a juggler and I never let my right hand know what my left hand does.' Or as someone else has written about FDR, he was accustomed 'to play his cards so close to his chest that the ink rubbed off on his shirt'.

People who met him felt he was very affable and a great, generous talker – he certainly had the gift of the gab. He would listen carefully to what they had to say, nod his seeming approval, and then when they had left, he'd forget them and take a totally different course of action. FDR could not be relied upon. As President Truman, his successor and one-time Vice-President, said of him after his death: 'FDR was the coldest man I ever met.'

FDR never allowed anyone to get really close to him. Even his wife and sons never seemed to know what was going on his great handsome head. As some commentators have noted, there appeared to be only one recognisable constant about his actions. It was that he wasn't really too interested in achieving individual goals. Everything he did had to be calculated on the basis of how he, the President, stood with the US electorate. In that Roosevelt seems to have established an unfortunate principle which has been followed by US presidents ever since.

Anyone with a taste for psychological speculation might suggest that Roosevelt's ambiguity of character dated to 1921, when he contracted polio, which turned him into a cripple for the rest of his life. In order to survive, he had been forced to hide his pain, his true feelings from everybody. But already before that time, the son of an elderly father and a strong-willed younger mother, the 'little milksop', as FDR was thought to be, had had it drummed into him that he must avoid all displays of emotion. The Roosevelts of the end of the 19th century aped the British in their belief in the 'stiff upper lip'. As his daughter Anna once remarked: 'None of us know what father feels.'

After 1921 when, as his son James stated, FDR became 'the father with the dead legs', the future President certainly needed that 'stiff upper lip', if he wasn't to crack up completely. Now he had to hide his true feelings from even his cousin and wife, Eleanor. She had already turned away from him on account of an affair he had had just before he contracted polio. Now she frequented the company of notorious lesbians, whom FDR called half-jokingly 'she-males'. Still his wife's coldness and the company she chose hurt. But as always FDR had concentrated on concealing his

4

feelings and got on with the extremely painful, harsh, often disappointing business of healing himself.

In 1922 he celebrated his 40th birthday in a painful hipcast. Weighing heavily on his paralysed lower body, it had been applied to stop his atrophied legs from curling up. If that occurred he would have to have them amputated. By 1923 this cast had been removed and he was fitted with heavy braces that stretched from his withered buttocks to his feet where they were clamped into his shoes. He hated the new stiff-legged walk that he was now forced to adopt, if he wished to move independently of the customary wheelchair.

Head forward, planting his crutches at an angle and then swinging his body level with the crutches, he progressed in a strange crablike manner, over and over again, until the sweat stood out on his forehead like opaque pearls and he was gasping for breath. Even though the crutches and calipers were intended to make him independent, he needed the assistance of an attendant or chauffeur. For if he slipped on a polished floor, for instance, he was rendered helpless: a strong upper torso on useless legs, surrounded by a mass of tangled crutches and locked calipers.

By this time FDR had discovered the power of water. 'Water made me sick', he often declared (he had contracted polio while swimming), 'water will heal me'. It didn't. But his relentless swimming in hot springs gave him powerful arms so that he could manage his chair and when necessary his calipers; and allow him to crawl, trailing his useless legs across the floor behind him. The most powerful man in the world-to-be was crawling like a helpless child.

But in a more cruel age than ours, he was always conscious of his disability. After all at that time, segregation of people with disabilities was enforced by city ordinances, called 'ugly laws'. In cities such as Chicago, these laws prohibited 'any person who is diseased, maimed, mutilated, or in any way deformed so as to be unsightly or disgusting . . . to be on the public ways . . . from exposing himself to public view'.

So it was that FDR always hid his legs, even when dressed and sitting in a wheelchair, with a newspaper or some such object. No one was ever allowed officially to photograph him in his wheelchair either (there are only a handful of such photos available). When he travelled, which in years to come he had to do frequently, the ramps needed for his wheelchair were always kept hidden from the press and the general public. When photographs were allowed of him standing, he was always seen using a cane and what was called an 'assisting arm', usually that of his son, Elliot.

It was what one of FDR's biographers, Hugh Gallagher, has called 'a splendid deception'. And it was a deception which worked, or appeared to. Things seemed to get done. Important visitors went away, feeling that they had impressed the President with their ideas and proposals; for wasn't FDR as always full of beans, a master of witty banter, one big toothy smile all the time? But, in reality, FDR was trying mightily to make those visitors forget that he was a cripple, virtually totally dependent on his loyal servants. More importantly, his visitors never seemed to realise that FDR just wanted to be liked and that, in fact, he *hated* making decisions.

But on this June Monday, six decades or more ago, President Roosevelt was going to make a decision, a very important one indeed: one that might have been occasioned by the news he had received just before his special train had left Washington. It was special information from the State Department which had made him angry. One hour before he had departed the capital, he had heard that the bombastic, flashy Italian dictator, Benito Mussolini, Nazi Germany's partner, together with Japan, in the so-called 'Pact of Steel' had joined in the war on the German side.

In an attempt to capitalise on Hitler's victories in France against the virtually defeated Franco–British forces, Mussolini had ordered his troops to march into southern France. With Paris abandoned by the French government, the British Army departing through Dunkirk and the demoralised Grande Armée fleeing southwards in shambles, Mussolini had decided to act. At six o'clock European Time on 10 June 1940, he had stepped on to the balcony of the Palazzo Venezia in Rome. There in full uniform, chin thrust out in a gesture oddly reminiscent of the way that Roosevelt stuck out his own chin when making a speech, the Duce had announced that Italy was at war with France and Britain.

On hearing the news, the British Legation in Rome had flashed a pre-determined code-word to the Foreign Office in London. It was 'Duplicity'. That code-word might well have summed up what FDR now felt about the Italian dictator's decision. As his train rolled ever closer to Charlottesville, FDR, pale and angry (and against the advice of his closest associates) altered his speech to fit in with the new situation in Europe. He wouldn't attack Germany in that speech – Germany was too powerful. But although it might lose him the Italo–American vote, he *would* attack the tinpot Italian dictator (whom, incidentally, his mother admired greatly, maintaining that Mussolini had 'the devotion of all classes').

The special train reached Charlottesville at five that afternoon. It was raining and over at the University's Memorial Gymnasium, where FDR would now speak, they were hard at it, preparing ramps so that the President's automobile could drive straight up, while camera crews fussed and the Secret Servicemen hurriedly scouted all the nooks and cranies where an assassin might lurk in this hastily changed new venue.

Despite the rain, however, the Memorial Gymnasium was now packed, not only with the graduating class, which included FDR's own son Franklin D Roosevelt Jr, but also with 'honored' guests, in particular

FDR's ugly wife Eleanor. The streets were packed, too, as the motorcade drove by the local cinema, with a separate entrance at the back for 'coloreds' and stores advertising the latest female styles, 'a deluge of dots ... flimsy sheers ... as new as television ... as cool as a cucumber'. However, those frocks couldn't have been all they were cracked up to be. For on the following day the Charlottesville *Daily Progress* (established 1892) commented: 'The rain wormed a special hardship on the women. Their dresses began to shrink.'

The comment was typical of a sleepy, southern, provincial town. But as the municipal band finished playing 'Hail to the Chief' and Roosevelt commenced his speech, it would be, as the *Daily Progress* pointed out, 'just as serious as any he has ever made. There was nothing in it that drew a laugh'. For this was to be a fighting speech, one in which FDR seemingly made a firm statement, without any double-talk, about his own position, and as the representative of the American people, that of the United States.

FDR's speech that Monday afternoon, with the rain pouring down outside, was full of the usual rhetoric that senior politicos customarily use. He pledged 'America's material resources' to the Allies. That didn't mean much. The US Army ranged below the Army of Bulgaria in military strength and in the year before it had received exactly six new tanks. As for America's 'industrial might', it had virtually disappeared after the 1929 crash. The basic tool industry had gone. When the Army wanted howitzers, there was no specialised machinery available to produce them; they had to be turned out on machines normally used for manufacturing streetcar axles.

Still that speech, which according to the *Daily Progress* was greeted by 'tumultuous applause', did mark a significant step forward on FDR's part. After pitching his address to youth, with the President saying: 'Again the young men and women of America ask themselves with earnestness and deep concern this same question: What is to become of the country we know?', he partially answered it. Not directly. He dared not do so. *Yet*.

What he did was to orate. 'On this tenth day of June 1940, the hand that held the dagger has stuck it in the back of its neighbor.' The hand in question was naturally that of Italy's Il Duce. Earlier he had been warned by Sumner Welles, Assistant Secretary of State, not to use the phrase; it was too provocative. At the time he had agreed. But on the train he had changed his mind. As Roosevelt recalled later: 'The old red blood said – use it.'

Now he had, and by doing so he had breached America's hitherto neutral position on the war in Europe. This first attack on a leading member of the Axis powers seemed, for once, to be a clear indication of the way FDR was thinking. Now he went on to say: 'Let us not hesitate – all of us – to proclaim that victory for the forces of hate will endanger the institutions of democracy in the Western World.' America could no longer remain an isolated democratic country in a totalitarian world, as represented by the Axis powers. 'Such an island represents to me . . . a helpless nightmare of a people without freedom, a people lodged in prison.'

Again Roosevelt was making a clear statement signalling a change of direction for the USA. As he saw it, the days of isolationism and neutrality were over. If democracy was to be saved in Europe and, perhaps, in America, too, the US would have to do something practical to save it. Seemingly the great talker, Roosevelt was maintaining the days of talk were over; the time for action had come!

The graduation day speech at that dusty little Virginian town caused a sensation, as FDR obviously hoped it would. The *Louisville Courier-Journal* reported: 'Mr Roosevelt was in a realistic mood . . . His words were precise; his meaning unmistakable.' The *Cleveland Plain Dealer*, another independent-democrat paper, stated: 'Mussolini has brought home to the American people the danger that threatens all free people.' Even Republican papers such as the *Pittsburgh Post-Gazette* recorded: 'This [speech] may not be neutrality in a strict sense, but the fact is the overwhelming majority of this country supports the President's position fully.'

Naturally in the isolationist America of 1940, there were many who *did not* support Roosevelt's apparent new course. Influential people such as Foster Dulles, Henry Ford, and Colonel Lindbergh, all of whom had links with Nazi Germany (Hitler was reported to keep a picture of Henry Ford on his desk, for instance) declared that America must keep out of the 'European War'. Lindbergh spoke at a mass meeting on the subject in New York, and when Churchill's name was mentioned in his speech, there was loud booing.

Even those closer to the action of that 'European War', such as the US ambassador to London, Joe Kennedy, a man Roosevelt privately thought `an appeaser . . . a pain in the neck', wanted America to retain her neutrality. He told the US Secretary of State, Cordell Hull: 'It seems to me that if we have to fight to protect our lives, we could do better fighting in our own backyard.' Not that the father of a future US President was going to do any fighting. As soon as the Germans started bombing London in earnest, he was quick to get out of the capital and return to America.

Surprisingly enough, this ground-breaking speech did not go down well among certain sections of the British people, whom FDR was proposing to help (the BBC had sent a special team to Charlottesville to record it). Some Britons thought his speech was simply part and parcel of Roosevelt's usual electioneering tactics, and had been motivated by his desire to be the only three-term President in US history.

Others, even at this moment of British defeat and despair, remained obstinately anti-American. They distrusted the 'Yanks' and their promises. Back in the '20s before the crash of '29, the US had presented a great challenge to Britain as the 'workshop of the world' and these Britons hadn't liked it. The great Depression of the '30s, when America had turned isolationist, concerned only with its own economic problems, hadn't helped either. The 'Yanks' talked a lot, but did little. As Neville Chamberlain, the British Prime Minister up to 10 May 1940, expressed it: 'It is always best to count on nothing from the Americans but words.'

But there was one prominent member of this establishment who was only too eager to believe FDR. He was Chamberlain's successor, half-American Winston Churchill. Shaving one morning and discussing his plans with his son, Randolph, home on leave from his regiment, the 4th Hussars, the new PM said: 'I think I can see my way through.'

'Do you mean defeat or beat the bastards?' Randolph asked.

'Of course I mean we can beat them,' Churchill replied, as if defeat had never entered his head, even at this most critical phase of Britain's war.

'Well, I'm all for that, but I don't see how you can do it,' his son said.

Churchill wiped the lather from his face and snapped: 'We shall drag the US in.'

This then was the manner in which the two pragmatists conceived what would be known thereafter, right into our own time and lynchpin of British policy, as 'the special relationship'. Thus it was that on that same day that FDR made his celebrated speech on the other side of the Atlantic, Churchill ordered his ambassador in Washington, Lord Lothian, to warn Roosevelt. The previous day, Lothian had enquired what would happen to the British fleet if Germany won the war, which seemed very likely that June. Churchill signalled Lothian to tell FDR that 'if Great Britain broke under invasion, a pro-German government [in London] might obtain far easier terms from Germany by surrendering the Fleet.' If that happened, it would make 'Germany and Japan masters of the New World'. Lothian was instructed to talk to Roosevelt in 'this sense and thus discourage any complacent assumption on the United States' part that they will pick up the debris of the British Empire by their present policy'. In conclusion, Churchill warned: 'If we go down, Hitler has a very good chance of conquering the world.'

On Monday 10 June 1940 the 'Iron Division' reassembled in the southern English counties of Wiltshire, Dorset and Somerset. Like the rest of the defeated British Expeditionary Force in France, they had been evacuated through Dunkirk eight days before. They had suffered, too, the same fate as their comrades in other divisions. There had been severe casualties. In the case of the 'Iron Division's' 4th Royal Berkshires, only forty-seven men out of the 800-odd, who had gone to France in 1939, returned. Most of their heavy equipment, lorries, Bren gun carriers, 25-pounders and radios had been destroyed on the beaches of Dunkirk. Years later German quarter-masters would still be handing out corned beef taken from abandoned British stocks when their own 'Old Man' * had run out. Just as was the case with most of the BEF, the 'Iron Division' had returned to Dover armed only with their personal weapons, rifles, Bren light machine guns and the like.

But there had been one major difference. The men who bore the divisional red-and-black triangle patch on their shoulders came home in military formations under the command of their surviving officers. As the historian of the Royal Ulster Rifles, one of the division's infantry regiments, recorded: 'There was no spirit of defeat when the battalion disembarked at Dover. Every officer and rifleman was convinced that the battalion had fought the enemy to a standstill, when it was allowed to do so. No section had lost an inch of ground, nor withdrawn a second before the appointed time.' Another officer, this time, Lt Col. Wedderburn Maxwell, CO of the 7th Field Artillery Regiment, remembered with pride: 'It was a great experience to see officers and men turn into veterans of the highest calibre in under three weeks and to serve in a Division that never lost cohesion nor its high state of discipline.'

The general, who had commanded the 'Iron Division' during the running three-week battle from Louvain in Belgium to the coast at Dunkirk in France, had been one of the few divisional commanders – there were twelve of them – who had not cracked up under the strain or made fatally wrong decisions that terrible May. He was small – some 5 foot 3, skinny, long-nosed with piercing blue eyes, and tended to look at people with his head cocked to one side like an inquisitive sparrow. He didn't look at all like his fellow generals, who tended to be the beefy, red-faced, hearty types detested by the poets of World War One.

Indeed, he was a different type altogether from those celebrated generals of the 'First German War', as the little divisional commander used to call the conflict of 1914–18. He possessed no inherited wealth, as Haig had done. He did not belong to the fashionable cavalry regiments as Gough and Plummer had. In fact, he had started his career in the PBI – the Poor Bloody Infantry; and a very unfashionable part of it at that – the Royal Warwickshire Regiment.

But in a way the commander of the 'Iron Division' was a mixture of two different types of Englishman: a forerunner of the new Englishman of our own time, and a survivor of the past.

There was something 'folksy' and plebeian about him. Sloppy in dress, he'd be the first general to wear the new 'battledress' instead of the usual general's elegant service dress. He would acquire an odd taste in hats and

---

* Tinned meat, reputedly made from the bodies of old men from Berlin's workhouses.

in the end he would be reprimanded by the King-Emperor, George VI, for his scruffiness, his non-regulation civilian corduroy pants and a 'green gamp' (umbrella). More clearly than any of his fellow generals at the beginning of World War Two he realised that you could no longer tell soldiers what to do; the modern conscript civilian soldier needed to have things explained to him. Naturally the common soldiers died in battle as they always have done, but at least the commander of the 'Iron Division' made them believe they knew why they died.

Not that he wasted men. His soldiers knew that, too; he was careful of their lives. Under his command in France and later over battlefields that ranged from Africa to Europe, he tried to keep casualties low; there would be none of the great bloodlettings such as Ypres or the Somme under his leadership.

All the same there was a great deal of the Victorian Imperial past in his make-up. He could sanction brothels for his troops in France (and nearly got sacked for doing so), but at times he was the worst kind of Victorian prig. Non-smoking, non-drinking, the son of a bishop, he orated just like one, with a mode of expression evocative of Kipling, the playing fields of Eton and the noble sport of fox-hunting, with an unfortunate upper-class tendency to lisp a little and make his 'rs' sound like 'ws'.

The 'Iron Division's' commander stood out in a profession given to drink, whores, profanity and killing birds. To his fellow generals, he seemed an ascetic 'little saint', popular with his soldiers, but definitely suspect. Soon he would be even more suspect to those red-necked, hairy-chested 'get up and go' 'cousins from over the sea' with whom he would deal for the rest of the war. With that inborn English feeling of superiority, which the upper-class English schoolboy absorbs with the very air of his public school, the 'Iron Division's' commander would seem to more than one senior Yank soldier 'as if he's Christ walking across the water'.

With his 'Iron Division' embarking from Dunkirk to Dover, the skinny little Major-General Bernard Law Montgomery (for it was he who had fought his Third Division as a cohesive force back to those bloody sands of the French port) had on 31 May 1940 gone to meet his future mentor and current corps commander, General Alan Brooke. The latter was going to relinquish his command, which Montgomery would now take over. Watching at some distance, the newly appointed Brigadier Horrocks, like Montgomery and Brooke a veteran of World War One, saw how Brooke, normally a hard-headed Ulsterman, suddenly broke down. Brooke could obviously not stand the emotional strain of the great defeat any longer. He laid his head on the shoulder of the newly appointed corps commander Montgomery and began to sob while the smaller man patted his back gently like a mother might comfort a broken-hearted child.

'I remained a silent and interested spectator of this astonishing scene,' Horrocks recalled many years later. It showed that Montgomery,

11

normally so businesslike and unemotional, had a heart after all. Then Brooke departed and Horrocks was called across by Montgomery. Unemotionally and with pathos, the birdlike little general, who would dominate his life for the next five years, started to rap out his orders for the day. Bernard Law Montgomery was in business.

Montgomery of the 'Iron Division' had seen the disaster in France coming right from the start. As he wrote later: 'The war was lost in Whitehall years before it began.' He commenced his one-man crusade to reform the British Army. He would start with his own division. Reassembled in southern England, the Division was given a complete replacement of weapons and equipment. There was only sufficient for one division, which showed in what desperate straits the Army found itself that June – and Montgomery's division got the lot. It was a sign that Montgomery was a coming man – and he knew it.

Back in the 19th century, General William Tecumseh Sherman, one of the US's great Civil War commanders, maintained that: 'There is a soul to an army as well as to the individual man and no general can accomplish the full work of his army unless he commands the soul of his men, as well as their bodies and legs'. 'Monty', as everyone would soon be calling him, realised that. Whatever his failings, and they were many, Monty now gave himself a mission. Not only would he reform the British Army, but he would win over their hearts and minds. After the terrible defeat at Dunkirk, he was convinced that he could inspire an army of conscripts from a democratic country to fight – *and win.*

On that 10 June, when his rearmed division assembled once more and prepared for battle, it was joined by a new formation. It was to replace the decimated 4th Royal Berkshires. The new outfit was the 1st Battalion the South Lancashire Regiment, once known as the 40th Foot. Although (in the past) the South Lancs had won three Victoria Crosses and would, in four years' time, lead the 'Iron Division' assault on the D-Day beaches, it was regarded in the Army as a provincial, unfashionable regiment recruited in the industrial north, which seemed to have seen most of its service overseas.* It certainly lost out when compared to the Guards who then made up part of the 'Iron Division' or the cavalry regiment, the King's Royal Hussars, attached to the division.

Indeed it could be said not much was known about the South Lancs even in the ranks of the Regular Army. For it had been formed from eight independent infantry companies stationed in pre-revolutionary America. Known as the 40th and 47th Foot in the 18th century, it had helped to capture Quebec under General Wolfe and had gained the nickname

---

*Each pre-war regiment in the Regular Army had two battalions. For three years, one served at home, the other overseas. They then swapped stations.

'Wolfe's Own'. Thereafter in the US War of Independence, it had taken part in the Battle of Brooklyn, which led to the capture of New York. After that came the Battles of Princeton, Brandywine and the ill-fated Saratoga Battle.

In the 19th century the South Lancs' forerunners spent half the century overseas, fighting everywhere, and served in the outposts of the British Empire, ranging from Afghanistan to Australia. By the time the 19th century was over, the South Lancs were entitled to more battle honours than any other regiment in the British Army except the 1st Regiment of Foot. In addition to their new name, the South Lancashire Regiment, they had also acquired a regimental motto, taken from Shakespeare: 'They win or die who wear the Rose of Lancashire.' This would be shortened in due course to 'WIN OR DIE'.

Soon the South Lancs would 'win', but they'd 'die' too in their hundreds. On D-Day, those who had joined Monty's division on 10 June '40 would suffer hellish casualties, leading the Army Commander's old division into battle. Their CO would be killed immediately. He was followed by two company commanders. In the end as they rushed the beach, leaving behind a khaki carpet of their dead and wounded comrades, the lead company would be commanded by a second lieutenant- and he wouldn't last long either.

But that was four years off. Now the main problem for this obscure regiment (recruited in the industrial north) was the same as for the rest of the British Army: to retrain and re-arm and prepare for what was to come, a probable German invasion of England's south coast.

How long could they last, however, on an island lacking food and war supplies?

For the beleagured country depended on imports from overseas which she desperately needed to continue the battle. But already Admiral Doenitz's U-boats blockading the island were putting a stranglehold on these urgent supplies. Soon, too, Goering's Luftwaffe would commence the serious bombing of Britain's cities, in particular the capital, London.

Churchill might well proclaim on 4 June that Britain would never surrender and 'give us the tools and we shall finish the job'. But the tools were still not forthcoming, in particular from the United States. This, as the pressure on Churchill's Britain grew ever more intense, gave heart to those who wanted to keep America out of the 'European War'. As the arch isolationist Senator Burton K Wheeler would say later in 1940:

I think we are doing Britain a great disservice in urging her to go on fighting till she is exhausted . . . Peace has got to come sometime and I don't think that there is any sane, intelligent military or naval officer who thinks that England can land troops on German soil and drive the Germans back to Berlin before that time arrives. And even if our

13

warmongers [the Senator meant Roosevelt] succeed . . . I doubt that the joint efforts of Great Britain and the United States could succeed in the project.

CHAPTER II

If it moves, salute it!

That summer of 1940, when Britain finally stood alone and would continue to do so for another year until Russia entered the war against Hitler, Churchill kept up his defiant rhetoric. Eight days after Roosevelt's key speech at the University of Virginia, for instance, Churchill gave his celebrated speech that opened with the words:

> Hitler knows that he will have to break us in this island or lose the war. If we can stand up to him, all Europe may be free and the life of the world may move forward into broad, sunlit uplands.

Those who heard this speech and all the others Churchill made at this time never forgot them: the bulldog growl, the timbre of his voice, the rhythm of his phrases, even his unique pronunciation of the word 'Nazi' (which he said as 'Nazzy'). As Oxford philosopher Isaiah Berlin remarked: '[Churchill's imposition] of his will and imagination upon his countrymen' was transmitted 'with such intensity that in the end they approached his ideals and began to see themselves as he saw them.'

There is some truth in that statement and that 'Battle of Britain' summer has lingered in the British folk memory as a time when they felt themselves something akin to heroes.

But while Churchill encouraged his virtually defeated people with another celebrated speech, proclaiming, 'We shall never flag or fail', and ending with that magnificently defiant 'we shall NEVER surrender', he was at the same time making an appeal for help to the American people, and FDR in particular. In his 18 June speech, for example, he referred to the price that would have to be paid by the USA if Britain did not defeat Hitler: 'But if we fail, then the whole world, including the United States . . . will sink into the abyss of a new Dark Age.'

Churchill might pull out all the stops in his defiance of Hitler, reiterating his intention to continue the war, whatever the cost. But at the same time he believed his efforts would be doomed to failure if he did not being Roosevelt's America into the great conflict on Britain's side. Thus it was that the great man – and Churchill was truly great that summer in the eyes of most of his people – now placed himself in the role of a suitor, deliberately wooing Roosevelt into doing what Churchill believed (probably wrongly) he should do: take the USA into the war, despite the opposition of a great many Americans.

Throughout the late summer and into the fall of 1940, Churchill badgered Roosevelt to send aid in the form of war supplies and food. He sent a British supply mission to Washington. He told Roosevelt in October that he was confident that Britain could fight on successfully, 'if we are given the necessary supplies'. Two months later he laid out the seriousness of Britain's economic position, her assets being sold in both North and South America to pay for supplies and, grovelling a little, telling the President he didn't think it right, nor would the President, if 'after victory was won with our blood . . . we should stand stripped to the bone.'

But although Churchill told it differently after the war, Roosevelt was strangely unmoved by the PM's urgent appeals. He did not take to Churchill's sentimental rhetoric. Indeed, Roosevelt thought some of Churchill's florid emotional outpourings were due to the Englishman's fondness for drink – a stiff whisky and soda for breakfast, etc. He even requested information from those Americans who knew Churchill about the latter's drinking habits. Most of them concluded that the British leader was an alcoholic, but he could hold his booze well. For the time being, he would consider the supplies to Britain issue, but American manufacturers could still go on bleeding the British white for anything they sold to the hard-pressed island nation.

It was said after the war, in particular by the British, that Churchill linked his military plans to the preservation of the British Empire, while at least until late '44, FDR had no specific post-war aims linked to US military policy. But that seems not to have been true. FDR's usual tactic of playing the game with his cards held exceedingly close to his chest obscured the fact that he did have definite post-war plans, which would not be in the British interest.

FDR certainly wasn't prepared to help maintain the British Empire. He wanted to end all imperialism. There had to be an end naturally to the new Japanese Empire. And the President also wanted the dissolution of the British, French and Dutch empires. There would be an end to trade barriers, resulting in open economic frontiers, which could only benefit American exporters.* In a way FDR, unwittingly perhaps, was paving the way for the US economic imperialism of our own time.

*When the US Army did go overseas in force, the soldiers always seemed to have with them American businessmen masquerading as staff colonels. Perhaps they were looking for post-war business opportunities in these foreign lands. It is a fact though that the great Ford works in Cologne survived the massive 1942 bombing raid and were providing dividends until 1943, two years after the USA went to war with Germany.

For the present, while Churchill played suitor to the man whom he thought would help save the British and their empire, and prepared to make virtually any concession as long as he got the USA into the war on Britain's side, American industry made the British pay through the nose for all the supplies their factories and mills shipped across the dangerous Atlantic. The Americans even demanded a complete list of all British assets abroad, and then went even further by ordering that Britain should sell them at once in order to pay for the goods America was supplying. Churchill dutifully complied with part of that demand. It seemed that the 'special relationship' that Churchill hoped for between the two English-speaking nations was not getting off to a very good start.

Back in the south of England that obscure divisional commander, now promoted to command a corps, the soldier whom another obscure US brigadier general named Patton would one day call 'that little limey fart, Montgomery', was busily engaged preparing for a German landing in southern England. He did so with characteristic ruthlessness, totally unconcerned by the fact that he was making himself very unpopular in some quarters. He sacked senior officers left, right and centre. He weeded out others who were too old or not 'up to scratch'. He played high-handedly with civilians and their houses, if he felt they and their properties were in the way of making a good defensive position, if the 'Hun' came.

Brigadier Horrocks, now commanding the 'Iron Division's' 71 Infantry Brigade, was surprised, not only by Monty's ruthlessness but also by his energy. As Horrocks recalled:

> Monty used to pay very frequent visits [to the Brigade]. 'Who lives in that house?' he would ask, pointing to some building which masked the fire from one of our machine-gun positions. 'Have it out, Horrocks. Blow up the house. Defence must come first.'

As Horrocks later recalled, Montgomery had the effect of a 'series of atomic bombs exploding all over this rural corner of England'.

He told Horrocks: 'I want you to go through the Corps HQ staff and report to me anyone who you think is not up to his job because I suspect that most of them . . . have been leading somewhat soft lives.' A week later, Monty was writing to his superior: 'A number of heads are being chopped off – the bag to date is three brigadiers and six commanding officers. Wives are being evacuated by trainloads; it is just a matter of whether the railways will stand the traffic.' They did and when those trainloads of wives and 'axed' officers reached the capital, people started to talk about this ruthless little general, ruling the south of England like some latterday Cromwell.

17

His reputation must have reached Churchill, for on 2 July 1940 the Great Man invited Monty to dine with him at Brighton. At the start of the meal, Churchill, who was preparing to commence his usual mixed tipple of whisky, wine, port and brandy, asked what the Corps Commander wanted to drink, Monty asked for water. As the Corps Commander told the story gleefully in his *Memoirs*: 'This astonished him. I added that I neither drank nor smoked and was one hundred percent fit.'

But Churchill was, as usual, quick to respond.

'He replied in a flash that he both drank and smoked and was *two hundred* percent fit!'

Monty had made an impression. Churchill had, too, on the soldier. Perhaps Monty compared his own feeling of being isolated and out of step with the time in which he lived with Churchill's pre-war role as the oracle of war that no one would listen to. As Monty wrote:

In those days I was not impressed by politicians. But I was keen to see this politician who for many years before the war had been telling a series of governments what would happen. They had not listened and now it had happened.

Hadn't Monty attempted the same with any senior military man prepared to listen? But they hadn't.

A common interest had been created. From now onwards, it seemed that Monty had a special line of communication to the PM. At all events he was promoted to lieutenant-general that same month and made a Companion of the Bath. Monty was on his way upwards.

Still he was not satisfied with the level of training and readiness for war in his new command. In particular, he didn't think very much of his Corps' 50th Division, which had also managed to get out at Dunkirk. Monty wrote of the northern Tyne-Tees Division:

There are men who have never in their lives fired more than five rounds with the rifle; there are men who have never fired the Bren gun. The men have done no drill, no P.T., no training. The men did not seem to be on their toes. I did not see the light of battle in their eyes.

Perhaps as 1940 gave way to 1941, the main reason Monty didn't see the 'light of battle' in the eyes of so many of his men, and indeed in the British Army as a whole, was the attitude of the Regular Army officers who trained these civilian soldiers. These 'Colonel Blimps', as they were beginning to be called, inspired by David Low's cartoons of portly colonels with the 'tea-strainer' moustaches of the Boer War, still believed in training recruits as if they were the illiterate farmhands and industrial workers of the turn of the century.

For them 'bull' for 'bullshit' reigned supreme. The recruits lived in spartan huts, where the beds were squared off, coal bunkers were white-washed a brilliant white, and where for the Saturday morning 'CO's inspection', the troops were supposed to dust off the leaves of any vegetation that could be seen through the hut's windows.

Here the regulation three blankets per recruit were squared off within the fourth blanket, each with the recruit's name, regimental number, etc. sewn into it and then the pile was lined up the whole length of the room. Around these blankets were arranged the man's kit-boots (instep polished black, regulation 13 steel studs burnished), helmet, mess-tins (also highly polished) and webbing, brilliantly blancoed. Woe betide the hut's inhabitants if the 'laid-out' kit did not meet with the squad sergeant's approval. Then he would go on one of those artificial rages that were fearful to behold. He'd go down the line, with his swagger cane, slashing to left and right, knocking the kit to the floor so that when he had disappeared the recruits had to go through the long-winded procedure all over again. 'If it moves,' the harassed young soldiers quipped, 'salute it. If it don't, *paint it!*

The hard-pressed recruits learned how to scrub a barracks room floor with a toothbrush, give their dull ammunition boots the look of patent leather through hours of patient spitting, polishing and buffing with a toothbrush handle (it was not uncommon, after this treatment, for the whole toecap of a boot to fall off when the boot was stamped down hard on the parade ground); burnish the metal buttons of their collarless shirts, even though these were hidden behind their battledress blouses. NCOs and officers were sometimes inclined to make the soldiers open their blouses and examine these buttons. After all, in the conscript British Army of the early 1940s, a soldier could get fourteen days' jankers* for having his boot-laces the wrong way round, revealing the raw leather below.

Of course this being the British Army drill reigned supreme. As Brigadier John Smyth VC wrote at the time: 'It has been found from experience that units which are good at drill and are well turned out rarely fail in battle.' In 1940, with invasion imminent, young soldiers were practising drill movements, some of which dated back to the 18th century. They learned how to slow march, march as if at a military funeral, execute the 'general salute' and half a dozen other antiquated drills that they would never need, especially in battle. While the German Army, the conquerors of Europe, were quietly dispensing with their own '*Gedaver-gehorsamkeit*' (the obedience of the corpse), the British were still learning how to salute on a bicycle while holding a package under one arm.

Even when they were allowed out from camp, after facing yet another inspection by the NCO in charge of the guard in front of a full-length

---

*Punishment for defaulters – in this case being confined to barracks with extra duties before daylight and after dark.

mirror which bore the legend 'ARE YOU A CREDIT TO YOUR UNIT?', they still could not completely escape the 'bull'. There were hard-eyed 'redcaps' (military policemen) patrolling everywhere in pairs, officers and NCOs too, who even when off duty would put soldiers on a 'fizzer', if they didn't think they were up to scratch. So the young conscripts swung their arms and walked in step as if they were still on parade; they didn't lounge or lean anywhere; and above all, they saluted anything and everything that looked like an officer. Cinema commissionaires were routinely saluted and more than one rookie swore blind he had saluted a uniformed dummy in the shop window of a multiple tailor!

The only place where they seemed able to find respite from 'bull' and its constant demands to conform was the pub. Their pay was low, but with the ten shillings a week that most recruits received (paid out by an officer who had to be saluted twice for his generosity, and carried away in the soldier's cap) they could afford a pint of beer at sixpence to wash away the week's hardships and indignities. It might be weak wartime beer – 'gnats' piss' – but it sufficed to get them red-faced and pugnacious, their caps at the backs of their cropped heads, bellowing out a defiant chorus of

> Fuck 'em all, the long and the short and the tall.
> Fuck all the sergeants and the WO1s
> Fuck all the corporals and their bleeding sons . . .
> For we're saying good bye to them all.

But not yet would they be saying good-bye to them all . . . not yet.

While Churchill, outwardly confident save when he was plagued by depression (his 'black dog'), steeled himself to meet the German attack without America's help. On the other side of the Atlantic, Roosevelt felt his way gradually. He knew that not only did he have to convince John Doe, the American man in the street, that it made economic sense to support the British, but he also had to convince him that America had the power to do something militarily if the worst came to the worst and the United States really had to fight.

On 17 August 1940 FDR inspected 94,000 men of the US 1st Army, which in four years' time would be the first American outfit to cross into the Third Reich at six o'clock on the evening of 11 September 1944. Eight times FDR was honoured by a 21-gun salute. Eight times he sat to attention, hat across his broad swimmer's chest, as military bands played the national anthem and the Stars and Stripes banner fluttered in the breeze and regimental and divisional flags were dipped in salute. It was all very impressive – at a distance. The reality, seen in close-up, was far less impressive. For the pomp and the glory were sabotaged by the true state of the US 1st Army.

It was hopelessly under-armed, with only five anti-aircraft guns. Its ground artillery was antiquated and dated back to World War One, as were many of the over-age officers, who commanded the First's formations. There seemed, too, to be few new tanks in evidence. Indeed in the previous year only six medium tanks had been built for the *whole* of the US Armed Forces. As a sardonic ditty of the time observed: 'Tanks are tanks and tanks are dear. There will be no tanks again this year.' But there were still plenty of horses about. There were, however, one hundred aircraft of all types involved, which seemed a lot then, though by the time the 1st Army finally went into action, a single corps would have that many to spot for its artillery.

Roosevelt quizzed General Powell of the 44th Division about his divisional equipment. The latter told him that it was 'pretty good, what there is of it. But we are using broomsticks for machine guns and rainpipes for mortars'.

FDR forced a laugh. He said everyone seemed to be in the same boat. That 'everyone' was naturally the British, who right up until 1944 would supply more fighting men in the line than the army of the USA, which had a population four times that of Britain.

It was clear to the President that the USA was in no position to fight this year, even if the country did enter the war. The US Army needed radically re-arming, replenishing with new recruits and the savage reducing in the number of over-age and unfit officers. The onus of keeping up the fight against fascism would lie with the British until America was ready.

That fall 16 million America men were forced to register for the draft. Those who were found suitable to serve would expand the Regular Army and the National Guard. However, by law, these draftees and newly federalised Guards units would be restricted to twelve months' service within the western hemisphere or US territories.

But the draftees were not an impressive bunch. Forty out of every hundred were restricted for one reason or another. For example, two million were eliminated for psychiatric reasons. As the cynical young soldiers quipped, the reason for this high rate was that 'the army doesn't want maladjusted soldiers, at least not below the rank of major'.

In the end, after an October '40 Gallup poll found the prevailing view of American youth to be 'a flabby, pacifistic, yellow, cynical and leftist lot', the army started to lower its standards and, as a new recruit told a reporter: 'The Army no longer examines eyes – *it just counts 'em!'*

But although the US Army seemed to be in a worse state than the British Army recently chased out of France, some American officers welcomed the changes, the new money being pumped into the Army, even the raw draftees, who more than once booed Roosevelt and his Chief-of-the-Army, General Marshall, when they appeared in the newsreel cinemas.

One such was a 52-year-old lieutenant-colonel of humble origins, who would consider himself lucky that year if he was offered a regiment in the 2nd US Armored Division soon to be commanded by his older friend, General Patton. In five years' time he would come back to the States, having been honoured by millions in London, Paris and New York, laden with honours, more than had ever been bestowed on any American, military or civilian, to tell the citizens of his mid-West hometown: 'The proudest thing I can say today is that I am from Abilene.'

He was of course Dwight D Eisenhower, to become universally known as 'Ike'. But in the summer of 1940, 'Ike' was an unknown officer, commanding a battalion of the 15th Infantry Regiment at Fort Ord, California. It was a new, rough-and-ready camp composed of primitive wooden buildings overlooking Monteray Bay and the soldiers it housed were, in part, just as rough-and-ready. For the 1st Battalion was under strength and had been forced to take in raw, untrained volunteers to fill the gaps among the regulars.

Not that Ike minded. He had been in staff jobs for far too long. Now he wanted to be standing behind a gun and not sitting at a desk behind a pen. As he wrote to a Lieutenant-Colonel Bradley, who would play an important role in his future just as Patton would: 'I am having the time of my life. Like everyone else in the army, we're up to our necks in work and problems. But this work is fun!'

But Ike didn't show that he was enjoying his first taste of ordinary duty in years to his soldiers. Instead he was here, there and everywhere, trying to instil into his soldiers, enlisted man and officer, a sense of urgency. This wasn't a summer camp for boy scouts, but a place where soldiers were being prepared to fight in the 'PBI' – the Poor Bloody Infantry'. Just as Monty was finding some five thousand miles away, this enlarging American army was still concerned with inter-battalion sports, traditional routines, drills. Ike wrote that it was difficult to 'eliminate an apathy that had its roots in comfort, blandness and wishful thinking'.

Still he tried to encourage a sense of urgency in his officers and men. Some of his men thought Ike and his attitude were crazy. This was a country that was fundamentally isolationist. Hadn't the President himself promised that he would never take the USA into a foreign war? But Ike made his attitude crystal clear. He assembled his officers and told them straight out:

If any of you think we are not going to war, I don't want you in my battalion. We're going to war. This country is going to war and I want people who are prepared to fight that war.

That speech might have gained the respect of his soldiers, but it did give the new battalion commander, the refugee from years of desk and staff jobs, a nickname. It was 'Alarmist Ike'.

In October 1940 FDR achieved a first in American political history. He beat the Republican presidential candidate, Wendell Wilkie, by a handful of votes and thus became the first US president to be elected for a third term. 'SAFE ON THIRD' Democrat banners proclaimed the victory using baseball terminology. But although Wilkie was defeated (he had lost his voice during the campaign after making 560 speeches), he was still dangerous. Wilkie set out to make the case that Roosevelt wanted to don the mantle of dictatorship and take the USA into the war raging in Europe.

Roosevelt, who had fought a fairly easy campaign, grew worried. On 30 October Wilkie charged in a hoarse speech: 'You may expect a war by April 1941 if he [Roosevelt] is re-elected.' Roosevelt, on the other hand, told another audience in Boston: 'And while I am talking to you mother and fathers, I give you one more assurance. I shall say it again and again and again. Your boys are *not* going to be sent into any foreign wars'. His speechwriter, Robert E Sherwood, the playwright, said later: 'I burn whenever I think of those words.' For he thought he was sure that, in due course. FDR would do the direct opposite; he *would* send those 'boys' to the war on some continent far from their homeland.

Naturally FDR's speechwriter would be correct. A little later he made the same point in Buffalo, stating: 'Your President says this country is not going to war.' Previously, he had always qualified such statements with 'except in case of war'. Now he didn't. Later it was said that this promise to keep the USA out of the war came to haunt him. But how would anyone know; hadn't he always held his cards close to his chest? Perhaps then Churchill, like some of the more astute Americans who knew Roosevelt better, should have questioned the motives and the morality of the American he was currently wooing so ardently. But he didn't. In due course Britain and its Empire would pay the price for the Great Man's lack of curiosity.

For a while after the defeat of Wendell Wilkie, things quietened down at the White House. His closest adviser, Harry Hopkins, felt that the President was thinking. 'I did not know for quite a while what he was thinking about, if anything, 'Hopkins confessed later. 'So I didn't ask him any questions.' Shortly thereafter, on Tuesday 3 December 1940, the President dropped out of sight. That day he sailed for ports unknown on the cruiser *Tuscaloosa*, cheered on departure by thousands of well-wishers and watched by scores of puzzled reporters, wondering what FDR was up to. On the presidential train taking FDR to Miami, the port of embarka-tion, he had chatted mostly about fishing and fishing tackle. He wouldn't even tell the reporters how long he was going to stay away. Some thought it might be fourteen days, a long time for a fishing trip.

At first the President did what he said he would do: he went fishing. He trawled for marlin, using pork rind on a feathered hook, as that year's best-selling author Hemingway had advised him by radio. He stopped off at the Bahamas and gave lunch to the Duke and Duchess of Windsor, whom Churchill had quickly transported there when it appeared that they had been making positive approaches to Hitler. In the evening he watched boxing matches on the lower deck, played poker and watched movies such as *Tin Pan Alley* with Betty Grable and *Arizona* with the handsome, up-and-coming young actor, William Holden. But during all this time, the President seemed to be waiting for somebody or something.

It came on Monday 9 December. Out of the sparkling sunlight two US Navy seaplanes dropped out of the sky and came gliding to a rest next to the elegant, white-painted cruiser. Harry Hopkins, who was watching, felt a heightened sense of interest; something was going on.

It was. In the mail pouch there was a long report from Winston Churchill who, back in November had promised FDR 'a very long letter on the outlook for 1941'. Britain had survived the debacle of 1940. Now Churchill would undoubtedly reveal how the country, all alone and under virtual siege by the German U-boat blockade, might cope with the coming year.

The prognosis wasn't good. The 4,000-word report told FDR that the beleagured island had already lost one million tons of shipping and that Britain would need an additional three million tons for 1941, if she was to survive. In one of the final paragraphs of this gloomy report, Churchill also pointed out that 'the more rapid and abundant the flow of munitions and ships which you are able to send us, the sooner will our dollar credits be exhausted'. This was 'the red light' that Roosevelt had asked be sent to him, once Britain reached the danger point. Now the time for talk and double-talk was over. FDR knew he would have to do something positive if he wanted to keep Britain in the war.

Indeed the position was worse than Churchill reported or knew. Imported fruits (bananas, grapes, oranges) were a thing of the past. Meat was down to a couple of ounces per person a week. In the nation's storage depots, there was enough butter for eight weeks; and for most of the British who ate 'marge', there were only three weeks' of that particular fat left. Eggs were rationed on the basis of 'one egg per person, per week, *perhaps*'. Even that standard dish of the country's working class, one which some experts argued had brought them through the 30s Depression, fish and chips, was endangered. Fishing smacks were refusing to venture to sea and face the danger of U-boats, mines and low-flying German aircraft. Thus, in the great industrial cities of the north, the humble patrons of the 'fishshops' were eating potatoes as chips and more potatoes fried in fish fat known as 'scallops'. Stodge on stodge.

Roosevelt finally acted. Harry Hopkins reported:

One evening he suddenly came out with it. The whole programme. He didn't seem to have any clear idea how it could be done legally. But there wasn't a doubt in his mind that he'd find a way to do it.

24

Lease-Lend – officially House Bill 1776 – what symbolism! The date of the American Revolution against Britain had come to represent her attempt to keep the one-time 'mother country' afloat – was Roosevelt's programme to supply the beleagured islands with goods and supplies for free. These items wouldn't be paid for in greenbacks, but in kind once the war was over. Roosevelt guessed he'd please two sections of the American people with this new, radical approach – the group which resented the fact that Britain had reneged, in part, on its war debts after World War One; and the other, heavy industry, which would now be reassured that the Federal Government would pick up the tab for the goods they supplied to Britain, come what may.

Roosevelt had guessed right. The new idea went down well with the American press and subsequently with most of the population. The British weren't going to get anything for free and, in addition, this new shot in the arm for industry would guarantee thousands more jobs for Americans. Cynics might have added that Roosevelt had not only helped Churchill, but he had also ensured that almost decade-long fight against the Depression ended that December day.

On the evening of Sunday 29 December 1940, as President Roosevelt prepared to give his last 'fireside chat' of the year to the nation, at a quarter past six, Greenwich Mean Time, the German fire-raisers started to drop their incendiaries on the almost deserted square of the old walled City of London. Most of the owners of the properties there lived elsewhere and had taken the keys of their premises home with them on Saturday night. Now as fires started to erupt everywhere, the harassed Civil Defence workers and the police were being forced to break into property after property in an attempt to extinguish the fires.

Two hours later, a westerly started to blow in. It fanned the flames higher and higher. The recipe for disaster was almost complete. Now the water drawn from the River Thames was getting lower and lower. The frantic firemen were forced to wade through the muddy shallows in order to draw water into their hoses – and the hoses were simply not long enough.

Some time later, with the city well alight, the Heinkel and Junkers bombers came flying in. As the flak thundered and the hopeless night fighters which lacked radar circled on the edge of the destruction, they dropped their loads into the centres of the blaze. The high explosives fanned the flames in what later became known as a 'fire storm'. The air was heated to temperatures of 1,000 degrees F. Men, women and children caught in this terrific heat were turned instantly into blackened pygmies, human cinders, through which the cracked flesh bubbled and burst in dull red patches of human gore.

Three hours after the 'fire-raisers' had come zooming in with their loads of incendiaries, almost 1,500 fires were raging. Despite all the 3,000 pumps being used by local and outside firemen, the fires were virtually out of control. Even St Paul's Cathedral, ringed by a circle of cherry-red flames, seemed about to be engulfed. It was a terrible sight and one of those watching helplessly was the Deputy Chief of the Air Staff, a hatchet-faced, bespectacled ex-pilot, Air Vice-Marshal Arthur Harris. That night he told his Chief Air Marshal, Portal: 'Well, they are sowing the wind.' In two years' time the man who became known as 'Bomber' Harris would ensure the Germans who had done this would 'reap the whirlwind'. But that was in the future. A lot of weapons and supplies would have to flow over the Atlantic before 'Bomber' Harris could coldly tell a young policeman, who stopped him for speeding and warned the hatchet-faced Air Marshal that if he went on like this he'd kill somebody: 'Young man, I kill hundreds of people every night.' Which he did.

On that Sunday night when Roosevelt was to speak to the nation, another two hundred-odd Londoners were added to the total of 30,000 British civilians killed in 1940, more than the British Army's casualties since the start of the war. Now Roosevelt would address a nation, still at peace for another year whose total civilian casualties would amount to exactly five, including one child, killed by Japanese-launched balloon fire-bombs.

For this last 'fireside chat' of 1940, Roosevelt had made his speech-writers, Sam Rosenman and Robert Sherwood work hard. For once it appeared FDR would not use his customary 'weasel words', as one critic had alleged. Indeed, the only phrase that had revealed his intentions – *perhaps* – and had given Churchill such hope was his 'stab in the back' reference to Mussolini back in Charlottesville. Now he planned to 'lay it on the line'.

For the first time FDR was going to mention the Nazis by name. He was also going to attack the isolationist stance: 'We cannot escape danger,' he would say, 'by crawling into bed and pulling the cover above our heads.'

It was going to be a fighting speech, that was certain. Still Hopkins, his closest adviser, wondered if it would go far enough. That same afternoon of 29 December, he suggested: 'Do you feel, Mr President, that you could include in this speech some kind of optimistic statement that will hearten the people who are doing the fighting?'

FDR pondered the request for a little while. Finally he puffed out his cheeks and started to dictate: 'I believe that the Axis powers are not going to win this war. I have this belief on the latest and best information.' Naturally Roosevelt knew nothing of the sort, but with typical politician's bravado, he was prepared to do anything to please his radio audience. Both his speech writers were intrigued by the President's statement. What was this 'latest and best information'? Roosevelt told them afterwards that he believed that his Lease-Lend Bill would pass through Congress, and when the arms and other war material started to flow to Britain, that would make an Axis victory impossible.

But would Lease-Lend make a British victory *possible*? FDR didn't tackle that thorny question. But one thing must have been clear to Rosenman and Sherwood after FDR had explained his choice of words. It was this. Roosevelt had no intention in 1941 of bringing America into the European war on Britain's side.

In the course of that 'fireside chat' on 29 December 1940, FDR used a phrase (probably borrowed from Frenchman Jean Monnet, the political father of the European Common Market, currently in the States at that time), which would go down in the history of World War Two. It was a statement that charted the course the President thought the USA should follow in the days ahead. It was: 'We must be the great arsenal of democracy. For us this is an emergency as serious as war itself . . .'

It was indeed a powerful phrase which found approval with many ordinary American citizens. But it was clear to some that, as Henry Stimson, the President's Secretary of State for War, phrased it: 'This was not a fireside chat on war, but one on how to keep America out of the war.' Stimson confided to his diary that the USA 'cannot permanently be in the position of toolmakers for other nations which fight'.

Churchill must have realised that too. For although he welcomed the speech and the subsequent Lease-Lend Act which followed it as 'the most unsordid act in the history of any nation', it did mean that Britain would continue to have 'to go it alone' (as the phrase of the time had it). The United States would not enter the war in 1941. So far, the Great Man, who was trying so desperately to woo Roosevelt into the European war, was not making much of a job of it. The 'Special Relationship', if such an undertaking did exist, seemed, as 1940 ended, to be very much a one-sided affair.

1941

When we get old and wear dark, baggy suits and slightly greasy bowler hats . . . we'll order more beer and begin painting this bitchy trull of a war until it looks like a latterday saint.
Cassandra (W Connor), 1943

CHAPTER III
'Lord Root of the Matter'

On 9 January 1941 Harry Hopkins, the President's most senior adviser and until now the most important American visitor to the war zone, arrived in England. He had come to ease any friction between FDR and Churchill, to report back to the White House what kind of man the PM really was, and generally find out the true state of Britain in this third year of the war. In his own words, he saw his mission as being a 'catalytic agent between two prima donnas'.

Naturally Churchill took him up in grand style. He stayed at the Premier's own home, where, among other things, he learned to admire his host for his drinking capacity, 'a bottle of wine for breakfast . . . two stiff whisky and sodas before nine in the morning'. He did not, however, like the freezing bedrooms that January, and before he left he promised one of Churchill's secretaries that a central heating system would be his 'personal victory present'.

Seemingly the two men got on well. Churchill knew of Hopkins' importance as FDR's alter ego and wanted their meetings to succeed. He nicknamed the wealthy American 'Lord Root of the Matter' for his candour and that supposed 'get up and go', of which all Americans are so proud, believing it to be a special attribute which distinguishes Americans from the fossilised denizens of the 'Old World'. However, even Hopkins had to admit that Churchill was 'something else'. Hopkins staggered back to his room at two o'clock on a freezing winter's morning, after listening to Churchill talk and watching the PM drink for hours on end, to collapse in a chair, muttering 'Jesus Christ'. . . . What a man!'

Hopkins went down well with Churchill, who underestimated his visitor's suspicions about British intentions, in particular regarding her empire. He said Hopkins was a 'true leader of men', whose 'love for the cause of the weak and the poor was matched by his passion against tyranny.' But big words of that nature did not, on the whole, go down well with Hopkins. Once when Churchill waxed poetic about Britain's war aims, stating 'We seek only the right of men to be free . . . we seek government with the consent of the people . . . But war aims other than these we have none', he asked Hopkins what FDR would think of such sentiments.

Hopkins, who liked to believe that he was a typical American who knew how to cut through the 'horse shit', replied: 'I don't think the President will give a damn for all that. You see, we're only interested in seeing that that goddam sonofabitch, Hitler, gets licked'. It was reported that Hopkins' words were greeted with 'loud laughter.' But the American was not as disingenuous as he appeared. He knew that the President had definite war aims and they wouldn't be all to Britain's liking. Still, Hopkins and Churchill got on well enough and many observers record that January, with its frequent meetings between the two men, as the real start of 'a special relationship'.

Five days before FDR announced that he was sending his adviser to London on a 'fact-finding mission', another future adviser to the President and US Ambassador to the Soviet Union got on the phone to Hopkins. He was a wealthy croquet-player, who had often enjoyed a game with Hopkins on their Long Island lawns. He begged to be allowed to go with him to London, maintaining: 'I've met Churchill several times, Harry. Let me carry your bag.'

Hopkins had been forced to turn down this fervent request. Perhaps he reasoned that Averell Harriman, the son of E H Harriman the ruthless and much vilified railroad magnate, who had built Union Pacific and had made a tremendous fortune doing it, was not the ideal companion for his forthcoming mission.

For Harriman senior had been one of those 'robber barons' who had industrialised the USA in the 1880s to their own advantage – and without too many scruples. Indeed, another Roosevelt had called him and his kind 'malefactors of great wealth'.

On the surface Averell Harriman was a different breed. He'd gone to Yale and, having dodged service in World War One, had used his position and inherited wealth to make a fortune of his own. Just like his father, however, he had not been over scrupulous in the process. Even before America had ended her war with Germany, the young Harriman had signed a shipping agreement with that country. A little later he made similar deals with Communist Russia, a country against which the USA was fighting. Indeed, when he had returned from Moscow in 1926, he told the press that the peasants had more freedom under Stalin than when they had been ruled by the Czars; and that Stalin was 'not a dictator in any sense of the word', but a 'kind of political boss of the US Tammany Hall mould'. In essence Harriman would do deals with anyone, as long as he made money.

Although he was a Republican, he did not line up with the party when it turned isolationist. For isolationism, he felt, might threaten his international business interests. In 1932, as a consequence, he started to support Roosevelt, the Democrat. It was yet another indication of Harriman's lack of national and political conviction. For him money and self-interest were his main concerns. A loner in business, he was the same in his private life. He devoted himself to polo as a rich young man, but later in life he took up bridge and even later the old man's game of croquet. Even though his second wife was vivacious and outgoing, with a love of parties and New York society, Harriman always remained a wallflower, an outsider even in his own home.

By December 1940, when he volunteered to carry Harry Hopkins' bag for him to London, he was a handsome, humourless, very rich man, whose only hobby of any importance seemed to be collecting rich or famous people regardless of their political inclination or background. Indeed, during the 1940 presidential election campaign, Harriman secretly backed both Roosevelt and his opponent Wendell Wilkie. He reasoned that whoever won, he would still be able to mingle with the rich and famous.

Snubbed by Hopkins, Harriman had now managed to become head of the new Lease-Lend co-ordinator office, with seventeen staff at his command, reporting directly to Hopkins who reported to the President. It was an ideal position for the man who knew Churchill and he jumped at Roosevelt's invitation to him to go to London in February 1941 'and recommend everything we can do, short of war, to keep the British Isles afloat'. For this task he would have the title of 'expediter'. That meant he could cut through red tape and circumvent the US State Department and the American Embassy in London if necessary.

Thus it was that Harriman arrived in the British capital on 17 March. The PM realised immediately that Harriman was exceedingly important, probably the most important American in the whole of the British Isles at that particular moment. He had Harriman rushed to Chequers to be wined, dined and wooed. Here Churchill told the American: 'We accept you as a friend. Nothing will be kept from you.' Indeed nothing was, including Churchill's pretty daughter-in-law, his son Randolph's wife.

'The Dorch' the Americans called it that year when they first started to arrive in London. In due course all of them, from Eisenhower to Hemingway, would stay there. For them, it was the 'in place'. For the Britons who frequented the Dorchester Hotel, either as permanent guests or for overnight stays when they were in the capital, the modern building was regarded as the safest hotel in London. It was supposed to have been built of ferro-concrete, which was pretty bomb-proof. It wasn't but that didn't matter, the guests and some who were not guests believed that implicitly.

'The Dorch' was attractive to the newly arriving 'Yanks' and others, not only on account of the supposed security it offered, but also because of its glittering social life and the rich and powerful people who lived and ate there. In such places in bombed, ravaged London, people still dined in evening dress or field service uniform, complete with highly polished Sam

Browne belt. They drank cocktails – gin fizz, martinis and the like – and champagne at 25 shillings a bottle. At places such as the Cafe de Paris, soon to be bombed itself, sophisticated entertainers like Florence Desmond gave an extra meaning to civil defence precautions when she sang: 'I've got a cosy flat. There's a place for your hat. I'll wear a pink chiffon negligee gown. I do know my stuff. But if that's not enough, I've got the deepest shelter in town.' And with that she'd flutter her long artificial eyebrows knowingly. She didn't need to. Every one of her admiring male audience knew that her shelter wasn't made of concrete.

In the Dorchester, where the supposedly secure lower floors were packed with residents frightened of the bombs, Emerald Cunard, the dissipated scion of the Atlantic shipping line, who had introduced 'rough trade' black men to London society ladies, held sway. Frequently among her guests was a pretty, buxom blonde who lived in one of the hotel's upper floors at a rent of six guineas a week, which she couldn't really afford. Not that the rent mattered. Even if she did get into arrears the management would never ask *her* to leave. After all, she did have one of the most powerful names in the kingdom. It was Churchill, of course.

This pretty young English girl had been born Pamela Digby in a castle, the daughter of an earl, who was now a general in the London War Office. Up to now she hadn't done much with her life, save to go school and spend a short spell in France polishing up her French until she had managed to get a job in the Foreign Office as a translator. Her father's title and position had helped there. Then by chance she had become entangled with Churchill's handsome son who, according to his sister, Mary, was 'spoiled rotten' by their father, who was probably compensating for the way he had been neglected by his own father and his American mother.

At the time they met, Randolph, already a gambler and heavy drinker (he died of drink in 1982), was sleeping with the actress Clare Luce and pursuing Lady Mary Dunn with an eye to bedding her too. Lady Mary Dunn was sharing a flat with Pamela Digby near Victoria Station when the former bumped into Randolph in the revolving door of the Ritz. Randolph asked Mary if she would have dinner with him. She refused, but said she had 'a red-headed tart up my sleeve called Pamela Digby'. As she told a friend later: 'She'll do anything for Randolph.'

Apparently she would. For within a matter of months Pamela of the splendid bosom, who was known as 'the dairy maid' in her circle, was married to the spoiled rotten scion of the Churchill family.

Winston was delighted. He had advised the young woman and her future husband: 'All you need to get married is a box of cigars, champagne and a double bed.' At first at least, that might have been good advice. Later Pamela, very quickly pregnant thanks to the 'double bed', thought differently. When their son was born, Churchill was ecstatic. He took them to Chequers and all four of them, Winston, his wife, the young

Winston and his mother slept in the same air raid shelter, troubled only by old Winston's persistent snoring.

Meanwhile Randolph went off to the Western Desert to fight the Italians. But he lost the first battle even before he reached the front. Gambling furiously on board his troopship, he lost £3,000, the equivalent of two years' pay. The young couple were broke and Pamela thought there was no way out for her but to get divorced. However, the 20-year-old of no education to speak of had a clever head on her young shoulders. She had already realised that if she attached herself again to an important man (something she would do for the rest of her long life, its high point as President Clinton's US Ambassador to Paris), she would ensure that they would not only be important but also wealthy – and generous with that wealth to boot!

Thus it was that one month after Randolph's departure, which would really signify the end of their marriage, she walked across the floor of Lady Cunard's suite at the Dorchester to where Emerald introduced her to the dark-haired new US Ambassador to the Court of St James, who had just replaced the unlamented Joe Kennedy; and also to the would-be bag-carrier Harriman. It was lust at first sight.

Naturally Harriman knew who she was and that she was in high favour with her father-in-law, Churchill. According to Harriman's own statement: 'Hopkins told me that she bore more information than anyone in England.' For her part, Pamela Churchill was surprised by the fact that the men 'who collected important personages' knew so little about the ruling British establishment. At all events, after Lady Cunard's dinner, Harriman suggested to the buxom young Englishwoman that she should come to his suite at the hotel and keep talking. How long she kept talking is a matter of conjecture. What is known is that she soon became Harriman's mistress and he her first 'Yank' lover, though before the war was over there would be a whole host of them, from Ed Murrow in '41 to Robert Capa in '44, with a few generals in between for good measure.

Naturally the war and the heightened sense of existence that conflict and danger bring with it had something to do with the relationship between Pamela and a man who could have been her grandfather. The capital was being bombed virtually every night, the men were away 'getting their knees brown' in some godforsaken desert and the 'Yanks' had a certain glamour about them, especially if they had plenty of money, as Harriman had. As people quipped at the time, 'London Society' was 'living for the day, fearing for the night'.

So Harriman would become the first of the important Americans who came to London that year and regarded English women as one of the 'perks' of the job. In the end all of them, even the Supreme Allied commander, Eisenhower, would do the same. But in the case of Harriman, his Pamela wasn't just a simple 'roll in the hay'; she was in fact an important source of information. In particular, because of her contact with Churchill and those who worked closely with him, she seemed to know more about high-level British policy than many a Whitehall mandarin or War Office brasshat. But it has been suggested by Pamela's biographer* that she might well have been a conduit for Churchill to transmit his own thoughts about the growing Anglo–American 'special relationship' through Harriman to his master, Roosevelt, in faraway Washington. In addition, the same American biographer maintains that she acted as a kind of a spy for the future Lord Beaverbrook, the Canadian owner of the *Daily Express*, who financed Pamela at times and was perhaps even her lover.

As Ogden records it, quoting several sources: 'The Averell–Pamela link was a very important tie that bound Beaverbrook, who was every bit as eager as Churchill to pull in the United States . . .' 'Max used everybody and Pamela was his catalyst on a hot tin roof,' said Tex McCrary, an American journalist and friend of Beaverbook. 'Beaverbrook was committed to getting closer to Harriman and Pamela was his link.' 'She passed everything she knew about anybody to Beaverbrook.'

If Pamela Churchill was indeed Beaverbrook's and Churchill's 'catalyst on a hot tin roof', it is a clear indication of how far Churchill would go to establish the 'special relationship' and ease the United States into the European war. In essence, Churchill was turning a blind eye, probably even encouraging his family favourite married to his spoiled son, into adultery for the 'cause'.

While the big shots intrigued and played their sordid, high-level games, the great mass of the British Army still waited for the call to arms one year after the defeat at Dunkirk. They were still training. For what, most of them didn't know, although they supposed in the end they would be going back to the continent to fight the 'Jerries' there.

Admittedly, despite the fact that 'bullshit reigned supreme' in a lot of the units, they were training harder since Montgomery had begun to set the standard for training. Now it was a rough and tough affair. When two battalions of infantry clashed on exercise, more often than not it resulted, as one 19-year-old recruit recalled,

. . . with rifles and bayonets [being] thrown to the ground and the men would fight with bare fists, while the officers stood by until things showed signs of getting out of hand. These dust-ups resulted in the first aid men, who were stretcher-bearers, having some *real* casualties to deal with as well as the imaginary ones labelled by the MO.

*Christopher Ogden, *Life of the Party*, Transworld, 1994

Men who had volunteered back in 1939 for the British Army, such as Lt Firbank of the Coldstream Guards, felt that this kind of training was 'like a breath of fresh air come to flutter the cobwebs of Army training'. Now, 'the soldier was being taught to be a mixture of poacher and gangster and yet remain a soldier'. But in common with many young soldiers in 1941, after three years in the Army, Firbank had seen no action and was beginning to think he never would.

The young soldiers of the South Lancs, which had joined Montgomery's old 'Iron Division' after Dunkirk, felt the same. The 1st South Lancs would indeed not see active service until 1944, save for some men who were transferred to other units sent abroad or bored young men, who volunteered for the new commandos and paratroops (which Churchill had ordered set up the previous year), desperate for any kind of action, however dangerous.

By now the South Lancs had expanded into several battalions, mostly based on pre-war territorial battalions. They were the 1/4th and 2/4 South Lancs, which just like their First Battalion had seen no active service and had been employed in the boring duty of guarding coasts against invasion, interspersed with training in Scotland. But when it had become clear that the threat of invasion had disappeared, these two battalions were mainly supplying trained soldiers for other infantry units being posted overseas, mostly to the Western Desert where the British Eighth Army was engaged in combat with the Italians and soon the Germans under the 'Desert Fox', Rommel.

In the spring of 1941, when the most important American in Europe was busily engaged in his affair with Pamela Churchill, the South Lancs were back to training and 'bull'. But as R W Thompson, the *Sunday Times* correspondent and ex-Infantry captain, noted, the real enemy was lacking 'and men did not choke in, drown in their own blood, gaps did not open up to leave men naked and lone, splattered with entrails, blood and brains of their friends where the coils of wire were littered with obscene offal of war'.

Montgomery, now a lieutenant-general waiting for an active employment, tried to inject even more realism into this boring round of training. Instead of throwing 'penny packets' into battle, in the form of a battalion here and a battalion there in traditional British Army fashion, he wanted training to be carried out by mass formations – 15,000, even 50,000 men – with armour, artillery and air working together as a battle team. He believed this was the way his 'reluctant heroes', many of them non-regulars, could beat the 'Hun', currently regarded as almost unbeatable.

As he told an audience of 200 officers, ranging from subaltern to brigadier-general:

The division is the fighting formation of all arms . . . I commanded a division in battle against the Germans [he meant the 'Iron Division'] . . .

> I never fought it in brigade groups once. I was never embarrassed by the Germans – nor do I propose to be in the future.

Very boastful indeed and, in general, true. He never was 'embarrassed' by the Germans save at Arnhem, where he proclaimed he'd really won a 'ninety percent victory', whatever that meant.

Unfortunately there were too few Montgomerys, and 1941 would see defeat after defeat for British arms until, in the following year, as a last-minute choice, the little general with his piercing blue eyes and beaky nose would be sent out to Egypt to command the British Eighth Army and commence that bold fighting career characterised by victory after victory.

Not everyone took to Monty's style of training. In addition to those young men who were sick of training altogether and longed for some desperate glory on the field of battle, there were those who thought Montgomery was over-doing it. Not all of them could take the strain, especially those who thought they were too senior, perhaps a little too old or unfit, to carry out his ordinary daily runs and strenuous PT. (The expanding US Army would soon face the same problem, especially with the National Guard outfits which had now been activated for federal service.) In 1941/42 there was a celebrated Monty story, which did the rounds of Army messes, about the portly staff colonel who reportedly complained to Montgomery that he would die if he were to run the weekly seven-mile course. Monty related in his *Memoirs*:

> I then said that if he were thinking of dying, it would be better to do it now, as he could be replaced easily and smoothly; it is always a nuisance if officers die when the battle starts and things are inclined to be hectic. His state of health was clearly not very good and I preferred him to do the run and die.

Funny in a way, but typically cruel as Monty so often was to those who could not hit back.

Those who thought Monty was not quite a gentleman, and who could hit back because they represented the establishment that Monty would never really belong to, continued in their old ways, as if Britain and its Army had not just suffered a series of catastrophic defeats with the fall of Tobruk and Singapore soon to come. Indeed, in one of his moments of despair, Churchill moaned about the British Army: 'Will they never fight?'

For example, the guards, although Monty would form some of their battalions into the Guards Armoured Division, still lived in the past, full of pomp, circumstance and upper-class privilege. Not only did the Guards continue to concentrate on bull to an extreme degree, with the men asking their officers, 'permission to speak, sir', as if this was the 18th century and not the 20th, but they spoke a language of their own creation – a kind of linguistic breviary of do's and don'ts.

'Service dress' was not a 'tunic'; 'batman' was not used. Instead the correct form of address for the soldier who 'did' for his officer was 'servant'. When off duty, the Brigade of Guards wore 'plain clothes' and not 'mufti'. As the adjutants of the Guards regiments admonished their new young officers: 'Those fellows who live among the wogs may wear mufti, but then the Brigade never serves east of Suez.'

If, as the ordinary British squaddie said cynically, 'bullshit baffles brains', this attitude among certain parts of an army still on home stations nearly two years after Dunkirk would not just amuse the Americans who would soon be arriving in their thousands and hundreds of thousands; it would also rile them, creating at officer level at least a great deal of bad blood. In the years to come, when finally the Americans began to outnumber the British in fighting troops, it would bring about a change in the 'special relationship' at the military level.

At the beginning there were many 'Johnnies-come-lately', as the first 'Yanks' into Britain called themselves, who were sympathetic to the British cause; some were outright anglophiles. But there would be changes. Many of the US staff officers who would serve in the 'Eisenhowerplatz' * would begin to doubt and distrust the British who served with them. These Americans would be suspicious of British motives and post-war intentions, just as Roosevelt, Hopkins and Stimson in Washington were.

Ralph Ingersoll, the editor of *PM* magazine, who would soon come to England again as a major on General Bradley's staff, would be one who was decidedly suspicious of the British. As he wrote immediately after the war:

> The British always first tried to be charming. If successful, they anglicized the individual to the point where in any Anglo–American argument he would be, at worst, neutral and at best, more frequently an active exponent of the British point of view.

But according to Ingersoll, who would be in the British capital three times as a journalist before he joined the US Army, there were Americans who 'experienced a sharp emotional revulsion against the British and their way of life'. But the perfidious British knew how to deal with such people. 'Let's be realistic,' they said. 'There are certain Americans who just can't abide the British. But we've got to work together to defeat the enemy . . . Therefore let's agree to get rid of them.'

---

* Grosvenor Square, the US High Command, nicknamed thus on account of Eisenhower's German-sounding name.

In time, Montgomery would become the focus of these patently anti-British Americans. He had presence, of course, just as Churchill did. But he did not inspire the same kind of respect that the PM did. Montgomery's presence was awesome, sometimes frightening. A cold ruthlessness shone from his eyes and he had absolutely no time for amateurism and lack of military know-how, which he thought was the cardinal fault of the US top brass.

But that was in the future. There were Americans already (secretly) present in the UK. Montgomery, however, had nothing to do with them. It would be another twelve months before he finally started to have contact with the 'Yanks' and those first meetings seemed to herald a stormy future between the little British general and his American counterparts.

As yet the United States was not in the war, and her army was in the same sort of disarray that the British Army had been back in the summer of 1940.

For the time being, Bernard Law Montgomery, the future star of the British Army, and Field Marshal Alan Brooke, his mentor and the new Chief of the Imperial General Staff, were in sole charge of the struggle against Nazi Germany.

CHAPTER IV
Will they never fight?

Just as Montgomery had attempted to do when he took over as corps commander after Dunkirk, the American high command was now kept busy trying to cut the 'dead wood' out of the regular army which would command the eight million soldiers that America would mobilise before the conflict ended. When the 'draft' commenced, the regular army had only 14,000 regular officers to command this vast host. Indeed one authority remarked that the inter-war US officer corps was 'so thick with dead wood that it was a fire hazard'; and that the officer's swagger stick, the symbol of authority in the old army, could be used as kindling for the blaze.

The situation was so bad that the War Department under General Marshall, who would now play the same role in Washington as Brooke did in London, instituted secret 'plucking committees'. These purged hundreds of regular officers who were too old, too tired or too set in their ways. The committees discovered that in 1941 there was not one single officer serving in the whole of the US Army who had commanded a unit as large as a division back in the 'Old War'.

Even the majors, who might now be selected for accelerated promotion to brigadier general, and command larger formations than a battalion, were found to have an average age of 48.

The situation in the various National Guard divisions, which had now been federalised for full-time duty, was even worse. Here a quarter of their lieutenants were aged over 40, and their senior ranks, especially generals, were often political appointees, tainted by nepotism, embezzlement and downright military incompetence.

When the new General Bradley took over the 28th Division, the Pennsylvanian National Guard, he found he was the division's third commander in the six months since it had been mobilised. As Bradley wrote after the war: 'It was . . . an outfit known as the "Iron Division" . . . a less fitting epithet than "iron" could not be imagined.'

His senior, General McNair, Marshall's hatchet men in those early days, wrote to his chief in Washington that the Guard had 'contributed nothing to National Defense', and that 'its history since mobilization . . .was one of

unsatisfactory training, physical condition, discipline, morals and par-
ticularly leadership.' McNair recommended bluntly that the 'National
Guard be dispensed with as a component of the Army of the United
States'.

But McNair had to face up to the realities of life in 1941. As he remarked:
'We didn't know how soon war would come, but we knew it was coming
. . . and we had to get together *something* of an Army pretty darn fast.'

It was becoming a tough proposition. Not only were the planners
having difficulty with an over-age, ossified officer corps, they were having
real problems with the draftees, called up initially for one year of service.
Morale and discipline suffered accordingly. These reluctant draftees
coined an acronym – 'OHIO' (Over the Hill in October (1941)). This they
scrawled on latrines and barrack walls, and elsewhere, to make the protest
visible. Hadn't Roosevelt told them in 1940 that America would never go
to war? So what are they doing 'playing sodjer' when they'd be better off
at home earning good money, after a decade of Depression, in one of the
new, booming war plants? As McNair summed it all up after inspecting
yet another of the US Army's troubled divisions: 'It's a case of 'the blind
leading the blind".'

But for the new *full* colonel, Dwight D Eisenhower, things were
definitely looking up. The culling of so many old officers had resulted in
Ike being given another staff appointment, but one he relished, for it was
with the troops. He had been promoted from lieutenant-colonel and given
the job of chief-of-staff to 62-year-old, German-born General Krueger,
who commanded the army that General Patton would one day make
famous – the US Third.

Just as Montgomery wanted to do, though he did not have the wide-
open spaces that General Krueger had at his disposal, the US Army
commander concentrated on large-scale manoeuvres. Not only would this
give the fledgling US Army an opportunity to fight and move in large
units, it would also help to weed out those commanders who could not
stand the pace or think fast enough on their feet when mobile warfare
demanded many new decisions.

In the end Krueger's Third Army beat its opponent, the US 2nd Army.
Eisenhower got the credit for devising Krueger's strategy, though in
retrospect the 3rd Army's strategy proved old-fashioned and not in tune
with the kind of mobile battle conducted by Rommel, America's first
opponent one year later in North Africa. Together Krueger and Eisenhower also helped to weed out useless or over-age officers, including the
two-star general commanding the Missouri National Guard and the first
cousin of the powerful senator for that state and future President Harry S
Truman.

During these protracted Louisiana manoeuvres, which were widely
publicised in the US press, Eisenhower 'discovered' a talent for dealing

with the newspaper men who came to the various camps and stayed overnight in tents, drinking whiskey, playing poker and trying to find *the* human interest story. Eisenhower, these cynical, worldy-wise civilians discovered, was quite different from most of the thick-headed regular army men they had to deal with. He was able to poke fun at himself and the army and give them interesting if unprintable stories about the 'risque' goings-on of the conscript soldiers with the New Orleans whores they had encountered in their brief time off-duty.

Naturally these men, who, because of their civilian status, felt cut off from the large number around them in uniform, took exception to this among the ranks of senior officers they had encountered so far. Although the correspondents got his name wrong, calling Ike Lt Col. D D Ersenbeing, he was well pleased. He was becoming known. He was particularly pleased when Drew Pearson, whose 'Washington Merry-Go-Round' column was read by millions, wrote that Colonel Eisenhower 'who conceived and directed the strategy that routed the Second Army has a steel-trap mind plus unusual physical vigor'.

Despite his military background, Ike knew that America, unlike any other nation in the world, thrived on publicity. American soldiers, hitherto, had not received much of it. But the Army wasn't immune to it, especially now that the erstwhile middle-aged majors and 'light' colonels, soon to be generals, would no longer be commanding companies and battalions, but divisions, corps, even armies. By the time the US Army went into battle in force, most of them would be sporting a catchy nick-name of their own invention – 'Vinegar Joe' Stilwell, 'GI General' Bradley, 'Blood an' Guts' Patton; and there would be a whole host of lesser generals, calling themselves 'Lightning Joe', 'Iron Mike', 'Wild Bill', 'Gentleman Jim' and so on.

To get on Ike reasoned, even in the Regular Army of the United States, one needed the support of the press; and to gain that support you would have to be 'one of the boys', a regular guy who had no upper-class airs and graces; who drank his whiskey from the bottle, lost his shirt at poker, and, above all, was just a decent, simple hometown *American*, yessir!

It followed, Eisenhower must have concluded after his first encounter with the press, that if you wanted to succeed in the war soon to come, you not only needed to win battles; you had also to ensure that the US press knew you had won because you were a regular American who had led equally regular American soldiers, fighting strictly for their folks back home in the good old US of A.

Later much would be made of Eisenhower's tact and managerial skills in keeping the difficult Anglo–American coalition – the military 'special relationship – together. But in the final analysis, if, with his 'good humor man's' ear-to-ear smile, he had to make a decision on any conflict within that coalition which might be detrimental to American interests (and to his own), he would be forced to make an 'American' decision. For the press would be always looking over his shoulder. In years to come, with battles fought in front of the media on a day-to-day basis, all American commanders would make the same sort of decision. It would always be American interests first.

On 15 June 1941 Churchill signalled Roosevelt:

> From every source at my disposal, including some most trustworthy, it looks as if a vast German onslaught on Russia is imminent. Not only are the main German armies deployed from Finland to Roumania, but the final arrivals of air and armoured forces are being completed.

Although the 'secret Americans' already in Britain had been shown around the British Government's top secret decoding centre at Bletchley Park, they had not yet been told about the ULTRA operation – that 'most trustworthy' of sources.

Five days later, on Friday 20 June, Churchill debated with himself whether he should deliver a broadcast on the Saturday night telling the world what was afoot. In the end he decided against it. For as he wrote later: 'The Soviet Government, at once haughty and purblind, regarded every warning we gave as a mere attempt of beaten men to drag others into ruin.'

On 22 June, after Hitler had attacked Russia at four o'clock in the morning, Churchill decided to broadcast to the nation. It must have been a difficult decision. He had always been an aggressive opponent of Soviet communism. Yet if Russia was now involved in the fighting with Germany, it meant that Britain was no longer alone. But if he supported Soviet Russia, the one-time arch enemy, how would it affect Britain's relationship with America, where many of Roosevelt's enthusiastic 'new dealers' were very close to communism themselves.*

That Sunday however, Churchill went on the air and stated:

> Any man or state who fights against Nazism will have our aid. Any man or state who marches with Hitler is our foe . . . That is our policy and that is our declaration. It follows, therefore, that we shall give whatever help we can to Russia and the Russian people. We shall appeal to all our friends and allies in every part of the world to take the same course and pursue it, as we shall faithfully and steadfastly to the end.

Russia was in. Now what of Roosevelt's America?

*It was only many decades later, when the 'Verona' decodes were revealed, that America learned just how many young men working for Moscow there were in top positions in the American government.

Roosevelt's top soldiers were pessimistic about the Soviet Union's chances in this new war. So far, Nazi Germany had steamrollered all opposition wherever the Wehrmacht went into battle. Why should Russia be any different, despite her huge army? Besides, what could Britain and especially America, with its armies still in the making, do to help the new ally?

By 1 July the prophesy of German Chief-of-Staff General Fritz Halder that 'we shall fight fierce battles for eight to fourteen days and after this we won't have to wait long for successes', seemed to be coming true. By that date, the Wehrmacht had occupied eastern Poland (which Russia had seized from Poland when Stalin was still Hitler's ally), the Baltic states, Byelorussia and the Ukraine. By 1 July 1941 more than 100,000 Red Army soldiers had gone into the bag and more were continuing to stream into the German cages in their thousands.

How could America help an apparently swiftly disintegrating Russia? Certainly not with troops. But what about supplies of food, ammunition, tanks, guns, airplanes? Would that be throwing good money after bad, if Russia was in a state of collapse? Besides, where would these weapons of war come from? The 'Arsenal of Democracy' was finding it difficult enough to supply Britain. It was a problem that greatly troubled Harry Hopkins, the President's chief adviser. He guessed that if FDR followed his hunch that Russia would survive the German onslaught, and decided to supply that far-off country, those weapons of war would have to come from America's Lease-Lend shipments to Britain.

On 11 July, nearly three weeks after the German attack and after a long discussion of the new problem, FDR sent his trusty aide to London to continue talks with Churchill. Hopkins' brief was to present the PM with two issues: the American aid programme, and the effect of this new conflict on the current British strategy in the Middle East, which many in the US military and civilian planners believed was the wrong one. If the USA was going to enter the war, she did not want to be wasting time battling on the outer fringes of the Nazi empire. America wanted to take the shortest route to Berlin, which was through France.

At first Churchill felt that Russia would 'assuredly be defeated'. Then he changed his mind, probably bowing to American pressure, maintaining: 'If Hitler invaded Hell . . . I would at least make a favourable reference to the Devil.'

That was Churchill's public face, part of his customary attempt to please Roosevelt. Privately, however, he knew that every tank, gun and plane that FDR sent to Europe would have to come out of the Lease-Lend supplies to Britain. Moreover, the main burden of transporting those weapons of war to the north Russian ports would rest with Britain's already ailing merchant fleet. In the end it would indeed cost the lives of some ten thousand British seamen sailing from the country's north-eastern ports, and countless ships on that terrible Murmansk run.

Churchill was torn two ways. In one sense he hoped Russia would inflict heavy losses on the invaders and thus take the pressure off the British in the Middle East. In another he felt the Russians would not survive very long at the rate they were losing men and territory. So why help the Russians? Concentrate instead in beefing-up the Eighth Army in the desert and win a victory there.

What Churchill did not know, though he might well have suspected it, was that Roosevelt was not one bit interested in supporting British intentions in the Middle East. As Averell Harriman claimed, Roosevelt saw Churchill as 'pretty much a 19th century colonialist'. Roosevelt thought that Churchill was so deeply involved in the Middle East because he wanted to protect British oil interests in the area, and maintain control of the Suez Canal, vital for contact with the rest of the Empire. But FDR was not going to allow himself to be talked into the defence of the British Empire or any other European colonial empire for that matter.

In January 1943, when he was about to take over command in London, General Eisenhower summed it up from the point-of-view of the military.

I am not so incredibly naïve that I do not realize that Britishers instinctively approach every military problem from the viewpoint of the Empire, just as we approach them from the viewpoint of American interest. One of the constant sources of danger to us in this war is the temptation to regard as our first enemy the partner that must work with us in defeating the real enemy.

This was a practical and pragmatic approach to the natural problems of the Anglo–American coalition soon to come. But it was already clear in that summer of 1941, after the German attack eastwards, that Roosevelt had taken another and third partner aboard – Soviet Russia. Until America finally got into the European war (if she ever did), FDR would try to keep the two endangered European states, Britain and Russia, afloat. But Churchill, FDR must have told himself, need not think that he was the more favoured partner. FDR distrusted Churchill as an old-fashioned colonialist. He once rounded on him:

You have four hundred years of acquisitive instinct in your blood and you can't understand how a country might now want to acquire land somewhere if they can get it. A new period has opened in the world's history and you will have to adjust to it.

The country that 'might now want to acquire land somewhere if they can get it' was obviously, in FDR's opinion, the USA. But in a way he also regarded Soviet Russia in the same light. Russia had no empire, so FDR thought. She, too, was a country of the future just as the USA was. Such countries would shape the post-war world. Britain, like France and the Netherlands with their empires, would not. For the time being he would support and use Britain. But when the time was ripe, Churchill would have to learn to toe the new post-war line. Or else.

Harriman, the man who 'collected' famous people, had established an even firmer relationship with Churchill's daughter-in-law, Pamela. By the early summer of 1941, he had set up an establishment, supposedly run by his daughter, Kathy. In fact, its centrepiece was Pamela. If Averell or Pamela thought this cover fooled those close to them, they were wrong.

Roosevelt's senior aide, Harry Hopkins, who got on very well with Harriman's mistress, told her that FDR knew all about the affair. Indeed the President got 'a big kick' out of it.

What Churchill knew about the relationship he kept to himself. But his principal private secretary, John Colville, soon to volunteer for the RAF, had seen the two lovers out early in the morning the previous April when they were examining the damage from the previous night's German air-raid and had guessed what was going on. Later Churchill asked Pamela about her relationship with Harriman, but she shrugged it off. One can be sure that the PM knew all he needed to know; after all, he'd have access to the MI5 reports on important people who might endanger national security; and Pamela was not particularly secure, something that Harriman naturally used to his advantage.

Still it stretches the imagination somewhat to find Churchill writing to his son that June:

Darling Randolph
Averell Harriman is travelling out to the Middle East . . . I hope you will try to see him when he arrives. I have made good friends with him . . . He does all he can to help us.

Perhaps the note to his cuckolded son shows just how desperate Churchill was to win over the most important American in Britain and keep those Lease-Lend supplies coming, even at the expense of his son's honour.

Dutifully Randolph did as his father requested. He squired Harriman around for ten days. At the end of this period in Egypt, he wrote to his father: 'I have been tremendously impressed by Harriman . . . He has definitely become my favourite American.' The cuckolded husband ended with, 'he clearly regards himself as more your servant than Roosevelt's.' Apparently, Randolph didn't know the half of it. Or did he?

Playing the field in Cairo with a mistress and several Egyptian whores in tow the young Churchill had plenty of contacts in the Egyptian capital at the British GHQ located there. Here people from London came and went all the time, bringing with them the latest gossip from Britain. Did

Randolph know what his wife was up to with the elderly American multi-millionaire? His father probably did. Was it then that Randolph prepared to sacrifice what was left of his honour (and that wasn't very much, it must be admitted) in order to keep those vital supplies, which Harriman controlled, flowing?

At all events, on the same day that Randolph wrote to his father about his 'favourite American', he also wrote to his wife, Pamela. He stated, perhaps with tongue in cheek:

> I found him [Harriman] absolutely charming. It was lovely to be able to hear so much news of you and all our friends . . . He spoke delightfully about you and I fear that I have a serious rival.

But the days of wooing the Americans, pondering and perhaps even pimping to them, were almost over. On Sunday 7 December 1941 Pamela Churchill, Harriman and Kathleen, his daughter, the trio of the supposed secret 'love nest', were present at a dinner in the Prime Minister's home at Chequers. Just before the Home Service's nine o'clock news, Churchill's valet, Harry Sawyers, came in. With him he brought a cheap US portable radio that Harry Hopkins had presented to the PM so that he could hear the news without going to the drawing room.

The chatter ceased as they settled down to the ritual of the news, read by an immaculate BBC announcer. These days he no longer wore an evening jacket and black tie, and he gave his name at the beginning of the news so that his listeners would know this was a genuine BBC broadcast. For of late a fluent English speaker from Berlin had begun to cut into the news to comment on the items read out from the German point of view.

While the others watched, Churchill rested his head in his hands looking as if he were again afflicted by one of his 'black dog' moods. But perhaps he was just weary. It had been a terrible, burdensome year for a man of his responsibilities. After the usual bulletins, the announcer's well-modulated voice rose somewhat. He said:

> The news has just been given that Japanese aircraft have raided Pearl Harbor, the American naval base in Hawaii. The announcement was made in a brief statement by President Roosevelt. Naval and military targets in the principal Hawaiian island of Oahu have also been attacked.

Churchill responded at once, almost as if he had been expecting and waiting for this news for a very long time. He slammed his hand down hard on the little bakelite radio. He pulled his bulk out of the chair. 'We shall declare war on Japan,' he announced, as if a new plan had only just sprung into his agile brain.

John Winant, the dark-haired US Ambassador who was present that historic Sunday objected with, 'Good God, you can't declare war in a radio announcement.' The new American representative to the court of St James did not know Churchill.

When, a few minutes later, the British Admiralty confirmed the BBC news report, the PM called FDR immediately. The latter greeted him with, 'We're all in the same boat now.' He went on to tell 'Winston', as he was now calling Churchill, that the next day he would go to Congress to declare war on Japan in his famous 'Day of Infamy' speech. Churchill again reacted immediately. He said he would do the same thing in the House of Commons, adding, 'This certainly simplifies things.' For now it did. But what of the future?

Back as an obscure schoolboy of 16 at Harrow, at the height of Victorian confidence in the British Empire, young Winston Churchill had told a fellow pupil:

I can see vast changes coming over a now peaceful world, great upheavals, terrible struggles, wars such as one cannot imagine and I tell you London will be in danger – London will be attacked and I shall be very prominent in the defence of London . . . I see further ahead . . . I see into the future . . . but I will tell you I shall be in command of the defence of London and I shall save London and the Empire from disaster.

But the 'tremendous invasion' young Winston envisioned and that he boasted to his fellow schoolboy he would beat to save London, Britain and the Empire would not come from an enemy, but from a friend. Now over five decades later, Churchill had achieved his 'special relationship' with the United States. He had saved his country and its 400-year old Empire, he thought. As he wrote later: 'I went to bed and slept the sleep of the saved and the thankful.'

1942

Vive la France . . . Lafayette, we are here again . . .
for the second time.
US General Mark Clark, 1942

CHAPTER V
Eisenhower? No, never heard of him

On the morning of Saturday 26 January 1942, a grey, drizzly day typical of Northern Ireland in winter, the flags were out everywhere at Dufferin Quay, Belfast. As the tenders started to nudge away from the transport ships, the *Strathaird* and the *Château Thierry*, which had braved the submarine-infested Atlantic to bring the newcomers to this Godforsaken place, the band of the Royal Ulster Rifles struck up 'The Star-Spangled Banner'.

Slowly the assembled dignitaries began to move forward through the murk ready to welcome the first man ashore. They were the real top brass: the most distinguished figures in the whole of the province. They included a Duke, a Prime Minister, a Secretary of State for Air, and a clutch of bemedalled general officers. There was even the Inspector General of the Royal Ulster Constabulary, whose men would have their hands full soon enough, trying to keep 'our cousins from across the sea' in line. But that was in the future. Today Mr Churchill wanted to ensure that these Americans received a proper welcome. After all, it had taken him a long time to convince their leaders, in particular FDR, that they should come to fight in the European War. They deserved a welcome.

The Secretary of State for Air, a key member of Churchill's cabinet, Sir Archibald Sinclair, a tall, lean man in a black suit and wearing a stiff wing collar, looked every inch the well-bred, upper-class English gentleman he was. He now addressed the new arrivals from the quay. He told them they had come from the prairies and teeming cities of the North-West over thousands of miles, not to soujourn among strangers, but among grateful friends. Their safe arrival here in Belfast marked a new stage in the war against the Germans.

Now the first serving American soldier to step on to British soil since 1918 came ashore. He was a slightly bewildered Private First Class, Milburn H Henke from Hutchinson, Minnesota. He belonged to General Ryder's 34th Infantry Division, which before the year was out would engage in America's first battles in the European theatre.

Not that PFC Henke was feeling very warlike at that moment. The Atlantic had been rough and the boiled sprouts and smoked haddock had not suited his stomach too well. Still, he allowed his hand to be pressed, his photo taken, while the military band played and he stood, laden down with his kit, old-fashioned World War One helmet tilted to one side.

Abruptly the local worthies were startled to hear another military band begin playing. It was accompanied by the soft shuffle of rubber-soiled boots so unlike the harsh stamp of British Army hobnailed ammunition boots. As one they turned, surprised.

Behind them a whole company of the 34th Infantry Division was marching off smartly. Somehow it had bypassed Churchill's reception committee and was on its way to the new camp for these 'Yanks', the first to return to the 'Old Country'. Ironically, PFC Henke's 'Old Country' was on the continent. It turned out that he was of German origin and he had more relatives on the other side of the Rhine than he had back in the States.

But the SNAFU – Situation Normal, All Fucked Up' – as the GIs called it, did not end there. A little later, a BBC reporter approached one of the newly arrived 34th Division and tried to get his impressions of his first moments in Britain. Unfortunately, the GI took the BBC man for a representative of an American radio station. He obliged with what he thought his American listeners would like to hear. 'Gee Mom, I sure wish I was back home.' One wonders if the BBC ever did broadcast that comment.

But Churchill was overjoyed. One full division in Britain, within six weeks or so of America entering the war. That really was cementing the special relationship between the two countries. Now, he knew more and more US divisions would follow. He even placed the 'Queens' at the disposal of the US Army, so that they could ship a whole division in one go across the Atlantic. Not that that impressed the average GI. One who travelled in the *Queen Elizabeth* told a crew member: 'Pity you Britishers can't build ships like this.' But there were plenty of 'Britishers' who were equally unimpressed by the new arrivals from the 'Land of the Free'.

In particular, British troops serving in Northern Ireland, who were the first to observe the 'Yanks' at close quarters, were not particularly fond of them, their ways and their ability as soldiers. The 'Yanks' wore smart uniforms with collar and tie, just as officers did in the British Army. They did not clomp around in the heavy boots issued to the British squaddie; instead they wore light, rubber-soled 'shoes' (they didn't even call them 'boots'). They wore decent coats or fawn-coloured civilian type raincoats in Ulster's persistent winter drizzle instead of the hated capes, or even worse, camouflaged gas capes of the British. But above all, the pay of the average GI was five times that of the average British squaddie. No wonder they got all the girls. They had the money.

As soldiers, however, a lot of their British 'comrades-in-arms' thought the Yanks hopeless. They called their NCOs, even some of their officers, by their first names. They did not march with 'bags o' swank' and plenty of 'swing them arms there' of the British soldier. Instead they seemed to saunter along in a casual, easy-going style. Their black soldiers even danced in a way, springing up and down 'like bleeding whirling dervishes', as some of the other British troops observed.

When the 'Yanks' mounted ceremonial guard outside their new camps of an evening, there was none of the traditional British Army 'bull'; no 'old guard' and 'new guard' commands, hands slapping rifles and gleaming webbing equipment in clouds of green blanco powder. Instead they leaned casually against anything they could find – Yanks always leaned – and chewed like contented cows with their cud, even in the presence of their 'OD' as they called their orderly officer. (The Yanks appeared to abbreviate everything.) All in all, the general opinion among the British troops in Northern Ireland of the Yanks could be summed up as: 'If this shower is typical of the whole of the US Army, then thank God for the Royal Navy.'

Nor were the GIs overly taken by the British. They thought them too class-conscious, that their traditional respect for authority verged on servility and that, as a June 1942 opinion poll discovered, 60% of Americans regarded the British as 'oppressors'. Even FDR had declared just after America entered the war: 'This distrust, this dislike, even hatred of Britain . . . is in the American tradition. The Revolution, you know and 1812.'

Above all the Americans of the US V Corps thought that, for all their martial outward appearance, these 'limeys' with their bullshit, had not yet won a decisive battle against the Germans. Since Dunkirk, the British Army had suffered defeat after defeat. As the GIs wisecracked in the local pubs.' 'Let's have a beer as quick as the British got out of Dunkirk.' This was widely reported and the standard British reply was 'Is that how the Yanks swam at Pearl Harbor?' When the sentimental favourite of the time 'There'll always be an England' was played at the troops' dances on the giant Wurlitzer organs in the cinemas, the GIs would snigger, 'Yeah, as long as we keep it there for you.' And perhaps these GIs were right.

In May 1942 the newly promoted Major-General Eisenhower, now on the staff of the most important man in the US Army, General Marshall, flew to England, together with an old friend, Major General Mark Clarke, in order to assess exactly what the American troops there were up to. At Paddington Station, the two were picked up by Kay Summersby, who when asked by a friend, 'Surely you've heard of General Eisenhower?', replied, shaking her pretty head: 'Eisenhower? No, never heard of him.'

But Kay Summersby and soon the rest of the Free World would hear a lot more about this low-ranking, obscure, two-star general, who still believed he'd be lucky if Marshall would allow him to go back to the troops and command an armoured division.

The two generals did a lightning tour of the US installations in the UK, including a trip to Northern Ireland to inspect the US V Corps, to which

Ryder's 34th Division belonged. Eisenhower was pleased with what he saw. Clarke was not. He thought the infantrymen 'seemed fat and podgy in contrast to the lean, hard look of the British soldiers'.

Although Eisenhower now started to worry about the state of the troops he found, when he returned to London the GIs thought they were a war-winning force. *New Yorker* correspondent Mollie Panter-Downes remarked that year in her tart fashion on 'the impatience of the American troops now in London, most of whom talk as though they were somewhat doubtful of being able to give the town a quick once-over before leaving to keep a date with von Rundstedt, which they seem to imagine will be around Thursday week at the latest'.

Churchill, who perhaps guessed the role Eisenhower might play in the future, and certain that the American general would definitely report to Marshall, who, in his turn would report to FDR once he had returned to Washington, made certain that Eisenhower saw the best British troops still in the UK. At the suggestion of Brooke at the War Office, Eisenhower was sent to see Lt Gen. Montgomery commanding a large 'scheme', i.e. military exercise, in southern England.

Kay Summersby, the red-haired divorcee and former model, who was rapidly becoming more American than an American, drove them there and deposited Eisenhower and Clarke at a large farmhouse with a map tacked to the wall. Here they waited the arrival of the British general, apparently known to everybody as 'Monty'.

Soon Monty came in. He 'was very abrupt', Clarke who was somewhat anglophobe, recalled later. Monty said: 'I have been directed to take time from my busy life to brief you gentlemen.'

Eisenhower, who by now was well on his way to becoming a chain-smoker (in the end he'd be smoking sixty a day), lit a cigarette, a heinous crime in Monty's eyes. The little general stopped his briefing immediately. He demanded, 'who is smoking?' Eisenhower answered, 'I am sir.'

Monty jumped on the American new boy. Monty told Eisenhower that he did not tolerate smoking in his presence. Beetroot red now, Eisenhower stubbed out his cigarette and the briefing continued.

Later Clarke stated that Ike had laughed the incident off. For his part, Eisenhower wrote in his diary: 'General Montgomery is a decisive type who appears to be extremely energetic and professionally able.'

Kay Summersby, who had taken a shine to Eisenhower (just as he had to her) told it differently. On the way back she overheard the two generals talking in the back of the sedan and caught the phrase 'that son of a bitch'. As she recalled:

[Eisenhower] was furious – really steaming mad. And he was still mad. It was my first exposure to Eisenhower's temper. His face was flaming red and the veins in his forehead looked like worms.

Ike and Monty had not got off to a good start. Neither did Ike with 'Brookie', Field Marshal Alan Brooke. They too met during the course of Eisenhower's whirlwind tour of wartime Britain. Brooke was very experienced and very professional. Just like Marshall he, too, had undertaken the re-organisation of a new British Army after the defeat at Dunkirk. Marshall's last experience of war had been in 1918, however, and the Ulsterman, with his dour manner and loner's habit of bird-watching, had little time for him. He said of the American, 'a pleasant and easy man to get along with', but 'not a great man'. But then Brooke and Montgomery underestimated these American staff officers, who had long learned that in Washington it was not enough to be a soldier; you had to be a politician too.

From the outset Brooke tested Eisenhower. The former knew that the Americans felt their first priority was to help the hard-pressed Stalin and his Red Army with a push through France. The British Chief-of-Staff and his political chief, Churchill, thought this unrealistic. Neither the British nor the very green Americans were in any position to accomplish this in 1942. Still Brooke had been ordered by Churchill to go along with the Americans' foolish notions and unrealistic strategy.

Brooke asked who should command such a force and Eisenhower, un-familiar with all the high-ranking officers sitting around the table waiting for his answer, said the commander should naturally be British as the British would provide the bulk of the troops. He then stated that Lord Louis Mountbatten, who had recently changed from commanding a destroyer flotilla in the Mediterranean to heading up Combined Opera-tions, i.e. the commandos, might be the man they needed.

Eisenhower, warming to his subject, said he'd heard Mountbatten was vigorous, intelligent and courageous. 'I assume he could do the job.'

Suddenly Eisenhower realised that his audience were not really taking his words in. There seemed to be a kind of embarrassment hanging in the air. Indeed, when he was finished, he was greeted by silence. Eisenhower wondered what he had said wrong.

The silence was broken by Brooke. Another man would have smiled and let Eisenhower have it easy. Not the stern Ulsterman, who would never think much of Eisenhower to the very end of the war. He en-lightened the newly promoted American general with: 'General, possibly you have not met Admiral Mountbatten? This is he, sitting directly across the table from you.'

It is not recorded if Ike (as Mountbatten himself would soon call him) went 'beetroot red' this time. But it is highly likely. For yet again, the future Allied Supreme Commander in Europe had been wrong-footed by these snooty limey generals.

Roosevelt was never much interested in military matters. He usually left such things to General Marshall. Unlike Churchill, he did not interfere in overall strategy. Churchill did, almost on a daily basis, much to the annoyance of Marshall's equivalent, Field Marshal Brooke. But in the summer of 1942 FDR realised he had to take a hand in the strategic planning of the war in the immediate future. America had been involved now for over six months, but she had done little for such a great power. She had sent troops to Britain, but the likelihood of their being involved in action before the end of the year seemed to be growing ever remoter. And there was the Congressional election process scheduled to start in November. Consummate politician that he was, FDR knew the Great American Public would by then be asking what kind of counterpunch was the USA launching against the Japanese and the Germans. As always in the USA, even when she is at war, politics are most important.

Although FDR had made up his mind that the battle against Nazi Germany should have priority over that against Japan, very little was being done in Europe. In particular, Russia was still reeling under the German onslaught and the Washington planners estimated that if Russia were defeated, not only would Germany gain access to the oilfields of the Middle East and the Russian Caucasus, but scores of German divisions would be released to the West. That had happened once before in spring 1918 when Imperial Germany had signed a peace treaty with Russia, and Germany had thrown the divisions thus released into the great March 1918 attack on the Western Allies. Then the Germans had come very close to victory.

Yet the British seemed lukewarm about a cross-Channel assault – one which in May 1942 Roosevelt had promised Stalin would take place before the end of the year, to take the pressure off the Red Army. Indeed some of FDR's navy chiefs were urging him to drop the British option and turn his attention to the war against Japan. The British, it appeared, wanted priority to be given to the Middle East, in particular to the Western Desert where the Eighth Army confronted a mere six German divisions compared to the estimated 225 German divisions attacking the Red Army. FDR's navy men thought the British were more concerned with preserving their Empire than winning the war. In particular, Admiral King, an anglophobe whom Roosevelt once accused of 'shaving with a blowtorch', predicted that British would never invade Europe 'except behind a Scotch bagpipe band'.

With his service chiefs in disarray, the Soviets suffering and the British still insisting on the Western Desert priority, and above all, with the November congressional elections coming ever closer, FDR knew he had to act. For him what mattered now was not the question of whom America should attack first, Germany or Japan, but that American troops went into action somewhere in the world. For the US voter demanded that of him, as the President. As he himself said that July: 'It is of the highest importance that US ground troops be brought into action against the enemy in 1942.'

On 25 July he completely surprised everyone by announcing that the 'second front', as it was now being called, was off in North-Western Europe for the time being. Nor was Japan to be attacked in force by ground troops. Instead US troops from both Britain and America would invade French North Africa. North Africa was now the US's principal military objective and the assault on the French colonies there would commence at 'the earliest possible date', preferably within two months.

It was a strange decision. The Americans were to attack French colonies, governed by Vichy Frenchmen, most of whom still supported Germany. What if they fought back? Then the spectre of Americans killing the people they had come to 'liberate' would arise. More importantly for the American voter, the French might well be killing Americans. What price Lafayette then?

And there was the problem of shipping the troops. A single armoured division needed forty-five troopships and cargo ships, plus naturally warships to guard the vulnerable merchant ships. Now perhaps six or seven US divisions would be needed for the landings and the follow-up, plus another two or three British divisions. Where was the shipping to come from? And how were they to get off the troopships to assault the beaches? Were they to use rowboats, for as late as May, Eisenhower was still asking: 'Who is responsible for building landing craft?' Indeed landing craft would remain in short supply right into 1945.

But the greatest problem raised by Roosevelt's snap decision, of which he informed Churchill on that same Saturday 25 July, was that in this invasion of North Africa, with all its looming military and political problems with the French, a million US troops and millions of tons of supplies from the States would be tied up in the Mediterranean for another two years to come. Effectively, FDR, who was supposedly committed to a 'second front' as soon as possible, was postponing the cross-Channel attack for another two years. Unwittingly however, he did save the US Army from what probably would have been what Churchill feared – a massacre – if the Americans attacked in France in 1943. But the American generals didn't see it like that. Cynically Marshall commented on FDR's July decision: 'We [himself and his fellow generals] forget that the leader in a democracy has to keep the people entertained . . .'

One American general was to profit from Roosevelt's choice of actions. He was Dwight D Eisenhower. For now his days as a staff officer at the Washington War Department were already numbered. Marshall was sounding him – and other generals too – out as to his ability to take over America's most senior post overseas.

Throughout late June and early July Marshall kept coming back to the

European Theatre of Operations, in particular the British Isles where a General Chaney controlled things. Not very well, it seemed.

Marshall consulted Ike about Chaney. But Eisenhower was wise enough not to recommend the relief of the man who commanded those first 'secret Americans' in London. That would have been a bad policy mistake. Instead he told Marshall:

It is necessary to get a punch behind the job or we'll never be ready by spring [of 1943] to attack [across the Channel]. We must get going.'

Thereupon Eisenhower drafted a plan for Marshall on how the growing US presence in Britain should be organised. Marshall accepted it, but still did not tell Ike his plans for him, as the future Supreme Commander. In the meantime other generals were recommending to Marshall possible alternatives. Still the latter did not commit himself, though he did think the other suggested candidates were too old. As always in the US Army, the West Point network was being used, testing candidates for senior posts on the basis that all of them had known each other since they had been 18-year 'plebes';* from the very beginning of their careers in the US Army, they had known each other's weaknesses and strengths.

At West Point they had spent the most formative four years of their lives in a setting of great natural beauty, with the Storm King Mountain towering over the Plain and the Hudson sweeping like a blue-grey ribbon around the Academy. Here they were a privileged class in superb physical shape and supposedly possessing the best brains in the USA. They lived an absolutely regimented existence, cut off from normal society, and very unlike the relaxed life of the British officer cadets at Sandhurst with their binges and weekend busts in London.

Here, although they claimed to have sprung from a democratic nation, they lived in an institution that was anything but democratic. They were pledged to honour a code of conduct which included the duty to report on a fellow cadet, and perhaps have him expelled if he infringed that code. They ate like Prussian cadets, with no speaking allowed, save 'pass the water' sort of thing, and sitting at attention. They sat down and got up on order. They even spoke a special language of their own, and those who were asked by Marshall to report on their onetime fellow cadet 'Ike' would say that Ike had once been a 'yard bird' (one who had to parade up and down the yard as a punishment), was 'a busted aristocrat' (a cadet demoted for misbehaviour), and that although he was a 'hivery' (one quick to learn), he had not been a 'file bones' (a cadet who tried to outsmart his classmates in exams).

Thus it was that Marshall asked Clarke, who had accompanied Ike to

*1st Year students at West Point

London that year, for his opinion about who should command in Europe. Clarke agreed with previous choices (like Eisenhower he was careful of voicing strong opinions in front of Marshall). Yet when asked for a name of a young officer for the job, he replied without hesitation 'Eisenhower'.

On 11 June Marshall probed Eisenhower about the future use of US troops in Europe. He asked: 'In your opinion are the plans as nearly complete as we can make them?'

Eisenhower's answer came back loud and clear: 'Yessir.'

Marshall did not smile; he wasn't a man given to smiling. He said simply: 'That's lucky because you're the man who is going to carry them out.'

Then Marshall asked Eisenhower informally whom he'd like to take to England as his deputy. Instantly Eisenhower replied: 'Clarke.'

Now Marshall allowed himself a wintry smile. Wrily he commented: 'It looks to me as if you boys got together.' And perhaps they had.

That night, eating supper with his wife Mamie, who was going to plague him for the rest of the war on account of her complaints and criticisms, Eisenhower was uncharacteristically silent (Montgomery always criticised Eisenhower for talking too much) until the time came for their usual coffee and cake dessert. Now he revealed that he was going to London again, this time for good.

'What post are you going to have?' his wife asked.

Now Eisenhower let loose his pent-up excitement. He cried: 'I'm going to command the whole shebang, Mamie!'

Two months after Eisenhower, an obscure American general who had never commanded so much as a platoon and had never heard a shot fired in anger, left for London and the job of Supreme Commander, an equally obscure British general, who had heard many shots fired in anger and had once been left for dead on the battlefield, was also on his way to command a new army. At last, after two years of waiting following Dunkirk, Montgomery was to be given his first fighting command.

In the desert, 'up the blue' as the troops called it, nothing much was expected of the 'new bloke'. After all, there had been four commanders of the Eighth Army within twelve months. What did this unknown, who'd spent the last two years in 'Blighty' know of desert warfare which had rules of its own? He had not even 'got sand in his shoes'.

But the birdlike new commander, with his brand new desert shirt and slacks, put it on the line when he addressed his officers in the evening cool of 13 August 1942. Indeed, his new chief-of-staff Freddie de Guingand recorded that his speech that evening 'was one of the greatest efforts. This effect was electric – it was terrific.'

Standing on the steps of his predecessor's caravan, while his listeners sat, Monty said:

I want first of all to introduce myself. You do not know me. I do not know you. But we have got to work together . . . I have only been here a few hours. But from what I have seen and heard since I arrived, I am prepared to say, here and now, that I have confidence in you. We will then work together as a team and together we will gain the confidence of this great Army and go forward to final victory in Africa.

The words were not in themselves 'terrific'. But the way Monty said them, in that dry sharp voice of his, hammering them home one after the other, was. Now, after the initial praise, he turned to the negative side of the Eighth Army, which he had taken over.

I do not like the general atmosphere I find here. It is an atmosphere of doubt, of looking back to select the next place to which to withdraw, of loss of confidence in our ability to defeat Rommel, of desperate defence measures by reserves in preparing positions in Cairo and the Delta.

His audience, suddenly very solemn, knew what the commander was talking about. Jokingly they called what the 8th Army had been doing for nearly two years 'the Benghazi Stakes', a mechanised horse race up to Benghazi and then the customary retreat towards Cairo. Up and down, with the initial victories always ending in the inevitable defeat. Monty finished his measured accusation with a firm 'All that must now cease.'

He turned again to a more positive, if defiant note, delivered in a very solemn tone:

The defence of Egypt lies here at Alamein and on the Ruweisat Ridge. What is the use of digging ditches in the Delta? It is quite useless; if we lose this position, we lose Egypt; all the fighting troops now in the Delta must come here at once, *and will*'. [He paused slightly as he approached the end of his fighting speech.] *Here* we will stand and fight; there will be no further withdrawal. I have ordered all plans and instructions dealing with further withdrawal to be burnt – and at once.

The news that all withdrawal plans were to be burnt must have shocked his listeners, especially those who were on the staff. For them plans were the holy of holies.

Monty took one last breath and then concluded solemnly with: 'We will stand and fight *here* . . . if we can't stay here, then let us stay here dead . . .'

CHAPTER VI
Next week we hit the Germans

They called it 'Operation Torch'. Naturally the code-name for the Anglo–American assault came from Shakespeare. Were they not coming this Sunday, 8 November 1942 to liberate the French in North Africa from the German yoke? This would light a torch that one day would purify, not only French Africa, but the whole of Nazi-occupied Europe with its sacred flame. Nothing but Shakespeare would do.

Now they prepared to land. They had brought their brass bands with them, their huge Stars and Stripes banners, their Class A uniforms. Their weapons they wouldn't need, of course. Hadn't they all learned to chant a slogan in basic French, telling those they would soon liberate who and what they were: 'Nous sommes soldats Americains! Nous sommes vos amis!' Even the limeys in the first assault wave would be wearing the new American helmet so that the French reception committees wouldn't recognise them as the sons of *Albion perfide*, that treacherous nation which had sunk the French fleet here in North Africa at Mers el Kebir in 1940.

But the French probably would not fire on the British even if they recognised them for what they were. They would be too elated. They would be too busy cheering, throwing flowers, bottles of wine, perhaps even given more of themselves, especially if they were French women – and everybody knew just how good *they* were in the hay.

They had seen it all in the Hollywood movies the Army had been feeding them on for the last year or so. The Nazi-occupied European countries with their heroic resistance movements, made up of men and women wearing striped jerseys and black berets, desiring nothing more than to be freed from those jack-booted, black-uniformed evil swine who bore the crooked cross of the beast Hitler on their uniform sleeve.

Now, one month after Monty had decided to stand and then win the Battle of El Alamein, Eisenhower, soon to be his boss, was attempting to make a success of his first battle in a long military career that dated back to before the First World War. It was a tremendous undertaking. Three separate but co-ordinated assaults were to be made by 107,453 soldiers who had to be ferried across U-boat infested waters from distances up to 4,500 miles in 111 transports escorted by no fewer than 216 warships.

The commanders of all three assault forces would be American, generals who had last seen action in WWI, including General Patton, who had not yet been let loose on an unsuspecting world. Included in the 'Eastern Assault Force', as it was called, commanded by General Ryder of the 34th Division, would be the British contingent: a brigade of the 78th Division and a commando. Once a beachhead had been secured, however, this force would become the British First Army which was to race 500 miles to capture the port of Tunis to prevent it from falling into German hands.

The problem of the logistics, immense as it was, was gradually overcome by Eisenhower's planners in London. But there was still the problem posed by the French. The French Army in North Africa, mainly under the command of officers loyal to the Nazi-allied Vichy Government in France, outnumbered the assault force by 50,000 men. What if this force contested the landings? As a worried Ike signalled Marshall in Washington:

> If this Army would act as a unit contesting the invasion, it could . . . so delay and hamper the operations so that the real object of the expedition could not be achieved, namely seizing control of the north shore of Africa before it can be substantially reinforced by the Axis.

In essence the success of 'Operation Torch' depended, at its start at least, on the reaction of the French North African Army. Marshall and Eisenhower believed they had established some understanding with the French generals, who would go over to the side of the Americans (not the hated British) when they landed. But neither of the two generals knew the real state of Franco–American relations, which had been worked out with certain French personages in Vichy. For as usual Roosevelt was playing with his cards held very close to his powerful swimmer's chest.

Back at the turn of the year, when Churchill had spent three weeks in Canada and the States, he had stayed at the White House. There FDR had had himself wheeled over to Churchill's room to discover that the Premier had just come out of his bath. There he stood, dripping water, coloured a delicate pink and minus his false teeth and looking like a toothless Buddha.

An embarrassed FDR had apologised and was about to withdraw. But Churchill, the scion of an aristocratic family which had no inhibitions about nakedness, waved for him to stay, lisping: 'The Prime Minister of Great Britain has nothing to conceal from the United States.' It was a typical example of Churchill's quick thinking and repartee. And it was the truth, too. Churchill, wooing FDR as ardently as ever, really hadn't anything to conceal from America and its President.

FDR was different. In matters French, Roosevelt was already playing a double game. He knew that Churchill had taken up Charles de Gaulle and had made him head of the Free French movement exiled in London. Hard-pressed as Britain was, Churchill provided everything for the immensely tall, prickly French general. For the British Premier, de Gaulle was the man who eventually would bring the mass of the French over to the side of the new Anglo–American alliance.

FDR thought differently. That month he had taken an intense dislike to de Gaulle. At first he tried to persuade Churchill to cut de Gaulle down to size. He suggested to Churchill that he should 'hit him [de Gaulle] in the pocketbook', i.e. cut his money sources. Churchill refused, although he thought that de Gaulle's Cross of Lorraine, the symbol of the Free French movement, was 'the hardest cross he had to bear'. FDR now took another tack.

While Churchill stayed loyal de Gaulle, whom he admired for his stubborn steadfastness, Roosevelt began to cultivate the Vichy Govern-ment, ignoring de Gaulle and his Free French movement altogether. The US ambassador Bullitt had already reported to Washington that the leaders of Vichy thought Hitler would win the war and they were pre-paring to set up a fascist state of their own some time in the future.

Perhaps the future didn't worry FDR. But it should have worried him that the world's greatest democracy was dealing with a regime that followed Nazi orders and carried them to unnecessary extremes. There was the question of the Jews for example.

After the fall of France, the local Vichy authorities in North Africa had placed severe restrictions on the local Jewish population, as was being done in Vichy France. There the Minister of the Interior had ordered all Jews to be rounded up and in due course sent to Germany, where thousands of them would perish in Nazi concentration camps. The Germans had not ordered the Minister to carry out the round-up; he had done it of his own volition. Now that same Minister of the Interior, Marcel Peyrouton had been appointed Governor-General of Algeria, one of the French North African territories the Americans would soon invade.

But FDR preferred dealing with these proto-Nazis than with de Gaulle. It was not just that he disliked the Free French leader. He distrusted him, too. For he felt, perhaps rightly as events turned out, that de Gaulle would, like Churchill, try to maintain the French empire, if he ever came to power. For the time being, however, de Gaulle, so FDR believed, was a British pawn, who would help Churchill to keep control of the Mediterranean. He observed: 'We've got to realise that the British look upon the Mediterranean as an area under British domination.'

To prevent that happening, FDR didn't want de Gaulle, Churchill's puppet, having any part in the operation now taking place in North Africa. Churchill, for his part, thought that de Gaulle would be the ideal person to rally the French in North Africa. When FDR told him that he did not want the general in Africa and that he intended to deal with the Vichy

French there and their generals, who regarded de Gaulle as a traitor with a price on his head, Churchill was shocked. At first he was not prepared to go along with the plan. How could he convince the British people and many in occupied Europe too that it was a political necessity to deal with Vichy appointees?

But in the end, regarding it as a price he must pay for American aid and participation in the battle for Europe, he gave in. He accepted FDR's decision that de Gaulle should not be told the date of 'Operation Torch'; nor was the Free French leader to be allowed to go to French North Africa until it suited Roosevelt for him to do so.

By the time the Allied troops began their landing, Churchill had, under FDR's pressure, abandoned all his reservations. When Admiral Darlan, a virulent anglophobe, proto-fascist and real ruler of Vichy France, made a surprise appearance in North Africa just before the assault, a resigned Churchill told Eisenhower: 'Kiss Darlan's ass, if you have to, but get the French Navy!'

On the eve of the first American battle in the west in World War Two, it was clear that Churchill had been overruled. Not only that, he had also been tricked by a machiavellian Roosevelt, who was working to a political agenda all his own.

In the Atlantic Charter, signed that year by Churchill and Roosevelt, it was stated that the UK and USA would 'respect the right of all peoples to choose the form of government under which they will live'. Churchill might have agreed to this formula, tongue in cheek. But FDR believed in it. Commenting on this business of Churchill, de Gaulle and the French North African colonies, the President stated:

> They're all interrelated. If one [colony] gets its freedom the others will get ideas. That's why Winston is so anxious to keep de Gaulle in his corner. De Gaulle isn't any more interested in seeing a colonial empire disappear than Churchill is.

That was probably true. But in the light of the events of that fall of 1942, the American partner in this 'special relationship' between the UK and the USA was committed to the free determination of nations to decide their own future only when he, FDR, decided who was going to make that decision.

The French in North Africa did not welcome their 'liberators'. Instead the Anglo–American troops met stiff resistance. The assaults were in the main a confused mess. Some American outfits marched off the beach with a large banner waving in front of them, and as one British soldier commented, 'they looked as if they might bring up a brass band playing the "Stars and Stripes For Ever" at any moment'. Others didn't even manage to get off their landing ships. They were slaughtered where they stood. Indeed, before it was all over, six thousand casualties, mostly American, were suffered by the assault force. It was a figure that was hushed up for the rest of the war.

In the confused fighting of the beach, a French *poilu* (footslogger) riding a bicycle was confronted by a bunch of tough-looking commandos with their faces covered in black camouflage paint. He was so surprised that he fell off his bike. Later he told the commandos' interpreter that at that moment he couldn't decide whether to greet the British with 'Heil Hitler, God Save the King, God Bless America, or three cheers for the blacks'; he was that confused.

This unknown French soldier could not have been more confused than General Eisenhower directing his first battle from the caves beneath the fortress of Gibraltar. For more and more unsettling messages were coming in all the time. Then his aides picked up a Vichy broadcast which unsettled Ike even more. The French stated that Admiral Darlan, the second man in the Vichy government, had been visiting his sick son Alain in Algiers. Now he was personally directing the defence of North Africa against the 'American invaders'.

Admiral Darlan was indeed in Africa, though it was doubtful that he was directing operations there. But he did have the power to overrule all French Army attempts to surrender, as Robert Murphy, Eisenhower's political adviser, was currently finding out on the spot.

He had just interviewed General Juin, the most senior French soldier in North Africa, when the latter told him that he, Juin, was hindered in any attempt to surrender by the unexpected presence in Algiers of his superior officer. 'He can immediately countermand any orders I issue,' Juin said. 'If he does, the command will respect his orders, not mine.'

Murphy was stumped. But twenty minutes later, the 61-year-old head of the French Navy, whose great-grandfather had been killed by the British at the Battle of Trafalgar and caused him to hate 'les Anglais' all his life, came in. Known to the Americans later as 'Popeye', Admiral Darlan did not appear to want to parley. He told Murphy: 'I have known for a long time that the British are stupid, but I have always believed Americans were more intelligent. Apparently you have the same genius as the British for making massive blunders.' This was the man, the mainstay of the Vichy Government, whom Roosevelt was prepared to do business with.

In the end a peace was arranged. Roosevelt, seemingly, was prepared to allow Darlan to rule on his own terms, which meant the suppression of the local native attempts at self-government and the continuation of the Vichy policy of anti-semitism. FDR thought it was worth the price. Let the successors to the local Vichy government continue with their fascist policy so that the French North African Army would fight against the Germans, who were now pouring in their thousands into Tunisia from the European mainland.

There was criticism of FDR's policy, of course. Ed Murrow, Pamela Churchill's newest lover, was angrily denouncing it from his London HQ over CBS Radio, declaring to his stateside listeners that he did not know 'what the hell Eisenhower was about, sleeping with the Nazis!' In the States, other critics maintained that 'victory [in North Africa] was a profitable tie-up with the current Congressional elections'. Even Churchill allowed himself some mild criticism. He wrote to the President explaining that 'very deep currents of feeling are stirred by the arrangement with Darlan'.

And when the opposition to Roosevelt's decision continued, Churchill was forced to call a secret session of Parliament. There he explained that since 1776 Britain had had no say in American policy decisions. Whatever Darlan was, the US deal with him had resulted in the Vichy French turning their arms on the Germans in North Africa.

Roosevelt took it all very calmly. He wrote to his son:

From what I hear of what has been happening in the papers, you are learning it is easy for a man to be a newspaper hero one day and a bum the next. The answer is that, just as one must not let his head be swelled too much by bit of acclaim, he must not get too irritated when the pack turns on him.

The heat on FDR lessened when four young French patriots, who had supported the American efforts to get the French North African Army to go over to the Allies, decided to act. They would assassinate Darlan and wipe out the stain on the honour of France – and America, too; for they regarded the US deal with the Vichy bosses as a betrayal.

The leader of the assassins, a fervent Free Frenchman, but somewhat of a dreamer, shot Darlan mortally and was apprehended almost immediately. The details of what happened next are still not clear. For not only the Vichy French in North Africa wanted to conceal them, but also some Americans as well. The killer was tried by a secret court-martial and shot at dawn. The 'Darlan Affair', scandalous as it was, was over.

Now the Anglo–Americans had their victory. For the Americans it was their first of the war, albeit against the French, the people they had come to 'liberate'. But that did not matter to the fighting troops. The men of the 34th Infantry Division and the US 1st Armored, both of which had suffered several hundred casualties, now celebrated their victory. As the French gave up, the men of the 1st Battalion of the First Armored Division went about slapping each other on the shoulder, shaking hands, congratulating themselves on their 'great victory'.

Their commanding officer, a West Point graduate married to the daughter of no less a person than General Patton, was not so sanguine. In the end he called his troops together and lectured them:

We did very well against the scrub team. Next week we hit the Germans. Do not slack off in anything. When we make a showing against *them*, then we may congratulate ourselves.

The future four-star general John Waters was right that November day in the desert. Within four short months, the battalion of which he was so proud would be destroyed and he would be on his way to Germany with several thousand other unfortunate US prisoners to spend the next two years behind the barbed wire of a POW cage.

The 1st Battalion, the British Parachute Regiment made its first combat jump of the war on the morning of 16 November 1942. The Regiment, which Churchill had personally ordered formed back in the dark days of June 1940, had waited a long time for this opportunity and all of them were determined to make it. As their transports started to roll down the field for take-off, a number of the 'Red Devils', who had been ordered to stay behind, were observed running after their aircraft, borrowed parachutes in one hand, weapons in the other. Some twenty of them were hauled aboard by their cheering, laughing, red-bereted comrades.

As the First Battalion historian recorded: 'It is not every man who will disobey orders to parachute into battle.' But then these were not ordinary soldiers. These 'Red Devils' were volunteers to a man. They had survived the tough, long selection process to join the Parachute Regiment. Daily they lived on their nerves, knowing that if they failed, they'd be sent back to the unit from which they had come with those terrible three letters stamped on their papers, ones that would stigmatise them – 'RTU' (Returned to Unit).

The Battalion landed in soft plough, formed up swiftly and began marching towards the village of Souk el Arbs. Here they met the retreating *poilus* of French General Barre's division which was withdrawing under German pressure. However, the villagers were in good heart. They turned out in full strength to welcome the British. They feted them with flowers, champagne and kisses from elderly men with huge white moustaches, sporting the battle ribbons of the 'Old War'.

They pressed on, rejecting (reluctantly) the offers of some of the younger female villagers, to another village where one of their number, Major des Voeux, who had broken his leg, located General Barre himself. He was spruce and trim, but looked 'incredibly old and down-hearted' to the young paras.

Colonel Hill, the CO of the 1st Battalion, decided to cheer the general up. He marched his 500-strong battalion round the village once in their red berets and then again in their helmets. He hoped this would make the general and his soldiers think there were many more Anglais on the ground than there really were. Whether the ruse worked or not, nobody knew. The paras had no time to find out. They were under direct orders of the British 1st Army commander, General Anderson, personally to march eastwards with all possible speed.

At the next 'village' along the line of march, Sidi N'Sir, which consisted of one solitary white house on a hill and a yellow-painted railway station, Major Cleasby-Thompson at the point located some huge black Senegalese soldiers. With these and their French officers they continued their march, heading for the town of Mateur. Fifteen miles short of it, as darkness fell with surprising speed, they halted, and bought some eggs and sheep from local Arabs, who seemed to be everywhere, scrounging and stealing and probably spying too for the advancing Germans (for many of them were anti-French and pro-German). Then they ate and fell into a deep sleep. But not for long.

Suddenly there was a burst of sten gun. They were awake immediately. One of their sentries had spotted something. The Germans were coming. Three enemy armoured cars and three scout cars were rolling towards them.

Hastily the paras prepared an ambush; and it was ideal country for ambushes. As one of the paras recalled long afterwards: 'On one side of the road, the hills rose steeply and on the other the ground was extremely boggy.' In other words, it would be very difficult for the Jerries to get off the road once they were attacked.

The sappers mined one end of the road in a hurry. Meanwhile, the Red Berets made arrangements to 'close the door' with more mines at the other end, once the Germans had entered the trap.

Tensely, their jobs done for the time being, the paras waited. Two young officers moved up the road a little. Lieutenants Mellor and Kellas clutched sticky bombs, known as Gammons. They would adhere to anything they hit. Now, hiding in the ditch at the side of the road, they could hear the motors of the six German reconnaissance vehicles approach in low gear. As yet they were still out of sight.

Suddenly an Arab appeared out of nowhere. He was riding on a skinny-ribbed donkey in the direction of the approaching Germans. Hastily, the two young officers ducked. They did not want him to see them and report their presence to the Germans. For a fleeting second they thought they ought to kill him. In the end they decided against it and he rode over the wires without exploding a single one of them!

A few moments after the Arab on the donkey had disappeared around the bend, the first German vehicle nosed its way cautiously into view. It was a six-wheeled, open reconnaissance car, its aerials swimming back and forth like silver whips. The paras sweated. They held their weapons in hands that were suddenly very damp. Would they pull it off? In a minute all hell would break out and most of them would have to kill a fellow human being for the first time.

Abruptly the front end of the recce vehicle rose into the air with a roar.

A ball of scarlet flame exploded beneath it. Next instant it had rammed its ugly snout into the rock wall. The trap was sprung.

Mellor and Kellas didn't hesitate. They leapt out of their hiding place and flung their sticky bombs. They didn't miss. Two other scout cars behind the first one came to a sudden halt. Already flame, greedy blue flame, was creeping up their steel sides, the paint bubbling in ugly blisters.

Now the paras' team, firing the ambushers' only mortar, sprang into action. The obscene snarl and plop of a mortar bomb being fired followed. The bomb sailed high into the sky. It seemed to hang there for a moment. Then it came hurtling down to explode in a shower of pebbles and soil at the end of the German mobile column.

Like a trained shepherd's collie forcing sheep into a pen, the mortarmen forced the German column ever closer to where the wrecked, blazing armoured cars lay. Another vehicle was hit. Two Germans fell to the road dead. Now the paras poured on the fire, hitting the trapped, panicking Germans from both sides of the road. Here and there individual Germans managed to save themselves. But soon the survivors surrendered. The First Battalion, the Parachute Regiment had won its first battle and the demoralised French were duly impressed. They felt that the Anglais had some kind of secret weapon which would knock out the heaviest German armour. It was recorded that 'suddenly the French commandant became whole-heartedly pro-Ally'.

But where were those other allies – the Americans?

Two days later, Hill and his Red Devils found them – four howitzer teams eager for action. They had gone through the British soldiers who had intended to guide them into positions overlooking Medjez. Waving gaily to the Britons and shouting mock insults at them, the men of General Ryder's 'Red Bull'* Division shot over a rise and disappeared, leaving behind them a cloud of dust.

For a while that heavy, brooding African silence reigned, seemingly typical of that empty continent. Then came the sound of heavy firing beyond the rise. A worried British officer reported 'guns of all calibres firing'.

Colonel Hill, who was present, became worried. What were the Yanks up to? Were they in trouble? He soon found out that the gun teams 'had worked it out that one of them should be the first American to fire the first shot against the Germans in this world war'.

In fact, as the 'Red Bull' men explained later, they hadn't seen any Germans, so they had fired at the Medjez church steeple instead. 'They [the Americans] had clobbered the innocent church well and truly.' Hill was philosophical. The colonel, who would see much violent action before the war was over and had no intention of racing for the honour of firing

*Thus named after its red bull divisional patch.

the first shot at the enemy, asked one of the young gunners why he had fired at the church steeple anyway. The reply was because he wanted to 'see if he hit it'. That answer, Colonel Hill concluded, 'seemed fair enough'.

But soon even the Americans would not by vying for that particular honour. Before this campaign in North Africa was over, some of them would see more than enough action.

Anderson now made one last attempt to break through before the reinforced Germans dug in for the winter – and winter in French North Africa was going to be a matter of freezing cold, mud, even snow. He threw in the 2nd Battalion of the Parachute Regiment, commanded by a battle-experienced CO, Lt Colonel John Frost, who was to win renown as the defender of the 'bridge too far' of Arnhem two years later.

The 500-strong battalion dropped twenty-five miles below Tunis with no transport, save for a few commandeered donkeys and carts and no heavy weapons. They headed northwards looking, as one para recalled, 'like a fucking travelling circus rather than a parachute battalion'.

Within hours the German panzers cornered Frost's battalion. They drew back, taking and giving casualties. Time and again they escaped German traps only to fall into another one. Now they were losing men rapidly. They were running out of food and water, too. Tormented by thirst, the paras of the 2nd Battalion licked the dew off the cactus leaves or the rain from their capes.

After three days trying to find their own lines, the retreating paras bumped into an American patrol. 'Doctor Livingstone, I presume,' Frost said with a weary attempt at British-style humour. The Yank didn't get it. But now it didn't matter. Frost knew it was over for the Second. The survivors had fewer than one hundred rounds of rifle ammunition left among them, and they had suffered 289 casualties in dead, wounded or missing. Half the battalion had been lost due to inexperienced generals and bad planning by staffs, who lived in great comfort far behind the front line.

Still, Colonel Frost, the big, burly para officer, who had made his first combat jump nearly two years before, formed the survivors up in ranks of three and in the best tradition of the British Army, they marched proudly into the nearby town of Medjez-al-Bab.

That was the end of the campaign in Tunisia for the year 1942. Two weeks later, Eisenhower's mentor in Washington, General Marshall, signalled Ike at his luxurious HQ in Algiers:

Delegate your international diplomatic problems to your subordinates and give your complete attention to the battle in Tunisia.

In other words: stop the jaw-jaw and get on with the war!

CHAPTER VII
North Africa will be defended

At the front, it rained, cold, grey drizzle, which together with the fog on the heather-covered hills, made the place look more like Scotland than Africa.

For weeks they had attempted to batter their way through the mountains. To no avail. German Fallschirmjäger, some veterans who had made the first airborne assault of the war on Fort Eben Emael back in '40, plus German tanks stopped them time after time. The French had been the first to attack, then the British and after them the Americans. None had succeeded in the 'bloody djebels', as the weary bitter infantry called those dank, wet African valleys where death lurked.

The 'Red Devils' had come out after suffering 1,700 casualties, well over half their strength. The PBI (Poor Bloody Infantry), such as the Hampshire Regiment, had gone into action, 800-strong. They were withdrawn with exactly six officers and 194 other ranks left (and of the latter there were 100 men who had been kept in reserve). The Americans had fared no better.

Now, in December 1942, the front had settled down into a moody, trigger-happy stalemate. The men dug in into the thick goo of Tunisian mud and tried to make the best of it. Food was not very plentiful. The mud was so bad that rations and other supplies had to be off-loaded on to mules two miles behind the front, which would then make their laborious progress, mostly at night, to deliver the rations and at the same time take away the casualties, which at times ran to 250 men, a quarter of the battalion, a day.

Australian war correspondent Alan Moorehead, who was there, described that terrible mud thus:

The dead were buried in mud and the living were in it up to their knees. They were wet to the skin day and night. They had mud in their hair and mud in their food. When the mud dried, it set like iron and had to be beaten off their boots with a hammer or a rifle butt. Before the astonished eyes of the commander, tanks went down to their turrets in mud. A spell of a few fine days made no difference – the mud was there just the same, and if you sent out a squadron of tanks, you never knew whether or not they would be caught in another downpour and so abandoned to the enemy.

But it was not only the mud that made life miserable for the man at the front that December. It was cold, for the nights were freezing. A B Austin, the correspondent of the British *Daily Herald*, heard one Louisiana GI complaining in 'his high-pitched Huckleberry Finn drawl':

Folks back home think Africa's warm. They should be here at night. Brrr! If there was rain, the puddles should be crackling.

'I have never been as cold ever since as that winter of 1942 in Tunisia,' said Captain Eric Taylor of the British 78th 'Battleaxe' Division:

All the infantry up front had was a hole and what they could carry or loot from the abandoned French colonial farmhouses. At night we crawled into our hole, wrapped in anything and everything we could find, including rugs and carpets looted from the farms and tarpaulins stolen from the gunners. For a couple of hours you could manage to keep reasonably warm, but by two or three in the morning the biting cold mountain air would steal into your very bones and you'd praying for dawn and first light, trembling in your hole like a young puppy, with the stars looking down on you icy and unfeeling.

But those young men, British and American, over sixty years ago, were hardy creatures. They had gone through the Depression of the '30s and had always known lean times. The war and the shortages everywhere had toughened them up even more. Now hundred of miles from the 'civilisation' they had once known – pubs and bars, baseball games and soccer matches, palais de danse and poolhalls – they lived a strange life, unimaginable to their folks back home. If they were in tanks, they lived a wandering nomadic life; if they were infantry, they existed like primitive cave-dwellers.

'We stood to mostly just before dawn,' remembered ex-Trooper Frankland of the 17/21st Lancers.

It was forbidden to brew up during the hours of darkness and we would be standing there above the 'flimsies', the 2-gallon petrol cans filled with petrol and earth, matches at the ready, trembling like leaves, just to get at the first hot brew of the char. There was always somebody who couldn't wait. Even before he was allowed to do so by the officer and NCO he'd drop his match in the mix. There'd be a soft whoosh of petrol exploding, a spurt of blue flame and suddenly all the other blokes would be putting their dixies and messtins on top of the cans to boil up the char. Naturally the bloke who had acted without orders would get a bollocking from the sarge. We didn't care. We were too busy opening up the compo ration boxes to get at the hard tack, which we'd smear with plum and apple jam before we got our dirty paws on the first free fags of the day (seven per man). Lovely grub!

Breakfast over and with a watchful eye for the German snipers, who were very expert, the men would 'take a shovel for a walk', with a wad of 'Army Form Blank' in their other hand. Or if they were lucky and sheltered, they'd go to the 'thunderbox', where they'd sit side by side on a pole suspended on two ration boxes above a hole. Even to take 'a shit' in peace was a great comfort under those harsh conditions.

Not always, however. For many of them suffered from the 'quick sits' (they had a cruder expression for it). For the virulent three-day bout of dysentery was epidemic. A wash. A shave in cold water. The face red and raw for the rest of the day (for this was the British Army). And the 'battle' could commence – swanning around the 'bloody djebels' hoping to catch 'Old Jerry' off guard. They rarely did, for 'Old Jerry' was a skilled soldier. And as the historian of the British 76th Division wrote after the war: 'The German troops in North Africa were highly trained, skilful, courageous and at their best in defensive positions and delaying fights.'

So they lived out in the wilderness. When there was no patrol activity, they 'lay doggo' in their pits, or as they called their slit trenches 'wanking pits' (though most of them didn't have the energy for that kind of sexual relief), talking about 'bints' (girls), 'desert chicken' (bully beef) and the 'flying dhobi wallahs' (Arab laundry men), who seemed to appear out of nowhere when the front was quiet, looking for anything of value they could lay their fingers on, including abandoned parachutes which they turned into ladies' knickers. Though who bought them, the soldiers didn't know, for most Arab women they'd seen didn't wear knickers (or so they had been told).

Nobody like the Arabs. At Tabassa, where the II US Corps was based, the natives brought large sections of the communications system to a standstill by cutting fifty-yard lengths of the US Signals Corps' wiring out in order to make clothes lines. At night the Arabs crept up and dismantled the hessian sacking screens around the men's 'crappers' to make cloaks for the men and rough sandals for their womenfolk. As the GIs cracked to one another about the habits of the locals: 'The Arabs have broken through and are bringing up vital supplies – of rugs and shoeshine boxes!'

One cynical writer on the US Army newspaper, *Stars and Stripes*, summed up the Arabs thus:

The truth will some day have to be told to our children. We, their fathers, will confess the North African campaign never really ended.

When leaving the continent, will go the story, we fell into a disorganised retreat with the Arabs on our heels; and we left behind to our opponents great stores of cigarettes, candy and GI clothing. '*Baraka*,' say the Arabs, meaning 'blessings'.

But if there was not much in the way of '*Baraka*' for the hard young men at the front, there was plenty to the rear where General Eisenhower had his headquarters in the Hotel St George in Algiers. 'A peacock, 'Churchill called it contemptuously, 'all tail.'

Chocolate, candy and cigarettes could buy everything and anything – even 'white meat', as the staff GIs called the local French women. Even as far back as Casablanca, where Patton was located, they were singing a dirty ditty on that subject. It was called 'Stella' and sung to the tune of 'Abdul-Abulbul-Emir' and its first verse went:

> Now every young tanker who was in Casablanca,
> Knows Stella, the Belle of Fedala,
> A can of 'C' rations will whip up a passion
> In this little gal of Fedala.

It was true certainly of Algiers with its famous Kasbah. There were plenty of brothels, mainly for the 'guys who brought up the Coca-Cola', as the frontline GIs quipped of the rear echelon: '*One* guy in the line and *five* guys to bring up the Coca-Cola.'

And the GIs had a lot of money. As a correspondent of *Stars and Stripes* wrote that December when the front bogged down, American soldiers and French civilians

> . . . are having a wonderful time getting acquainted. So far everything's as rosy as a honeymoon in Utopia, with the French trying hard to explain how glad they are to have us here and the Americans reciprocating by spending *beaucoup* francs and passing out unheard of quantities of such previously unobtainable titbits as chewing gum, candy bars and cigarettes.

In fact the Top Brass was not 'having a wonderful time getting acquainted'. Eisenhower, in particular, had been spending up to two thirds of his time – until he received Marshall's signal of 22 December – dealing with the French. In the end he would become heartily sick of the French politicians and their generals with their permanent concern with 'me, me, me', as a harassed Ike put it.

The situation was not so acute with the British generals under Eisenhower's command. But there were problems. Anderson, commander of the British 1st Army, was obviously a failure. His Christmas message to his troops stated: 'You have done splendidly and fought most gallantly. Keep up your efforts and I know we shall surely win.'

The reality was different. In a private letter to Field Marshal Brooke, Anderson wrote:

I felt deflated and disappointed, but it's no use getting depressed, it would be all too easy if we all attempted everything and succeeded, and the Almighty is much too wise to spoil us mortals that way.

When Eisenhower heard of that letter, he commented that Anderson 'blew hot and then blew cold'. He never knew where he was with the man. But Anderson, who would soon disappear from the history of World War Two, was just another problem for the sorely tried Ike.*

He had to face the fact that most British officers didn't think very much of the 'new boys', the Americans, and even less of him as the Supreme Commander. By now a lot of the British were calling the Yanks 'Alice', (signifying 'sissies'), which was not a very complimentary term. With that he could cope. But Eisenhower found it more difficult to deal with the criticisms of Brooke or even the British political adviser Harold Macmillan, whom he regarded as a friend and who would one day be British Prime Minister after he, Ike, had become President.

Macmillan, who like Churchill was half American, said for example to another British officer:

You will find the Americans much as the Greeks found the Romans – great big, vulgar, bustling people, more vigorous than we are and also more idle with more unspoiled virtues, but also more corrupt.

He added, as if the British were still in full control of these new 'Romans' which they weren't: 'We must run AFHQ (Allied Forces HQ) as the Greeks ran the operations of the Emperor Claudius.'

As if it wasn't enough that Ike had problems with the French and the British, he also had plenty on his hands trying to keep his West Point friends, the top American generals, in line.

Proximity to the British over the last three months had deepened the latent anglophobia of several leading US generals, including Patton, Clarke, and later Bradley, who took his cue from Patton. The British (with the exception of Field Marshal Brooke) were circumspect in their complaints about the 'Yanks'. Not the American brass, however. By now the Americans realised that they were being patronised by the British. The

---

*In the end Montgomery got rid of the general he called the 'good plain cook'. When, two years later, Anderson tried to visit the British Army in Normandy, Monty was so outraged that he had to be stopped from having Anderson arrested.

latter had been fighting the war for three years (not very successfully it must be admitted, with the exception of Monty's victories). But the British thought they knew enough about fighting the 'Huns' that they could look down in scorn at the Americans, whose last experience of combat had been back in 1918.

In many ways, Eisenhower realised that the British critics of the American generals were right and justified. US troops had suffered (and soon they would suffer even more) on account of inadequate planning by their leaders.

US generals didn't seem able as yet to assess the enemy correctly, and more often than not they carried out very sketchy reconnaissance and the like before they attacked. Indeed, generals such as Patton seemed to regard the campaign as some kind of game, an ego-trip for an ageing warrior.

But the major problem for Eisenhower, as 1942 came to a close, was the man who was working the closest with the British that December. He was Major-General Lloyd D Fredendall, commander of the US Second Corps. Aged 59, a veteran of World War I, he was a cocky, opinionated officer, who was a 'Marshall Man'. He had arrived in Africa believing that Eisenhower didn't want him because he outranked him. For a little while he languished as the military governor of Oran, where one of his acts was to give an airfield contract to a Vichy fascist despite the Frenchman maintaining he was against 'The Jews, the Negroes and the British'.

That statement must have pleased Fredendall, for when he took over II Corps Headquarters, taking its tone from the corps commander, the HQ became a hotbed of anti-British sentiment. The staff officers mocked the plummy accents of visiting British officers and cupped their fingers around their right eyes, as if they were wearing monocles. They even created a little bit of doggerel, which went:

When the British First got stuck in the mud
And settled down for tea*
They upped and beckoned for the Fighting Second
To help in Tunisee

In fact the headquarters of the 'Fighting Second' was established eighty miles behind the front. It was located far up a canyon that could only be

*In all the US accounts of WWII, there is much mocking of the British Army's habit of taking time out of battle to drink tea. What the Americans didn't or wouldn't realise was that water discipline was very strict in the British Army. It was a relic of colonial wars in waterless areas. In the British Army under combat condition, a soldier took water from his waterbottle only with an officer's permission. In the US Army, soldiers could have a drink any time they wanted.

reached by a single, fairly impassable road constructed specially by II Corps engineers. There Fredendall had his engineers labour for three weeks to dig bomb-proof chambers underground, while the staff went around in steel helmets, carrying pistols as if the Germans might well emerge from the surrounding pine trees at any moment. 'Most observers who saw this command post,' the reporter recorded, 'were somewhat embarrassed and their comments were caustic.'

Even Colonel Carter, in charge of the tunnelling, was embarrassed by the waste of labour and material involved. He tried to dissuade Fredendall, but the cocky little general wouldn't have it. As Carter wrote later:

> To make digging as unpopular as possible in an effort to have it stopped, I made sure the blasting was done at night to keep everyone awake. But that didn't stop it.

Now Fredendall, whom Eisenhower had welcomed to North Africa despite his misgivings, had become a major headache. Not only was the elderly general an anglophobe, he also seemed to hate his own subordinates. Now he was turning his HQ, officially known as 'Speedy Valley', but called by his contemptuous troops in the field 'Lloyd's Very Last Resort', into a laughing stock among those in the know.

For it seemed that Fredendall was primarily concerned with his own safety. Not only was he having the massive underground system con-structed, but he had ordered an armoured Cadillac, similar to the one used by the Supreme Commander, and was constantly on the phone to Oran asking whether the automobile had arrived from the States. It was said when aeroplanes were heard overhead, Fredendall's gaze would shoot towards the sky and he would intone: 'I hope they're some of ours.'

Now in the last days of December, Fredendall was supposedly organising his Second Corps for battle. As Eisenhower had instructed him, he was 'to provide a strategic flank guard for our main forces in the north [Anderson's First Army],' and later, 'to undertake offensive action in the direction of Sfax and Gabes in an effort to sever Rommel's line of communications with Tunisia.'

In other words, this anglophobe, who was commanding his corps from far to the rear, was to take part in America's first serious encounter with the Germans, working closely with the British. How would he do? Would his fears and prejudices undermine this first major US effort with disaster and was disgrace a possibility if they did? For Eisenhower knew that if the USA had been at war for a year, and had not achieved a victory in North Africa, heads would roll, his in particular.

He had realised already that the most senior British soldier, Field Marshal Brooke, had little confidence in him. Eisenhower would have been even more depressed if he had known what 'Brookie' was writing in his personal diary for 28 December.

> Eisenhower as a general is hopeless. He submerges himself in politics and neglects his military duties, partly, I am afraid, because he knows little if anything about military matters.

As for his own chief and mentor, Marshall, he had already warned Ike, as we have seen, to forget the politics and get on with winning the battle for Tunisia. But could he win it, burdened as he was, not only with green soldiers, but also with a cocky, loud-mouthed, opinionated Fredendall, who might well be a coward to boot?

That December Eisenhower could not function like the victorious, vain Montgomery, who possessed tunnel vision. Monty ignored all other considerations, political, personal, the power of the press, in order to carry out his plans. He wanted to 'kick the Hun out of Africa' and everything else had to take second place to that objective.

As we have seen, Eisenhower was preoccupied with political considerations and the administration of an area of a million square miles, inhabited by nearly twenty million people. Ever since he had worked with General MacArthur and later with Marshall as a senior staff officer in Washington, such considerations had figured largely in his life. By their mid-40s all important American generals would become 'political' generals. The result was that Eisenhower did not have the single-minded preoccupation and sense of purpose that all great captains need. Eisenhower had not yet learned to bend people and events to his purpose.

Naturally Eisenhower was clever enough to know he was not doing his job properly. He had read enough military history to know how a great captain should act. It riled him. Once he burst out with: 'For Chrissake, do you think I want to talk politics? Goddammit, I hate 'em.' Now, sensing rather than knowing that he was failing and Roosevelt was harbouring private doubts about his ability to continue in supreme command, he snorted (aware that if he were dismissed he'd return from being a three-star general to his permanent pre-war one of colonel): 'Tell Roosevelt I'm the best goddam lieutenant-colonel in the US Army.'

On the last day of 1942, one year after the United States had gone to war, General Eisenhower held a dinner party in his commandeered villa in Algiers. Prior to it, during the afternoon, although he was suffering from flu and had spent part of that day in bed, he dictated his thoughts about the campaign in French North Africa. He said: 'On the whole I think I keep up my optimism very well, though we have suffered some sad disappointments.' Eisenhower realised of course that 'only the sissy indulges in crying and whimpering' and that 'the need now is to get tougher and tougher'. A commander had to take losses in his stride and 'keep on everlastingly pounding until the other fellow gives way'.

Then Eisenhower forgot duty for a while and, although he didn't feel so well, he 'partied'. All his 'little gang' were there, including Kay Summersby and their dog Telek. There were a couple of 'visiting firemen' present, too, such as Sir Ian Jacob, Churchill's deputy adviser on military matters. The latter thought that he ought to make a little speech to cheer Ike up. For his master Churchill still thought Eisenhower was the best American to have in command and under his control some day in the future in London. As Jacob noted in his diary: 'He [Ike] has such an exuberant and emotional temperament that he goes up and down very easily.' He thought his speech 'might well have a large effect in restoring his self-confidence'.

Apparently it did. The drink and the vivacious presence of Ike's 'chauffeuse' did as well. The Supreme Commander forgot his worries about 1943. He mellowed. Around midnight, after all the kissing and shaking of hands, the slapping of backs, toasts and 'Auld Lang Syne', the men started playing bridge.

Eisenhower opened the bidding and made seven hearts. It was a good sign. They continued to play and drink. Finally, at one thirty on the morning of 1 January 1943, Eisenhower wound up the proceedings by making a grand slam vulnerable, which, as Jacob noted, 'put the seal on his happiness'.

Writing in his journal the next morning, Ike's PR man, a hung-over Lt Commander Harry Butcher, remarked, 'I could use ... some aspirin today.' All the same it had been 'a swell evening' and Ike's luck at cards seemed to Butcher to be 'a good omen for the coming year'.

A thousand miles away, on the other side of Africa, another commander was ill and despondent that New Years Eve. Field Marshal Rommel, the 'Desert Fox' and for two years the commander of the Afrika Korps, now in retreat after Monty's great victory at Alamein, was suffering from fainting fits and dysentery. He had lost a lot of weight and his face was covered with desert sores. But unlike Ike he had no Kay Summersby to cheer him up. Card playing he thought a waste of time and he was not particularly fond of drink.

Once he had been a great popular German hero. The press had lauded him. Hardly a day passed without his photo appearing in the Goebbels-controlled papers. Girls and women by the score had sent him fan letters. They had even sold picture postcards of his hard, tough face at newspaper kiosks as if he were some movie star like Johannes Hesters or Wolf-Albach Retty.

But that had been before his defeat at El Alamein and the long retreat westwards with what was left of his battered Afrika Korps. Now Rommel was virtually a pariah, starved of supplies and men, while to the east, facing the British and the Americans, General Juergen von Armin was receiving both in great quantities, ready for the coming confrontation with the Allies in Tunisia.

A month earlier he had flown to Germany to plead the case of his army with the Führer personally. But Hitler was in no mood to be tolerant and humour his one-time favourite. He attacked the 'Desert Fox', asking why he had allowed himself to be defeated at El Alamein. 'You had better material, stronger artillery, more tanks and air superiority,' he snorted.

Lamely Rommel had excused his army by saying, 'We ran out of fuel, mein Führer.'

'Fat Hermann', as Reichsmarschall Hermann Goering was known behind his fat back, who was present, had sniggered and said: 'Yes, but your vehicles fled back along their coast in their hundreds. You had enough petrol for them.'

Rommel had kept his temper with difficulty. What did the fat fool with his drugs, jewels and fancy uniforms, which he changed a dozen times a day, know about the war? 'We had no ammunition, Herr Reichs-marschall,' he replied.

'All the same you left shells by the tens of thousands behind at Tobruk and Benghazi,' Goering countered.

Rommel had flushed at that. He snapped, 'We didn't have enough weapons either.'

Hitler had jumped on him for that. 'Your men threw them away,' he had barked. 'Anyone who doesn't have a weapon must croak.'

So, in angry outburst, Rommel had let them have the truth. It was nothing short of a miracle, he said, that his army had managed to escape this far from the English. Unless it was not withdrawn to Italy it would be destroyed – and so would all German and Italian forces in Italy, once the enemy succeeded in setting foot on the continent of Europe.

The outburst had been too much for Hitler:

Marshal, I don't want to hear any more of that kind of nonsense from your mouth! North Africa will be defended like Stalingrad is being defended. Eisenhower's invasion army must be destroyed at Italy's door, *not* in the Sicilian living room.

Rommel said it was a good idea. But he needed more tanks, more fuel, more men. In the last twenty months, he explained, he had never received enough supplies to defeat one army, the British Eighth. Yet now he was expected to defeat two.

Hitler cut him off. 'North Africa will be defended, Generalfeld-marschall,' he snapped. 'That is an order.'

Rommel had said no more. Angry and frustrated, he had flown back to Africa, landing near the stone marker at El Agheila, where the great

German African adventure had started in early 1941. Time and time again he had defeated the 'Tommies' until he had almost reached Alexandria and the Delta. Those had been great days, with victory following victory.

But they were over. Victory was only a dream now. His Afrika Korps would never quit the continent. His men would leave their bones to bleach in the African sun. There would be no Dunkirk for him. He knew Hitler. He would order the Afrika Korps to fight to the 'last round and the last man'. Russia had shown just how ruthless the Führer could be even towards his most loyal soldiers.

Two days earlier Rommel had written his New Year letter to his wife Lu, back in Stuttgart. He had phrased it almost as if it was a Soldier's *Abschiedsbrief* (letter of farewell):

Our fate is gradually working itself out . . . It would need a miracle for us to hold on much longer. What is to happen now lies in God's hands . . . We will go on fighting as long as it is at all possible.

Now as he lay in the truck that served as his home, sick and shaking with the jaundice that had plagued him over the last year, Erwin Rommel considered what he should do. Already he had lost one of his best units, the 21st Panzerdivision which had gone to von Arnim in Tunisia. More would follow. In the end Hitler would probably convince the Italians to send their armour over to Tunisia. Then he would be left with his infantry only. They would be easy meat for Montgomery's tanks when he made his final attack.

Perhaps, in the end, Hitler might save him from the disgrace of the defeat that was inevitable and fly him out of Africa before the final debacle. After all, the Führer knew he was a sick man. Indeed, he was the only one of his original staff who had come to Africa with him to be still in the field; the others had long since returned to the Reich on sick leave or to hospital. Yes, Hitler could pull him out, if he wished, on the grounds of illness.

But what then? He couldn't return home to be put on the 'Führer Reserve' list, which had been the fate of so many other top German generals who had incurred Hitler's displeasure: men such as von Manstein, von Rundstedt, Halder and all the rest who the Führer thought had failed him. If he was to return home without his army, which was likely, he had to do something to show his men, the nation and his fellow officers that he had tried to the very end – that he had achieved something before illness had forced him to return to Germany. But what?

On that last night of 1942, the seeds were being sown for a victory from which would come defeat for German arms in Africa. For the first time since 1918, the Greater German Army would commence a major attack on the US Army. Part of that army would break and run in panic. As one intensely patriotic US general* who fought in both wars would claim, it would be 'the first – and only – time I ever saw an American army in rout'.

In a way that victory from which came defeat would mark a turning point in the Allied war. Thereafter there would be only Allied victories and defeats for their German enemies. But the battle to come would also mark a change in that 'special relationship', which Churchill believed existed between Britain and America. The roles of the two partners would begin to change drastically. Britain would become the junior partner; and if, as Roosevelt suspected, Churchill thought the victory in Africa would ensure the continuation of the 400-year-old British Empire, the PM would be mistaken. Roosevelt had plans for colonial empires, including the British. With the USA emerging as the senior partner, and FDR calling the shots, Churchill, who had declared he had not become the 'King's First Minister' to preside over the end of the British Empire, would have to learn otherwise.

Out at the front, far from the machinations of the 'base wallahs' and the devious plotting of the politicos, the little man, French, British, American – and German, too – who did the fighting and the dying, slept. Here and there a flare shot into the night sky to burst into bright, blinding light, then to fall spluttering like a doomed angel. Now and then a machine-gun might chatter nervously for a few moments. Tracer might zig-zag between the lines in a lethal morse.

But as the night wore on and it became increasingly colder, the only sound became the singing of the sand – the millions of grains contracting in the night cold, rubbing against one another to give out a strange, hunting melody.

It was the year of decision. It was 1943.

* Major-General Ernest Harmon.

1943

Don't tell me when they take off. It makes me too nervous. He is the truest friend. He has the greatest visions. He is the greatest man I have ever known.
Churchill, North Africa, 1943, on President Roosevelt's departure by air for the United States

CHAPTER VIII

He aint gonna jump no more

Back in the UK, most of the British Army was still in training, supposedly for the cross-Channel attack the Americans had proposed for the new year. Since Dunkirk, the six infantry and four armoured divisions, which were ready for action, had not fired a shot in anger. The several battalions of the South Lancashire Regiment were no different from the rest. Most of their soldiers didn't really mind the life.

After all, most of the non-regulars had lived on and off the dole for months, even years, before the war. Now at least, they had a regular wage (very low), three square meals a day and a roof over their heads, and, if they were married, an allowance for their wives and children. Every six months they would be entitled to fourteen days' paid leave (more than they'd ever had in peacetime), and most nights, if they weren't on a 'scheme' and could get a pass, they could go to the nearest NAAFI, 'Sally Ann' (Salvation Army) canteen, or pub and get a cup of tea or a pint to wash down their 'treat' of egg-and-chips or beans on toast. It was all very routine and boring, but at least it was safe and predictable.

Naturally some men didn't enjoy the boredom of it all. They had joined up to fight, have adventures, see a different world from the humdrum one of their previous civilian existence, with its endless routine of pub, pictures and palais de danse. These men volunteered to join the commandos, the new paras or the even newer Reconnaissance Corps, in which to live a fast life if a short one.

There were even men who deserted to go to fight the enemy, almost single-handed. Such was the case of 55-year-old Sergeant Peter King and 26-year-old Private L Cuthbertston of the Army Dental Corps, stationed at Aldershot. Refused permission to join a combat unit, they armed themselves with stolen grenades and revolvers and headed for the coast. Here they 'borrowed' a boat and headed for Cherbourg, two years before the US V Corps took the French port city. Here they sniped at Germans, stole their paybooks, etc. and to everyone's surprise returned safely to England with their booty. The authorities were so impressed that the charges of stealing government property and desertion were dismissed and the bold couple were allowed to join a combat formation. Later, Sergeant King was killed in action.

But the beginning of 1943 saw the Army reaching into this safe, almost peacetime world, looking for 'bodies' to replace the casualties suffered in North Africa and build up the assault formations such as the commandos and, above all, the paras.

In their bold but failed attempt to beat the Germans into Tunisia, Colonel Hill's Para Brigade had in a few short weeks suffered 1,700 casualties, well over half the brigade. Now that brigade had to be made up as part of the British 1st Airborne Division, which would spearhead the assault on what Churchill called 'the soft underbelly of Europe' (GIs would quip cynically 'tough old gut', but that was later). In addition, Churchill, the founder and advocate of airborne troops, wanted a new airborne division formed in England by the early spring of 1943. This would be called the 'Sixth Airborne', to fool the Germans that there were four more between the 1st and the 6th. But where were the troops to come from? It took time to train paras; therefore the men, all volunteers, could not come from the already trained assault divisions waiting, in theory, to invade France.

So the Army authorities turned to those infantry battalions which had not been integrated into divisions and which had spent the time since Dunkirk in coastal defence and suchlike duties. One of these was an obscure battalion of the South Lancs, the 2/4. In 1941, together with its sister battalion of 1/4th, it had been turned into part of the 164th Infantry Brigade, which was part of the 55th Division, and was fated never to go overseas.

For nearly two years the 2/4 had moved from town to town, shaking down time and time again, doing guard duties and supplying reinforcements for units going overseas. Thus it was that it took months before the South Lancs were sent to Aldershot with the rest of the 55th Division for actual fighting training. This had come as a shock to many of the civilian soldiers. But at Aldershot, the home of the British Army, they had at least learned the discipline and how to bear themselves as 'real soldiers'. In the years to come, some of them would prove in combat that they had learned those lessons all too well – those few of them who survived.

But by early 1943 the days of 'bullshit reigning supreme' were about over.

The South Lancs were going to depart from the ordinary infantry and be asked to volunteer for what was then the most elite regiment in the British Army, the newly created Parachute Regiment; the men who bore the red beret so proudly and the blue wings of a trained para on their brawny shoulders.

At the time, two new parachute battalions were created to join the new 6th Airborne Division, the 12th (Yorkshire) and its rival, the 13th

(Lancashire). The future 13th Parachute Battalion, still known as the 2/4 South Lancs, were called together by the CO Colonel Russell and asked if they would volunteer for parachute training. There are no surviving eye witnesses of the occasion, but one can guess what those young men must have felt, as they stood there in the parade ground at the 'at ease' position with the CO looking down at them intently.

Most of the South Lancs, poor men who had probably never spent a night away from home until they had been called up, had never been inside an aeroplane before, probably never seen one at close quarters. Now they were being asked to jump out of one suspended by a piece of white 'knicker silk', as they would come to call their chutes. It must have been a tremendous shock for them. In a moment they would have to make that overwhelming decision in front of their comrades, who might well judge them to be brave or yellow depending on what kind of decision they made.

Perhaps that was the reason the authorities had urged Colonel Russell to assemble them thus en masse and put the question to them in front of their fellows. We don't know. What we do know is this. Out of 500-odd infantrymen, 220 volunteered to join up as parachutists and enter that unknown and very lethal world of the elite 'Red Devils'.

The 13th Parachute Battalion was in being and, as the men were dismissed, the volunteers, instinctively separating themselves from those who had refused, must have wondered if that 'thirteen' was going to be unlucky for them. For many, as we shall see, it would.

Hurriedly, aware of the fact that most of those who went to war by air were a superstitious lot, with their lucky rabbits' feet, teddy bears, good luck charms and the like, the CO tried to lighten the unfortunate connotation of number 13. As we have seen, the South Lancs had taken their regimental motto from Shakespeare's phrase 'They win or die who wear the Rose of Lancashire' and had abbreviated it to 'Win or Die'. Now the newly formed battalion took it a little further. They created a new motto from the old one. It was '13th Battalion, unlucky for the Hun'.* They would, in due course, live up to that new motto. But the butcher's bill for doing so would be very high.

Now the two hundred-odd South Lancs, plus volunteers from other regiments, set about the dangerous and back-breaking task of becoming paras. First of all they were sent to Hardwick Hall, the Airborne Force Depot, to be toughened up. All of the young South Lancs were A1, the Army's top fitness category. But if they thought they were fit, they had another think coming.

Under the leadership of those feared fanatics of the Army's Physical Training Corps, shaven-headed hard men in white vests, under which

* Based on the bingo call, 'unlucky for some'.

their muscles bulged, they were chased 'at the double' from one exercise to another watched all the time for the least sign of weakness or lack of determination. Naturally the failure rate was high which led to the fate that all the new boys dreaded 'RTU' (Returned to Unit). But those who succeeded in passing the two weeks of living hell went on to undertake parachute training at No. I Parachute Training School at Ringway, near Manchester, the site of the present-day International Airport.

Here the course also lasted two weeks. The trainee para learned how to exit correctly from a plane, control his chute and how to land without injuring himself. In the great hangars at Ringway, there were grouped the fuselages of Whitleys and then later Dakotas from which the fully fledged paras would really jump later. From these the trainees would learn to exit without 'clocking' themselves on the edge of the hole as they did so.

Thereafter, the trainee graduated to the 'fan'. This consisted of a drum around which was wound a steel cable attached to a parachute harness. When a trainee jumped from a platform twenty feet high, his weight caused the drum to revolve, taking him down to the same impact he would experience when he jumped for real.

'The 'tower' came next, one hundred feet above the ground. From the 'tower' the trainee would launch himself into the air to find himself suspended in mid-air beneath a canopy. When he was able to adopt the correct position for landing, he was then lowered to the ground.

Relentlessly the training continued, getting tougher and tougher by the day. The trainees were now subjected to the balloon, which even trained parachutists hated. Four men sat around a hole in the basket of a tethered balloon some seven hundred feet above the ground. On the command 'Go', the first man of the 'stick' would launch himself through the hole to drop a stomach-churning 120 feet before his chute opened with a startling, frightening crack. After two drops from the balloon, those who had not already flunked out, were almost relieved to start their five jumps from a real aircraft.

However, these descents were not without their hairy moments. In 1943 the Army was still using converted bombers. Unlike the Dakotas that the 13th Parachute Battalion would use in combat, there was no side exit and the paras had to jump through a hole in the floor. If they did this incorrectly, they received a nasty blow to the mouth or the jaw. The result was that a good few young men in their prime would be wearing false teeth before they were finished with Ringway.

Then there were the problems of the 'twists' – the front and rear rigging lines getting intertwined, so that the canopy would not open correctly; the 'blown periphery', when the canopy rolled up like a skirt; and finally 'the streamer', when the canopy did not open at all so that the para plunged to his death in what these hardened young men called half-fearfully, half-cynically the 'Roman Candle'.

By the time it was all over and they had done their seven jumps, which qualified them for the red beret and the right to wear the blue wings of a trained para on their shoulder, they had become a tough cynical lot indeed.

Bawdy songs, that made light of their fears, included:

> Jumping thro' the hole
> Jumping thro the hole
> I'll always keep my trousers clean
> When jumping thro' the hole

and

> He jumps through the hole with the greatest of ease
> His feet were together and so were his knees
> If his 'chute doesn't open, he'll fall like stone
> And the blood wagon will take him away.

The worst of them, 'What a Lovely Way to Die, ended with:

> There was blood upon his lift webs
> There was blood on the floor
> And there he lay like jelly in the welter of his gore
> . . . and he ain't gonna jump no more.

Before it was all over there would be many of these new boys of the 13th Battalion, the Parachute Regiment who weren't 'gonna jump no more'.

While new efforts were now being made in Britain to build up more combat battalions, including parachute ones for the newly formed 6th Airborne Division and the existing 1st Airborne, which would experience its first action as a complete division soon, the 'Invisible Soldiers' were arriving in the UK in their thousands.

In 1942 the US Army decided they'd send whole battalions of these 'Invisible Soldiers' to Britain, not as combat soldiers, but as service troops to carry out camp construction, maintenance, transport and general quartermaster duties. Unlike their fellow Americans of the infantry and armour who were now also arriving in divisional strength, they were not welcomed by military bands or politicians and generals making speeches of congratulation. Instead, like the Invisible Soldiers that they were, they almost sneaked into the country, as if the leaders who had sent them to the UK were ashamed of them.

In reality those leaders were not ashamed of them. These 'Invisible Soldiers' had important roles to play overseas, if only to free their white

comrades to do battle with the enemy, from which they were officially
barred. These 'colored' soldiers of the Republic belonged to an army
which had been virtually segregated for almost half a century and their
military leaders had grown up believing them to be inferior, not worthy
of bearing arms for the country of their birth, the greatest democracy in
the world, or so it proclaimed itself.

General Marshall, their military chief, thought little of them. He
maintained that the best postings for 'colored' troops would be Alaska
and the Aleutians, where the sun shone far into the night; for when it got
dark most black soldiers would panic and run away. The Supreme Commander, although he didn't express his opinions on the subject publicly,
routinely called his soldier servants, who were black, 'my darkies', as did
most of his contemporaries. Surprisingly enough, the only senior US
general who would accept US soldiers into combat units was that epitome
of prejudice, General Patton, who maintained that any black man who
volunteered for his Third Army could tell his grand-children that he
fought for his country and didn't 'shovel shit in Louisiana'. Even the US
Army's Commander-in-Chief, President Roosevelt, was not exempt from
racial prejudice, despite the Atlantic Charter of 1941, which had proudly
proclaimed that all people had a right to freedom and self-determination.
But all those lofty aims, supposedly advocated by FDR, did nothing to
advance the cause of the black American race within the USA's own
borders.

Every now and again Roosevelt would trot out the Atlantic Charter,
which Churchill had also signed, to air his views on the 'Four Freedoms',
which were supposedly the basis for his wartime and post-war
philosophy. In fact the Atlantic Charter, according to Roosevelt, didn't
exist, as he once told reporters. He and 'Winnie' had dictated bits of it to
their secretaries. The rest had been put together by American and British
officials. As he told a bunch of chuckling reporters: 'There is no copy of the
Atlantic charter, as far as I know. I haven't got one. The British haven't got
one.' As far as his black soldiers went, that was true.

Up to that time there was little anti-black feeling among the general
British population. Indeed most Britons had never seen a 'negro' before
the 'Invisible Soldiers' arrived. As the US soldiers' newspaper *Stars &
Stripes* reported: 'The Negroes have found a people [the British] ready and
willing to make them feel at home.' As one witticism of the time had it: 'I
don't mind the Yanks, but I can't say I care for these white chaps they've
brought with them.'

A letter from a British canteen helper working with the Americans was
opened by the censor and was found to read:

We find the coloured troops are much nicer to deal with; in canteen life
and such, we like serving them, they are always courteous and have a

very natural charm that most of the whites miss. Candidly, I'd far rather serve a regiment of the dusky lads than a couple of the whites.

But although his wife Eleanor was passionately concerned with the plight of the 'coloreds' (though she still used words such as 'darkies' and 'piccaninnies', which gave offence to the Blacks), FDR was again selective in his choices of 'freedoms'. Just as he had preferred to deal with the Vichy antisemites and neo-fascists in North Africa, he concerned himself very little with the lack of freedom for those hundreds of thousands of his black citizens who were drafted just like their white comrades and deserved the same treatment and rights. Again FDR's sense of real politik and knowledge of the US electorate (after all his Democrat Party relied largely on the Southern vote and the South was anti-negro) overruled all other factors. US foreign policy, as always, would be dominated by domestic issues and the need to win the next election.

Now in this January of 1943, Roosevelt had other and more pressing problems than a rearrangement of the post-war world and what role the 'Invisible Soldier' might play in it. Although FDR, unlike Churchill, Hitler and Stalin, concerned himself little with the day-to-day running of the war – in his case he left that to Marshall – he did realise that something had to be done about the stalemate in North Africa and Allied strategy for 1943/44.

Thus it was that he decided to run the risk and terrible strain of making the long, wartime journey to the African continent, despite the poor state of his health.

It is said that President John Kennedy relied on a frightening cocktail of drugs, including methadone and codeine, to kill the pain of his various ailments. In addition he took Ritalin and thyroid hormone to liven him up and librium and barbiturates to calm him down. We know this, in part, thanks to the Freedom of Information Act.

In the time of FDR no such act existed. His medical records were kept by two naval doctors, Admiral McIntre and Commander Bruenn. Thus they were able to classify what they knew as naval secrets that were only partially made known many long years after President Roosevelt's death. What we do know of the President's health during the wartime period is explained by just what lengths his aides and secret servicemen went to conceal the extent of his crippling illness from the general public and the press in particular.

Throughout his long journey, whenever he had to be moved, with his wasted lower body often concealed in a large naval cape, he would be wheeled hurriedly to some sealed off place, stripped completely, his underwear soaked in sweat, to be given a rubdown, a change of clothing, especially underwear, plus a stiff shot of whisky to revive him.

Yet FDR was prepared to undertake such a challenging journey because he knew that not only military decisions were needed in the Middle East, but also political ones. As Churchill would remark to him when they met, they were there 'because we have no [suitable] plan for 1943'.

So finally FDR arrived at Casablanca at the suburb of Anfa, where Patton had prepared a new camp for the President and other illustrious guests. The villa complex, fragrant with the smells of mimosa and begonias, ran down to the sea. It had a bombproof shelter, especially made for the President, and housed so many secret service agents to protect him that Patton protested.

Indeed the whole area was so luxurious that the GIs who visited the place from combat zones called it 'the Ice-Cream Front' and there were so many whores that even the most innocent of GIs could lose his virginity within five minutes of stepping off the 'deuce-and-a-half' (two and a half ton truck), which had brought him here. Still the local authorities assured worried US generals that the VD rate in the local Moroccan brothels had long stayed 'absolutely steady' – at one hundred percent! The new camp at Anfa and the surrounding area of Casablanca were the first of those 'little Americas' which the US Army would take with it everywhere it went for the rest of the 20th century, in some cases, a complete replica of 'back home America'; and as cut off from the 'economy', as the local civilian world was known, as the earth is from the moon.

And so the 'VIPs', as such persons were now being called, arrived. The chiefs-of-staff came with six truckloads of trinkets for trading with the 'natives', as well as parkas, arctic gear and snowshoes just in case their plane missed North Africa and crashed somewhere farther east, say in the snowy wastes of the Russian winter. General Marshall, for his part, went to the opposite extreme. He had been warned that malaria was prevalent in Africa and that he should take proper precautions. Thus, to the surprise of the British officers, dressed in khaki drill and shorts, waiting to greet him, the US Chief-of-Staff stepped off his plane in mosquito boots, gloves and a floppy, veiled hat like that worn by beekeepers.

So the Americans, obviously not too well prepared for the world away from Washington, came to plan the future, and now for the first time they would be dealing not only with Churchill, but also his chiefs-of-staff and the relative dark horse, who would now become first a nuisance and then a definite irritant, even a threat to Eisenhower, for the rest of the war. The recent victor of El Alamein, Field Marshal Montgomery, was about to take his place centre stage.

CHAPTER IX
Wollt Ihr den totalen Krieg?

At two thirty on the afternoon of Friday 15 January 1943, General Eisenhower faced up to a dozen senior Allied generals of the Anglo–American Chiefs-of-Staff. In the outer world that day, things were moving. At Stalingrad the beleagured Sixth German Army had refused to surrender. Now it was under attack by the Red Army. In Africa, two thousand miles away, the British Eighth Army was on the attack again. Now they were within two hundred miles of Tripoli. In the air too there was considerable activity; German-occupied ports and submarine bases on the French coast were undergoing heavy bombing, while the weakened Luftwaffe in that same country launched another of their 'tip-and-run' raiders on England, attacking two schools and killing several children. No one paid much attention to that raid, save the grieving relatives. Nearly eighty thousand British civilians had been killed or badly injured in such raids already. Death, even of children, had become commonplace in Britain over the last three years.

Flushed and replete with good food and wine for those who wanted it, the generals took up their places in a high-ceilinged conference room, full of dappled sunbeams and the fragrance of flowers. It was a world away from that of the fighting fronts. Now, however, they were assembled to hear from the 'new boy', Eisenhower, how he intended to plan the rest of the campaign in North Africa, defeat Rommel and allow the chiefs to get on with the rest of the war.

It was not going to be an easy task for Eisenhower, although he was a highly articulate staff officer, used to briefings. But now he wasn't facing a staff conference, back in Washington, lecturing officers whose combat experience was like his own – nil – or limited to a few months of trench warfare back in France in 1918. These bemedalled generals had fought in wars over three continents in a dozen countries ranging from India to Ireland.

Nor did Eisenhower look very impressive this warm Friday afternoon. He was haggard from overwork, was suffering from high blood pressure, not made any better by the four packs of cigarettes he was now smoking a day, and there were deep purple bags under his eyes. FDR commented:

'Ike looks jittery.' He was and his mood was not helped by the fact that he had spent the last fifty miles of his flight to Casablanca standing at the door of a faulty Flying Fortress with his parachute in his hand, ready to jump.

Now, speaking with notes, he went straight into his plan for the next phase of the African attack, 'Operation Satin', only to discover that he had jumped with both feet right into a mess. Brooke rounded on Eisenhower almost immediately. While Marshall, Eisenhower's boss and mentor, seemed to be dozing after a heavy lunch, he started to tear the helpless Eisenhower and his plan to pieces. He gave chapter and verse why it could not succeed.

An embarrassed Eisenhower went on the defensive. He forgot the plan. He said he faced the dilemma of allowing his troops 'to deteriorate by remaining inactive in the mud or suffering some losses through keeping them active'. The latter, Eisenhower believed, 'was the lesser of two evils'. It was not an argument to impress Brooke. An experienced commander didn't keep his men 'active' by throwing them into some useless operation that could only result in casualties.

Eisenhower could see he was getting nowhere with Brooke. Nor was he getting any support from Marshall. So with his face set and grim, he saluted and beat a retreat. In due course 'Operation Satin' would be hastily buried and forgotten.

Brooke confided to his diary that day that Eisenhower was 'deficient of experience and of limited ability'. Even his old friends and supporters thought that Ike had performed badly and that, perhaps, his days in command were numbered. Patton sat up with him, trying to console him and cheer him up, until one thirty in the morning. Later, however, Patton wrote in his diary: 'He thinks his thread is about to be cut. I told him to go to the front. He feels he cannot, due to politics.' Commander Harry Butcher, his PR man, was even less sanguine about his boss's chances. He wrote in his celebrated diary: 'His [Ike's] neck is in a noose and he knows it.'

When Ike had first gone up to the front in Tunisia with the much decorated British airman, 'Broadie' Broadhurst, he had spotted a dead guardsman hanging on the barbed wire after the fierce Battle of Wadi Akarit. Surprised, Eisenhower had exclaimed: 'Say Broadie, that's the first time I've seen a dead body.'

For people such as Brooke and Montgomery, that type of reaction marked the difference between them and the American Supreme Commander, soon to be Montgomery's boss. By the time Ike had graduated from West Point in 1915, together with General Bradley, one of the Englishman's greatest enemies, Montgomery had been a severely wounded and decorated major. One year later, when Ike married his Mamie, on 1 July 1916, sixty thousand British soldiers had been killed and wounded in a matter of hours on the first day of the Battle of the Somme.

But Montgomery was to go further than even Brooke, his mentor, in this criticism of the Americans and of Eisenhower in particular. Fearless and sometimes foolhardy, the victor of El Alamein was not afraid of being unpopular. If there were unpleasant things to be said about his fellow British officers (whom he criticised more than he ever did the American generals) and the Americans, he would say them. No one, save perhaps Brooke, intimidated Montgomery. He stood up to Churchill, who never developed the warmth with Montgomery that he did with Alexander and Eisenhower. At times he might have had Churchill's ear, but in private the PM said of the future field marshal that he was 'indomitable in retreat, invincible in advance; insufferable in victory'.

Now this little gadfly of the British military establishment was learning of its doubts about the man who might well soon be his boss; the same American he had told off for smoking in his presence a few months before. More importantly, his own Eighth Army, readying for victory, was getting ever closer to the Anglo–American force commanded by Eisenhower. But where was the co-ordination of the two efforts in Africa?

As Montgomery wrote at the time:

> Vested interests are beginning to creep in. We want some very clear thinking; the object must be kept very clear and pursued ruthlessly; we must not be led away on ventures that do not help in achieving the objective.
>
> We really want unified command; you cannot conduct operations in a theatre of war with a committee.

Montgomery was probably right. But the fault in his argument would be the same that continued right up to the end of the war in Europe. Vain and self-opinionated as he was, Montgomery believed that the 'committee' would have to be replaced by one single commander. It goes without saying that that man had to be Bernard Law Montgomery.

One the whole, the British top brass ended their part in the Casablanca Conference of January 1943 well satisfied. They had thrown out Eisenhower's plan for an attack in North Africa,' Operation Satin'. They had avoided being committed to a cross-Channel attack in 1943. Instead they had convinced the Americans to commit its first troops in Europe in Churchill's 'soft underbelly': first Sicily and then Italy proper. In essence, while Eisenhower's command would be committed still in North Africa, it would really only provide a supporting operation to help the new star of the British Army, Montgomery, in the kudos of final victory in that continent. After nearly three years of defeat, victory, defeat in the 'Benghazi sweepstake', Monty's Eighth Army would rightly be honoured by finally defeating the 'Hun'.

However, Churchill and Roosevelt had not finished talking about the more political aspects of the war. After settling (so he thought) the problems of the French and in the course of doing so making more of an enemy of de Gaulle than ever (a French enmity which would last into our own time, fuelled by a seemingly permanent Gallic suspicion of Anglo-Saxon motives), Roosevelt addressed the reporters present at his last news conference. He said:

> I think we have all had it in our hearts and heads before, but I don't think that it has ever been put down on paper by the Prime Minister and myself, and that is the determination that peace can come to the world only by the total elimination of German and Japanese war power.

He continued by guessing that even the British reporters present would know the story of U S Grant of Civil War fame, demanding at Appomattox in April 1865 that Robert E Lee of the South should surrender unconditionally. Whether the British knew that fact or not, they were certainly puzzled about what the President was leading up to. Now he told them.

FDR said that similar terms seemed fitting in this war.

> The elimination of German, Japanese and Italian war power means the unconditional surrender of Germany, Italy and Japan, but it does not mean the destruction of the population of Germany, Italy or Japan, but it does mean the destruction of the philosophies in those countries which are based on conquest and subjugation of other people.

Roosevelt paused, gave the reporters one of those flashing, toothy smiles of his and added that the reporters might even consider calling this conference at Casablanca 'the unconditional surrender meeting'. In fact, that conference had been called specifically to plan the military strategies for the rest of the war and was not intended to engage in political discussion about a war that was not won yet by a long chalk. Roosevelt's statement had indeed caught Churchill completely off guard; he had known nothing about it in advance. But as always the Great Man, despite his age, was a quick thinker. Swiftly he nodded and pontificated:

> I agree with everything that the President has said. The Allies must insist upon the unconditional surrender of the criminal forces who plunged the world into storm and ruin.

Later FDR maintained that the concept of unconditional surrender had 'just popped into my head'. It was typical of his secretive nature, as always playing the game with his cards held close to his chest. In fact, it seems, he had been considering the matter for several months. Indeed, the US Chiefs-of-Staff had already briefly discussed the concept a few days before, when German-born US General Wedemeyer had warned his fellow generals that 'unconditional surrender would unquestionably compel the Germans to fight to the bitter end'. It would also 'weld all of the Germans together'.

Wedemeyer was to a large extent right. The concept which had just popped into FDR's head was taken up immediately by the Nazi 'Giftzwerg' (poisoned dwarf), Dr Josef Goebbels, known thus on account of his vitriolic tongue and small stature. The Minister of Propaganda and Public Enlightenment would henceforth use it to urge the German people and armed forces to ever greater efforts to win the war. If they didn't, there would be no future for a beaten Germany. *'Wollt Ihr den totalen Krieg?'* he would shriek at a select audience in 1943. 'Do you want total war?' and the Germans would yell back *'JA'*.

Roosevelt, as always with his mind on other aims than those of his fighting men, and who would shed their blood to achieve them, had not done his soldiers a service with the supposedly off-the-cuff declaration. But such matters worried FDR little.

As he saw it, the demand for unconditional surrender had tied Britain in to continuing to fight against Japan, even if Germany surrendered first. It had also soothed Russian fears that the Western Allies might sign a separate peace with Germany, the kind of crooked deal that the USA, primarily, had just made with the murdered Admiral Darlan. To FDR's way of thinking, the three Allies, Britain, America and Russia were tied in to fighting the war to the bitter end, cost what it may.

Back in the UK, the wartime press made little of the 'unconditional surrender' announcement. The conservative *Daily Telegraph* was fairly typical when it reported on Tuesday 26 January:

President Roosevelt and Mr Churchill have met in North Africa to decide on future Allied operations . . . addressing a press conference at the conclusion of the ten days' discussion, Mr Roosevelt said that peace could come only through unconditional surrender by Germany, Italy and Japan. Mr Churchill claimed that the enterprise of this conference had altered the whole strategic conception and conduct of the war.

That was about it.

But there were those in positions of power in the UK who were not happy with 'unconditional surrender' and any of the President's pronouncements, which former Foreign Secretary, Lord Halifax had already warned were 'pretty inchoate' and both 'explosive' and 'feckless'. Foreign Secretary Eden was perhaps the most important. He thought that FDR was taking too pro-Soviet an attitude in order not to appear to Stalin to be taking the British side. 'We felt that, just as in WWI, the USA would abandon Europe once the war was won.' So Britain needed powerful European allies, in particular France. Churchill had warned Eden against promoting de Gaulle, whom the PM considered 'our bitter foe'. He begged the Foreign Secretary not to 'allow our relations with the United States to be spoiled through our supposed patronage of this man ... whose accession to power in France would be a British disaster of the first magnitude.'

But Eden was not going to follow the PM's advice in this matter or in other areas of foreign policy. He saw more realistically than Churchill, so grateful to the USA for this 'special relationship', which he and FDR enjoyed, that in 1943 Britain could still influence events. She was still providing the manpower for the battles to come – it would be 1944 before the USA could equal Britain and then exceed her in the number of soldiers it provided. Once the balance had turned in America's favour, however, the USA would really start calling the shots.

Eden believed that Britain could still carve out a policy, which would allow her to keep an empire – it was clear that FDR was intent on doing away with it, especially India – and stabilise Europe under some sort of Franco–British alliance, which would present a common front against Stalin's territorial ambitions. To do this, Britain would have to work for Great Power co-operation to ensure a stable world *now*. Unfortunately Churchill was not interested in working now for a post-war world. As he often mocked when such matters were raised, one had not to overlook Mrs Glass's Cookery Book recipe for jugged hare – 'First catch your hare'. Win the war first and worry about such matters then. Ironically enough it was Eden, when he became Prime Minister, who presided over the final stage of the dissolution of the British Empire after Suez in 1956. Back in the war he had warned, if something was not done, Britain might become 'the penurious outpost of an American pluto-democracy or a German *gau*'.* But Churchill wouldn't have it and his successor would pay the price.

On the last Sunday of Roosevelt's visit to Casablanca, FDR and Churchill were given a splendid dinner by the senior American diplomat in Marrakesh, Kenneth Pindar. They sang and drank well into the wee small hours. At about 8.00 am FDR was wheeled and driven to the local airport. Churchill, who was going to stay another two days in Marrakesh, insisted on accompanying him, wearing a black dressing gown, slippers and with an air marshal's gold-brimmed cap at a rakish angle and naturally smoking a huge cigar. This he brandished at the waiting photo-graphers, snarling: 'You simply cannot do this to me.' But they did, despite the fact that he had forgotten to put in his false teeth.

The two great men said their good-byes and, as the African sun started

* Nazi province

to rise above the mountains to the south-east, Churchill got back in his car, as Roosevelt's plane began to warm up for take-off. Now the PM clutched Pindar's arm saying: 'Don't tell me when they take off. It makes me too nervous.' He paused and added emotionally, 'If anything happened to that man, I couldn't stand it. He is the truest friend. He has the farthest vision. He is the greatest man I have ever known.'

'Smiling Albert', otherwise known as Field Marshal Albert Kesselring, arranged the meeting between the two ground commanders, Rommel and von Arnim. The big, burly overall commander in the Middle East was smiling as usual as he met them on 'neutral' ground at the Luftwaffe base at Rennouch, Tunisia. But he had never felt less like smiling. The situation was grave and now at this eleventh hour, he had to get two prima donnas to agree on a plan of attack before the 'Tommies' assaulted in strength.

It was eighteen years since Erwin Rommel and Jurgen von Arnim had last met. Now, on this Tuesday 9 February 1943, nothing had changed between the two officers; they still disliked each other as general officers just as they had as lowly captains. That was why there had been virtually no contact between them since the previous December. The time for temperament, as 'Smiling Albert' saw it, was over. That was the reason he had arranged this meeting at which he would dictate to them *his* plans.

All the previous month von Arnim had been battering away at Anderson's British First Army. The week before he had changed the direction of his attack and had started to assault Koeltz's 19th French Corps and its attached Americans with some success. It had hit Ryder's US 168 Infantry Regiment and had taken 1,100 prisoners.

Now the senior intelligence officer of von Arnim's 21st Panzer Division maintained that the morale of US prisoners was high, though they seemed very inexperienced as soldiers. The French POWs, on the other hand, were very bitter about their new allies, 'les Americains'. They claimed that the 'Americans sent us to the front line, while they stayed to the rear'. The intelligence officer ended his briefing by remarking that both French and British officers were contemptuous of the Americans, referring to them as 'our Italians'. It was a point well taken by Rommel, who had had to fight with the Italians, badly armed and badly led, for two years now.

As he listened, Rommel guessed what Kesselring would suggest – an attack on these natives of what the Germans called the 'Land of Boundless Possibilities', the Americans. A few minutes later 'Smiling Albert' confirmed Rommel's guess. 'We are going to go all out for the total destruction of the Americans,' he said. 'They have pulled most of their troops back to Sbeitla and Kasserine. We must exploit the situation and strike fast.' Swifly he sketched in his plan. Rommel would attack the Americans to the south, at the oasis town of Gafsa, and von Arnim would do the same to the north at Sbeitla. Once through the mountain passes, the two German armoured divisions involved would head for the port of Bone, supported by the remaining Italian armour. This bold stroke would remove the threat to the Afrika Korps' flank and might even cut off Anderson's First Army. Above all, however, it would give them a victory. Leaning across the desk, the burly Luftwaffe Field Marshal, his gap-toothed smile vanished now, said somberly: '*Meine Herren*, after Stalingrad our nation is badly in need of a victory.'

An hour later Kesselring was in his plane, heading back to his HQ in Rome. Now it was only five more days before the German Army commenced its first major attack on the American enemy in World War Two.

CHAPTER X

Fredendall's no damned good

At four o'clock on the morning of 14 February, St Valentines Day, 1943, Colonel Waters, Patton's son-in-law, commander of the 1st Battalion, the US 1st Armored Division, rose early as he usually did. He climbed straight to his observation post on top of Djebel Lessouda. There he exchanged a few words with the shivering, unshaven GIs of his unit, who had spent the night up there. He peered through his binoculars across at the Haid Pass.

He could see nothing. Overnight a fierce wind had blown up. It had swept across the mountains straight from the Sahara. With it the wind brought flurries of razor-sharp grains of sand. They stung the colonel's face, making him blink and obscuring his vision. Indeed it was difficult to hear anything over its howl and whine. In the end Colonel Waters gave up and went back down the hill to his tent.

Just as he reached it, the field telephone rang. It was his commander's second-in-command'. What's that shooting?' he demanded

'What shooting?' Waters answered.

Apparently firing had been reported on the road between Faid and Lessouda. Waters told the second-in-command he'd check it out. He hung up and tried at once to contact the troops in that area by radio. No answer. He sighed and set off to climb the escarpment once more. Up on top he again could not hear or see anything. Then came a sudden break in the keening of the desert wind. Now Waters heard it. The ominous rumble of artillery. There was a fire fight going on down there. Did it mean the Krauts were coming at last?

They were. Two whole battle groups of the German 10th Panzer Division were advancing on the positions of the 1st Armored's CCA. With them they were bringing Germany's new secret weapon: the sixty-ton Tigers of the German 501st Heavy Detachment. Before them they were driving everything back. Indeed, the handful of armoured infantry and artillerymen, which Colonel Waters had in position down there, were already retreating in near panic, uttering the cry that would become familiar to many Allied servicemen in the years to come, flung from mouth to mouth, 'TIGERS . . . The Tigers are coming!'

Waters, the West Point graduate, was as steadfast as he had been the day before when he had met the 'first team'. He didn't hesitate. He ordered up fifteen of his light Honey tanks to confront the attackers. A futile gesture. His Honeys armed with a 37mm popgun were no match for the German tanks, carrying massive 75mm and 88mm cannon. One after another they were blasted to pieces. Their shells bounced off the Germans' thick steel hides like white-glowing pingpong balls.

Now German Messerschmitt fighters joined in the battle. They came hurtling out of the morning sky, yellow-painted noses whirring, cannon chattering as they attacked at zero feet. Swiftly the noise of the battle grew to a crescendo, and as it did, Waters realised to his alarm that the Germans were sneaking in on both flanks. He ordered his command post – jeep and a White scout car – to pull back farther up the djebel. As he did so he counted eighty-odd German vehicles including tanks milling around in wild confusion. With a sinking feeling he realised he was surrounded and already Arabs, who as usual had appeared from nowhere, were pointing out his little command group to the Germans. Colonel Waters knew instinctively that time had nearly run out for his First Battalion.

It was the same for much of the US 1st Armored Division's CCB. Bravely Colonel Hightower, commander of the Division's 2nd Battalion, an officer who would one day command an American army himself, tried to stop the rot. He sent his Shermans forward. The new battle commenced. Solid AP shot zipped back and forth in a lethal morse. But more often than not, the burning blurs of white bounced off the thick shells of the German Tigers and Mark IVs. One single shot from the Germans, however, striking anywhere near the Sherman's rear sprocket would set the US tank's petrol engine ablaze immediately. No wonder their US crews called them 'Ronsons', after the well-known lighter.

But Hightower's men were also beginning to give. A whole reconnaissance company, a hundred men or more, simply raised their hands and surrendered tamely. Others took off their helmets, raised them as if in salute and cried the only word of German they probably knew – 'Kamerad'. Artillery support crumpled. The gunners began to abandon their pieces without even trying to break the weapons' firing pins. Officers tried to stop them, using their pistols. Others held out their hands like children playing tag in a playground. In vain, the panic-stricken men simply pushed past them.

Watching these terrible scenes, Colonel Drake of the CCB called its commander General McQuillan and cried over the racket: 'They're running away General. Your men are running away.'

McQuillan gasped: 'You don't know what you're saying . . . They're only shifting position.'

'Shifting position, hell,' Drake cried angrily. 'I know panic when I see it.' With that he slammed the phone down and waited for his own positions to be swamped.

By this time, his own tank hit and abandoned, Colonel Hightower had managed to get back to HQ to discover that he had exactly seven tanks left out of an original fifty-one. Like Waters' First Battalion, his own was effectively wiped out. Now, with the two tank battalions destroyed, it was the turn of Colonel Drake's infantry. By mid-afternoon the 600 men of his 2nd Battalion were cut off under the command of young Major Robert R Moore. Moore feared Drake more than he did the Germans all around him. In fact Drake had told the young battalion commander that any soldier who attempted to leave his position without orders should be shot. So despite German pressure, Moore held on, even though he had already seen what was left of the 1st Armored Division's tanks fleeing to the rear.

At dusk, however, Moore thought his luck was about to change. A light plane flew over his position and dropped a message signed by no less a person than the divisional commander, General Ward. It read:

Tank destroyers and infantry will occupy positions at 2200 tonight to cover your withdrawal. You are to withdraw to position ... where guides will meet you. Bring everything you can. Ward.

Moore made his plan immediately. They would move out in an extended column, making no attempt at concealment. That way Moore thought the Germans might take them for their own troops in the darkness. All wounded and prisoners would go with them. If the POWs made one wrong move, they'd be bayoneted in cold blood.

They moved. They bumped into German artillery position almost immediately. A German called out something. In the van Moore ignored him. The artilleryman shook his head and sat down again. They went on. After a mile, Moore heard voices to his front. His heart leapt. It had to be the guides that General Ward had mentioned. He was wrong.

The voice called something in German. Moore tried to bluff it out. This time his luck had run out. Somewhere to the flank a German machine-gun opened up. There was no mistaking that high-pitched, hysterical burr of the German MG42. Moments later silver flares started to sail into the night sky. Moore reacted at once 'Scatter,' he yelled. 'Run like hell!'

That did it. The men started running, dropping their equipment, and the wounded, as they did so. Thirty-six hours later Moore and twenty men reached the US line to hear a voice cry: 'Are you that lost infantry bunch?' Moore gasped they were, adding: 'Oh boy, am I glad to hear your voice.'

But his elation soon vanished when he was taken to the nearest HQ and told that only 300 of his men had reached safety. He had lost half his battalion.

Colonel Drake, the regimental commander, fared no better. Leading his own command and stragglers back, he was overtaken by German tanks. A German in a scout car ordered him to surrender. Drake snorted 'Go to hell', and turned his back on his would-be captor. But in the end he had to. His men were surrendering on all sides, letting themselves be looted by the triumphant Germans. Like so many of his men of the US 168th Infantry Regiment, he was heading for the cage, where he'd remain behind barbed wire for the rest of the war.

As that bloody first day of the Battle of the Kasserine Pass, as it became known, drew to a bloody close, it was clear that the Germans had achieved a great victory. In the US Second Corps' first engagement with the enemy, the Americans had suffered grievous losses.

Two days before, when Eisenhower had visited II Corps, the US 168th Regiment had 189 officers and 3,728 enlisted men. Now, even though one battalion had not been engaged in the fighting, it had only fifty officers and 1,000 soldiers left. General McQuillan's own command had fared no better. He had lost fifty-two officers and 1,526 men, including three colonels 'missing, presumed dead'.

The full extent of the German victory on that bloody St Valentine's Day was made even clearer when an American reconnaissance plane flew over the Faid pass to discover forty-four US trucks abandoned by their drivers and burning like torches. Now as the battle continued into its second day, the US Army would suffer a defeat unmatched in American military history during WWII until the December debacle of 1944, when the last German counter-offensive of the campaign in Europe caught the American forces completely by surprise.

'What happened during the night of 19–20 February,' states the official US history of the campaign in North Africa, 'cannot be clearly reconstructed from the record.'

Very true. The situation was totally confused. In a matter of less than a week, the US II Corps had retreated or withdrawn eighty-five miles, much more than the American forces would do in the Ardennes. Parts of five US divisions were involved in the battle, commanded in some cases by complete strangers, absorbing 800 reinforcements daily, all of whom seemed over-aged and poorly trained. British officers led US outfits, as well as their own. Soldiers of America's premier division, the 1st US Infantry, 'the Big Red One' ('There's the Big Red One and then the rest of the US Army,' they boasted proudly) surrendered as easily as any green rookie rushed to the front to make up numbers.

US General Ernie Harmon, a barrel-chested, gravel-voiced veteran of World War One, was being rushed up to Fredendall's HQ to take over his shattered 1st Armored Division. Trying to fight off sleep, he allowed Eisenhower to do up his shoes for him (afterwards he always boasted that a President of the United States had once tied his shoe laces). But once he got to the front all sleepiness vanished. For he was appalled by what he saw. As he wrote in his memoirs:

I have never forgotten that harrowing drive; it was the first and only time I ever saw an American army in rout. Jeep, trucks, wheeled vehicles of every imaginable sort streamed up the road toward us, sometimes jammed two and even three abreast. It was obvious there was only one thing in the minds of the panic-stricken drivers – to get away from the front, to escape to some place where there was no shooting.

Nor was he impressed by the state of mind of those men's commander, Fredendall. He found the corps commander sitting on a chair near the stove, drinking. Fredendall's words shocked Harmon, who regarded himself as unshockable. Fredendall said: 'We've been waiting for you to come. Shall we move the command post?'

In his deepest bass Harmon replied: 'No sir. We will let it stay here.'

The corps commander seemed happy with that. He handed Harmon a type-written sheet ordering the latter to take over command of the battered 1st US Infantry Division and also the British 6th Armoured Division, over which Fredendall had no authority. Harmon, who believed he was sent up by Eisenhower to take over command of the equally battered 1st US Armored Division, was now completely at sea. Still he kept his cool. He kept his opinions to himself. Thereupon Fredendall, who clearly thought Harmon was in charge, told Harmon that he was expecting the Germans to give him their 'Sunday punch' soon; staggered off to bed and fell asleep. Harmon must have wondered if he had not just landed in a madhouse.

Later, however, Harmon would report to Ike that Fredendall was 'no damned good. You ought to get rid of him'.

The Supreme Commander then asked Harmon if he wanted to take over II Corps. The latter said no; it wouldn't look good. Harmon then said something that opened the way for a new player in the battles to come, right up to 1945, one who would be instrumental in helping to destroy any special relationship that might have existed between the British and American military. Harmon added: 'My recommendation would be bring in Patton here from Morocco. Let me get back to my 2nd Armored. That's the best way out of this mess.'

But before Patton could explode onto the battlefield, another soldier, British this time, stepped in to take over the whole of the Tunisian campaign – General Alexander, who was known universally in the Army, and even to his wife, as simply 'Alex'. A dashing figure like Patton, he had none of 'Ole Blood an Guts' bluster. Indeed he appeared the exact antithesis of the American general. Yet he had seen much more bloody battle than Patton ever would. Wounded three times in World War One, he had been both the youngest lieutenant-colonel and general in the British Army. After that war he had commanded German troops fighting the Bolsheviks and had been at the disaster of Dunkirk, the last man off the beaches.

Now Alex was to take over ground command in Tunisia, leading General Anderson's First Army, the Americans, and Montgomery's Eighth. Officially Eisenhower was his boss and he listened dutifully to Ike's instruction: 'Your mission is the early destruction of all Axis forces in Tunisia.' In reality he was there under Churchill's protection (he was Churchill's favourite general) to put some backbone into the Anglo–American force in North Africa. Now, after seeing Fredendall, he signalled Eisenhower: 'In view of the situation I have assumed command.' He didn't give any detailed reasons why. But in a note to Montgomery, who didn't like Alex and thought him 'an empty vessel', he wrote that he was 'very shocked. There has been no policy and no plan. The battle area is all mixed up with British, French and American units.' In another signal to Brooke and Churchill, he added: 'Real fault has been the lack of direction from the very beginning.' That pointed to Eisenhower. But it was the latter's subordinate commander, the anglophobe Fredendall, his staff and his troops who came in for most criticism.

Fredendall was 'utterly shaken', his staff were 'dithery'. As for his soldiers, they appeared 'soft, green and quite untrained. They lack the will to fight. My main anxiety,' he wrote to the War Office in London, 'is the poor fighting value of the Americans. They simply do not know their job as soldiers and this is the case from the highest to the lowest.' Unless the US Army pulled itself together, he warned Brooke, 'it will be quite useless and play no useful part whatsoever,' in the coming invasion of Europe.

Most of Alexander's criticism of the Americans, both commanders and troops, did not become known until after the war, but some did get through to the Americans at the time. Even the ordinary GI might have wondered why his Second Corps was now placed directly under Alex's personal command. Why under such a high-ranking commander and a Britisher to boot, they must have asked themselves.

But American generals, such as Eisenhower and soon Patton, could have enlightened them even in that spring of 1943. The reason for this special attention for the four US Divisions involved, the 1st Armored, the 1st, 9th and 34th Infantry, was because the British generals, and Churchill, lacked confidence in the Americans as soldiers. They'd run away at the Battle of the Kasserine Pass. Now they had to be taken in hand and shown how to be real soldiers – by the British. It was something that would rankle among the Americans and give rise to a more virulent form of anglophobia especially in the person of the new II US Corps commander, General George S Patton.

General Omar Bradley, 'The Tentmaker',* as Patton sometimes called

*On account of his Arabic-sounding second name, Omar.

his future deputy corps commander contemptuously, watched him arrive at Le Kouif, where the new corps commander would set up his headquarters. With sirens shrieking Patton's arrival, a procession of armoured scout cars and half-tracks wheeled into the dingy square opposite the schoolhouse headquarters of II Corps at Djebel Kouif on the late morning of 7 March. As Bradley recounted, in the lead car, Patton stood like a charioteer. He was scowling into the wind and his jaw strained against the web strap of a two-starred steel helmet. Undoubtedly Patton was trying out his 'war face number one', which he sometimes practised in front of a mirror. But if he was, he certainly made an impact that day. As one young captain expressed it: 'Patton sure scares the shit out of me!'

In his time Patton had been known as 'Flash Gordon,' the 'Green Hornet' and 'Gorgeous George'. But now and until he died in 1945, he acquired the nickname by which he is still known today, 'Blood and Guts' ('*Our* Blood, *His* Guts', his hard-pressed troops quipped). For Patton was an old-fashioned, autocratic soldier, out of step with his time. He believed in the flag, self-sacrifice, bravery, Indeed, the 1970 film *Patton* has turned Patton the legend into Patton the folk hero. Just like the cowboy hero of the Old West (also the creation of the Hollywood movies for the most part), he has stepped into history, the symbol of an older, simplistic America, untouched by social change, political doubts and the uncertainties of our own time.

In reality, Patton the man was something of a foul-mouthed bully. He might cry at the drop of a hat, but he could send men to their certain death without hesitation. He might ride roughshod over the rules himself. Yet he took his soldiers to task and punished them for even trivial offences. Patton was indeed a very complex man. As Bradley expressed it: 'Patton is the strangest duck I have ever known.'

But after the shameful defeat of II Corps at Kasserine, with 6,000 of its soldiers dead or in German captivity, Patton was the right man at the right time. Reputedly he swore that he and his new corps would 'kick the bastards [the Germans] out of Africa', but he needed officers who 'can sweat, get mad and think at the same time' to achieve that bold aim.

To do it, he bullied and punished the officers who served under him. They would all display their badges of rank prominently on their helmets, although they knew that these badges served as 'aiming stakes' for the excellent German snipers, who would routinely take out Patton's frontline officers.

He sent his 'Gestapo' (the US military police) stalking through the II Corps' encampments looking for soldiers, even though they might be in the frontline, to check if they were correctly dressed. If they were without ties, they were fined. Unpolished boots also drew a fine. Every night after a day touring his troops, a scowling Patton would return to his schoolhouse HQ, carrying the woollen caps that he had forbidden his soldiers to wear. It was said that even men killed in action would not be buried by the blacks of the Graves Registration Units if they weren't wearing leggings and a tie.

But while this old-fashioned type of discipline started to produce results, Patton's own lack of discipline, that would cost him his army command in Sicily six months hence, was already making itself noticeable. A few days after he had arrived to take over command of II Corps, Patton visited the corps field hospital at Ferina (it was something that Patton didn't like doing, visiting the wounded, but he steeled himself to do it). Here he strode from bed to bed, saying the things that generals always say to their wounded soldiers, handing out purple hearts here and there. Things were going well until he stopped at the cot of one of the injured GIs and asked him how he had been wounded. The man answered that he had been shot while trying to surrender. That did it. Patton spun round and marched away, his lean face contorted with disgust. 'Serves him right,' he snorted bitterly, while the accompanying doctors looked aghast. 'That's what he gets for giving up.'

Patton was impressed by his new boss, Alexander. He knew the English general's brave reputation in two wars and exclaimed 'what a man'. Alex for his part, felt the same about Patton. The Englishman was especially impressed by the turnout and welcome given him by the guard of honour when he first visited Patton's HQ. As an ex-Guards battalion commander, he enjoyed such things. All the same Alex was not prepared to let Patton's 80,000 Americans of II Corps take part in major operations for the remaining two months of the North African campaign.

He still thought the Americans too green and their commanders too ham-fisted. And as the British were supplying the majority of the troops under his command, both the British 1st and 8th Armies, Alex called the tune.

Naturally this rankled with Patton and his subordinate divisional commanders, who found to their dismay that Eisenhower, their fellow American and West Pointer, was inclined to side with the English and not give them the support that they expected from him.

Patton's Corps won the Battle of El Guettar, which was a significant and first victory for the US Army in WWII, but as the battles of that war went, it was a minor engagement. As one participant remarked: 'Probably the greatest training benefit of the Battle of El Guettar was learning that the opponent was not ten feet tall.'

Patton and his generals thought differently. The corps commander's resentment grew apace when the final plan for the last attack in Tunisia gave the British the main effort, with his II Corps relegated to the minor role of flank protection for the British. As Patton wrote in his diary on 7 April 1943:

After having spent thousands of casualties making a breakthrough we are not allowed to exploit it. The excuse is that we might interfere with the Eighth Army . . . One can only conclude that when the Eighth Army is going well we are to halt so as not to take any glory. It is an inspiring method of making war and shows rare qualities of leadership and Ike falls for it.

A little later, when the British commander of the 1st Army's 6th Armoured Division criticised Ryder's US 34th Infantry Division, Patton fumed with rage. He wrote in his diary:

God damn all British and all so-called Americans who have their legs pulled by them. I will bet that Ike does nothing about it. I would rather be commanded by an Arab. I think less than nothing of Arabs.

One day latter Patton was still seething with rage, moaning: 'Ike is more British than the British and is putty in their hands. Oh God, for John J Pershing.'*

But by mid-April Eisenhower felt that the situation in Tunisia was stabilised enough to allow Patton to go back to his command in Morocco and prepare for the next Allied objective after victory in North Africa – the invasion of Sicily. Patton then gave up the II Corps, turning it over to his second-in-command, General Bradley, 'the GI General', as he was being called by the American press. In fact, however, there was little of the 'GI' about him. He had spent most of his career in officers' schools, principally teaching dry-as-dust maths; and even now when he had an active command, at last, after thirty years in the US Army, he rarely went out into the field to meet his fighting soldiers.

Although Patton praised Bradley warmly (at first), Bradley didn't think much of Patton. Bradley maintained that Patton's command of II Corps had not been his 'finest hour'. Patton had restored control and order to the II Corps but all he and his men had done in North Africa had been to learn 'to crawl, to walk – and then run'.

In part, Bradley thought this was due to the British, who wouldn't let the II Corps fight, aided by an Eisenhower who was 'too weak, much too prone to knuckle under to the British, often . . . at our expense'.

Now with Bradley in command of America's only battle-experienced corps in the West, a little anti-British cabal formed in the II Corps, which would one day spread to a whole army – the US Third – and finally to an army group, Bradley's 12th. Bradley's anglophobia commenced in Tunisia, hardened in the battle of Sicily to come and would flower in full

*The WWI US army commander in France, who stood up to French attempts to integrate his troops into the French Army.

force in 1944, focused, in the main, on the one man who was now the centre of attention.

Of these anti-British generals, and in due course, Patton would become one of them when his and Bradley's roles changed and he became the latter's subordinate in 1944, only Patton had yet met Monty. He had attended one of Montgomery's 'briefings' after the Battle of El Alamein. Here Montgomery had noticed him and characterised him as an 'elderly, grey-haired man'. Yet they all detested him for what he stood for. He had beaten the Germans in a major campaign. He had won a major battle too – El Alamein – that Churchill had praised as a turning-point in the British war. He ordered the church bells to be rung back in Britain to celebrate the victory.

Now, although Ike, the 'best general the British have', as the cabal would have it, had his reservations about Montgomery (he wrote in a secret and confidential memo to Marshall: 'He is so proud of successes to date that he will never make a single move until he is absolutely certain of success'), Montgomery would, in essence, be in charge of the next major Allied undertaking – the invasion of Sicily.

For on 2 May 1943, with victory in North Africa achieved and the wrangling about the planned Sicily invasion still going on, Montgomery cornered Bedell Smith, Ike's chief-of-staff, in the lavatory at the Allied Forces HQ in Algiers. Here standing side by side in one of the stalls, Monty said he wanted the original plan changed. He led Bedell Smith to a steamed-up mirror and outlined with his finger what he wanted doing. Then he insisted that Eisenhower should be told of what had to be done immediately. Thus the crucially important decision was orchestrated in an Algerian privy. Ludicrous at first sight, but with implications, far from funny, which would last until the end of the 'special relationship'.

CHAPTER XI
Soft underbelly, my ass

The thirty-day campaign in Sicily in July/August 1943 could be regarded as a military success and a political defeat. It did indeed lead to the downfall of the Italian dictator Mussolini and Italy leaving the Italian–German Axis and becoming what the Western Allies called a 'co-belligerent'. But the Germans remained in control in Italy and forced the Allies to fight a bloody eighteen-month campaign up the 'boot' of that country. What Churchill had called the 'soft underbelly' (of Europe) became what the troops who did the fighting would call 'a tough old gut'.

But unknown to the general public at the time, that month-long campaign increased the animosity between the Anglo–American allies and added to Patton's and Bradley's latent anglophobia. For both of them felt that the US Army, which Patton commanded with Bradley as his deputy, had been relegated to a mere flank guard to Monty's vaunted 8th Army. The victor of El Alamein, so the two US generals thought, wanted the kudos of victory in Sicily. To them, it seemed, the battle for Sicily was going to be a repeat of the unfortunate Tunisian campaign, approved yet again by a fellow American, Eisenhower, who in Patton's phrase was the 'best general the British had'. As Patton summed up the whole situation in the Mediterranean that summer: 'So far this war is being fought for the benefit of the British Empire and post-war considerations; no one gives a damn about winning it for itself now.' That remark clearly illustrates Patton's political naivety. All wars are fought for some sort of political gain or other.

At first, however, Patton knuckled down and accepted his role. Despite the fact that Monty had seemingly taken over the Sicilian campaign and placed his imprint on it, the Seven Army Commander regarded the future 'little Limey fart' as 'a forceful, selfish man [who] I think is a far better leader than Alexander.' He wrote to his wife, Beatrice: 'Monty and I had quite a conference and got on fine. I should hate to be married to him in either meaning but as a partner we will be fine.'

But egged on by Bradley, who thought little of Monty and even less of his erstwhile boss Patton (Bradley felt Patton was 'primarily a showman.

The show always seems to come first') he soon started to change his original opinion. He wrote in his diary that summer:

> Only an act of God . . . can give us a run for our money. On a study of 'form', especially in the higher command, we are licked. Churchill runs this war . . . the thing I must do is retain my SELF-CONFIDENCE. I have greater ability than these other people and it comes . . . [from] a greatness of soul based on a belief – an unshakeable belief – in my destiny. The US must win – not as an ally, but as a conqueror. If I can find my duty, I can do it. I must. This is one of the bad days.

As yet Patton did not know just how bad those days in Sicily were to become. Now, however, he decided he would no longer play second fiddle to Monty. He could win the race (as he saw it) between his Seventh Army and Monty's Eighth. He would capture the two keys objectives of Palermo and Messina, at whatever cost, and Monty be damned. It was now that the legend of the race between the two military prima donnas was created, though all the evidence seems to show that Monty wasn't even aware that he was supposed to be racing Patton to capture Messina first.

On 28 July, after capturing Palermo and feting Montgomery there with a guard of honour and a military band, Patton signalled General Troy Middleton, the commander of the US 45th Infantry Division, to push hard to Messina. 'This is a horse race,' he told the portly, bespectacled Middleton, 'in which the prestige of the Army is at stake. We must take Messina before the British.'

In the event Patton did. Not that Monty seemed to notice. Years later, his chief-of-staff, the loyal and long-suffering Freddie de Guingand, commented on the 'race' as portrayed in the film based on Patton's life:

> There was no race. None. It was all balls about who was going to get to Messina first. We were *delighted* when we heard that Patton had got to Messina first – and about that fictious scene in the film *Patton*, it was absolute cock . . . Monty marching at the head of his Highlanders – all balls.

A little while later the alleged race for Messina was soon forgotten in the uproar caused by Patton's slapping two of his soldiers who were suffering from combat fatigue. Patton was relieved of his command and justly held in his Sicilian *palazzo* in a kind of exile, gloomily wondering if he would ever be given another battlefield command.

Bradley, who seemingly hated Patton more than he would, in due course, hate Monty, felt his army commander had got what he deserved. He noted: 'I would have relieved him instantly and would have had nothing more to do with him.' Monty, however, supposedly Patton's great rival in Sicily, showed great magnanimity. As Warwick Charlton, the editor of the Eighth Army's newspaper, recalls, he had reported what Patton had done and was immediately ordered to report to the Commander-in-Chief personally. There:

> I got one of the two raps from Monty – that he was very upset – that he didn't think it was right, that Patton was a good man although it was true that there was this report (on the slapping incident), that I should have checked back because he had his responsibilities and it reflected badly on him.

While the Anglo–American force moved on to tackle the 'soft underbelly' which would soon become the 'tough old gut', and Patton languished in his Sicilian exile, the authorities began to look at the role of the airborne divisions which had led the assault on the island. Already Eisenhower had written to Marshall in Washington: 'I do not believe in the airborne division'. Shocked by what had happened to the 82nd US Airborne and the British 1st Airborne in Sicily, Ike felt the US Army's existing four airborne divisions should be broken up. He was supported by General McNair, the US Army's Commander of Ground Forces. The latter had concluded: 'My staff and I have become convinced of the impractically of handling large airborne units.'

The reason for this concern about the future of large-scale airborne units centred on the four airborne operations which had take place in Sicily that July. Not one of these missions, which had been launched in the first four days of the campaign, had been a success. Indeed two of them had been downright fiascos, which had resulted in a great loss of life due to 'friendly fire' and sudden panic, perhaps even cowardice on the part of the American pilots taking the British airborne of the 1st Division into battle.

When the transport planes brought their bloody cargoes of dead and wounded 1st Airborne men back to their base in North Africa, Brigadier Hackett of that division had to confine his remaining paras and glider pilots to camp in order to prevent a mass 'slugfest' with the supposedly guilty US pilots.

Accusations and counter-claims flew back and forth that summer. The Army blamed the Navy for the tragedy. They had fired at their own planes. The Navy blamed the Air Force for not observing the rules while flying over the invasion convoys. In its turn, the Air Force blamed both the Army and the Navy. Monty, being his usual opinionated self, laid the blame fairly and squarely on the American transport pilots. So did 'Hoppy' Hopkinson, the general commanding the British 1st Airborne. He was still bitter about the Americans when he was killed in action a month later in Italy.

General Matt Ridgway, the commander of the US 82nd Airborne, felt the fiasco was due to faulty planning at Eisenhower's HQ. There he saw the chief culprit as being the elegant ex-Guardsman and husband of novelist Daphne de Maurier, General 'Boy' Browning, who was Ike's senior airborne adviser. In due course Ridgway, one day to be a corps commander in Europe, would be yet another anglophobic US general.

For Colonel Frost, commander of the British 2nd Parachute Battalion, the future hero of Arnhem, and probably the most outstanding parachute commander of World War Two on the Allied side, the valuable talents of his volunteer soldiers had been squandered by incompetent staff officers. As Frost wrote long afterwards: 'It was yet another humiliating disaster for the airborne forces and almost enough to destroy even the most ardent believer's faith.'

Another outstanding paratroop commander, Colonel Gavin of the US 82nd Airborne (he'd be one of the few American generals in Europe who wasn't anti-British) was so soured and embittered by his experiences in Sicily that he wrote to his daughter at the time:

When this war is over, I think I would like to be a curate in an out-of-the-way pastorate with nothing to do but care for flowers and meditate on the wickedness of the world.

Naturally Joe Public wasn't told what had happened to the airborne in Sicily. Even the *Daily Telegraph* correspondent had written:

Paratroopers were dropped from the skies under cover of darkness. The enemy seems to have been taken by surprise, for the airborne troops were practically over their Sicilian targets before any flak was encountered.

General Hopkinson of the British 1st Airborne, his glider ditched, was swimming for his life in the Mediterranean, and Colonel Gavin, commanding the 82nd's first wave of paras, was groping his way through the darkness, accompanied by only six men out of the 3,000 'All-Americans' who had been dropped an hour before.

US paras were scattered all over Sicily; and not only over Sicily. Some landed in Sardinia, in Malta and even in the mountains of southern Italy, where their mouldering skeletons were found years later. Gliders and towing planes were shot down by the score by 'friendly' guns. Gliders were ditched far out to sea with some 300 British paras drowning before they had even spotted their objective. Next night the assistant divisional commander of the 82nd Airborne was shot by his own side and a whole parachute regiment virtually disappeared.

As Colonel Frost wrote:

1. Pamela Digby Churchill Harriman with Harriman on his 90th birthday in 1981. Shortly afterwards President Reagan appointed her US Ambassador to Paris.

2. Ike's driver, Kay Summersby, in North Africa, 1943.

9. Paras of the (British) 6th Airborne Division under fire at Bure.

10. Canadians crossing the Rhine, April 1945.

11. 101st A/B Div. Trooper Wilbur W Shanklin with a German prisoner, 1944.

12. Still friends. 'Georgie', 'Ike' and 'Monty', summer 1943.

Although the press at the time was complimentary and made out that many wonderful feats of arms had been achieved, it is doubtful whether this airborne operation had any effect on the success achieved by the initial landing from the sea.

Montgomery was even blunter. In his diary he commented laconically on two of the four airborne operations, the ones carried out by the British 1st Airborne: 'The glider operation ... failed badly', adding that the parachute drop 'also failed'.

'The big lesson,' he wrote at the time, 'is that we must not be dependent on American transport aircraft, with pilots that are inexperienced in operational flying; our airborne troops are too good and too scarce to be wasted'. For as Monty saw it: '... the [American] pilots ... were frightened off their job by the flak'.

In the end Washington decided to keep large-sized parachute units and ended the war with five whole airborne divisions. The scandal of the Sicilian operation was hushed up. It offered urgent lessons about such missions. But they were never really learned, as both the Arnhem and Rhine drops later showed.

Naturally the new boys of the 13th Parachute Battalion, formed from the South Lancs, knew nothing of these deliberations about the future of airborne operations and the scandal of the Sicilian mission. By now the new battalion was up to full strength and had received a new commander in the shape of Lieutenant-Colonel Luard, an experienced parachutist.

Luard, in his mid-30s, looked the typical British regular officer. Heavy-set and sporting a thick black moustache, he was keen on smart turnout and discipline. But at the same time he was a typical para in that he expected his men to be top fit for the arduous duties that he guessed would soon lie ahead of them in the coming year of 1944. He thought nothing of ordering his men out on a surprise route march, weighed down with half a hundredweight of equipment, covering thirty miles without even the traditional five-minute break at every hour; or sending them on a 'speed march' in battle gear, with the red-faced, sweating paras marching for twenty miles at a rate of five miles an hour. Luard might be given to 'bull', but he also knew that speed and fighting fitness were more important than drill.

Naturally 'Luard's Own', as the 13th now called itself, were trying to develop an individuality that would distinguish the new battalion from the others of the newly formed 6th Airborne Division, to which the 13th belonged. First, they decided the battalion should wear a red lanyard – red for the red rose of Lancashire – which would distinguish it from the 12th Yorkshire Battalion. The 13th acquired a dog, too, as a mascot. It was a German shepherd, called 'Brian', given to them by the then teenager Betty Fetch.

But this was no ordinary mascot. As the only dog in the whole of the Sixth Airborne Division, 'Bing', as it was now renamed after Bing Crosby, was being trained for what the battalion called 'special duties'. Its trainer, Ken Bailey, who had been a professional dog-handler in civilian life, wanted it to be used on patrol to warn the men of approaching Germans, the presence of enemy mines and the like. Moreover, Bing and its successors would jump with the battalion, using a special harness and a static-line parachute. In due course, Bing would jump into Normandy and later across the Rhine in Germany, winning the 'canine VC', the Dickens Medal, for bravery. Today the model of Bing is a treasured possession of the airborne museum.

The 13th Battalion was also acquiring a set of characters among recruits who came from all walks of life and who were of all ages. Lieutenant Jack Sharples, for instance, had served in the Guards. Being sick of all the Brigade of Guards' bull, he had volunteered for the paras although he was an old man in his mid-30s. At the other end of the scale was 15-year-old Private Robert Jones, who had lied about his age to join up. In a year's time he'd be dead, killed in Normandy at 16, the youngest British soldier to be killed in that battle. Indeed, within the next eighteen months, as 1943 drew to a close and their baptism of fire grew ever nearer, most of those men, all volunteers, would be dead.

For now the commanders who had fought the North Africa battles and the first on the European mainland in Sicily and southern Italy were coming home to lead the new ones in north-west Europe. One by one they would relinquish their commands on the battlefields of the south and return to Britain – Eisenhower, Montgomery, Bradley, even eventually the disgraced Patton, followed by a host of lesser generals who would do the actual fighting in the invasion of France to come.

Supposedly they were comrades-in-arms, welded together by their common experiences in the Middle East and the Mediterranean. Unfortunately for the alleged 'special relationship' between Britain and America, the exact opposite was true. For the most part, their time on the battlefields of that region had not brought them closer; instead it had levered them farther apart, nurturing their original prejudices and adding new ones to boot.

But it was not only American officers such as Patton and Bradley and their US divisional commanders who had become virulently anti-British and anti-Montgomery. There were British officers on Eisenhower's staff who were actively opposed to Montgomery, who would become the outstanding advocate of the British position and British strategy.

There was Air Marshal Tedder, for example, who would soon become Eisenhower's deputy. He had never forgiven Montgomery for having taken the full credit for the victory of El Alamein and overlooking the important role that the Royal Air Force had played in the desert battle. Tedder remarked of his fellow Englishman, Montgomery, that he was 'a little fellow of average ability who has had such a build-up that he thinks of himself as Napoleon'. Like several senior British officers at Eisenhower's HQ, he felt that Monty was pompous, vain and a glory-seeking egomaniac, forgetting that the general was also trying to fight a battle, not against the German enemy, but against an America that was taking over the role of senior partner in the conduct of the war: an America that was primarily concerned, naturally, with American interests. The relationship between the airman and the soldier was not helped much when the latter became aware that Tedder and his former mistress and now wife, the Belgian divorcee known as 'Tops', were returning to England in a plane that contained the load of a three-ton truck. The pair intended to smuggle these unheard of goodies in wartime Britain through customs without paying duty.

Another anti-Monty Britisher at Eisenhower's HQ was the clever chief-of-intelligence Brigadier Kenneth Strong. Probably the best senior intelligence officer on the Allied side – he had worked in Berlin and Germany before the war and knew many of the Wehrmacht's senior officers personally – he had been seduced by the American way of life and had grown accustomed to their way of doing things. As one former colleague of Strong's, Major Noel Annan, reported after he rejoined the Chief-of-Intelligence in 1944, Strong's (who had grown fat on the American way of life), 'intelligence appreciations were tuned to justify Eisenhower's policy'. This meant that anyone who criticised Ike's strategy, in particular Montgomery, would come in for censure from Strong and a little British, anti-Monty cabal formed at Supreme Headquarters.

Officers such as Tedder, Strong and the Assistant Chief-of-Operations, Brigadier John Whiteley, of whom Monty stated that 'he is no good; he proved a failure here' (i.e. in North Africa), had all found a very comfortable niche in Ike's HQ. They had grown accustomed to the kind of major headquarters life of wine, women, though not too much song, which was vastly different from what they would have been forced to endure if they had been posted to Montgomery's austere HQ, centred on a couple of caravans in the middle of a field. It is perhaps understandable that these British officers serving with an American supreme commander and living the good life, might have felt a little guilty and that that sense of guilt turned them against the 'little limey fart' who always knew better than they and their American boss did.

At all events, as American power in the field grew (three soldiers for every British soldier in battle), and with the influx of US officers who had fought with their British allies in the Middle East and the Mediterranean and had grown to dislike them and their methods, Britain's role started to change. Now she was being relegated from senior to junior partner. As

1943 progressed it would appear that, although Churchill fought for British interests as best he could while still trying stoutly to maintain the 'special relationship', the only major figure who seemed to oppose US-led strategy and concepts was 'Montgomery of Alamein'.

On 31 December Montgomery relinquished command of his Eighth Army in Italy for good. He journeyed to Marrakesh in Morocco, where Churchill was convalescing after a bout of pneumonia. Here the PM gave him the current plan for the coming cross-Channel invasion which Marshall and the senior US generals had been demanding almost from the day America entered the war.

A day later Montgomery presented his assessment of the plan to Churchill. Naturally Monty being Monty didn't like it. He wrote in the last sentence of his somewhat hurried analysis: 'My first impression is that the present plan is impracticable'.

While Monty was in Morocco, Eisenhower was in Washington on a short visit. Here he met Roosevelt. The latter asked Ike how he felt about being named Supreme Commander of the coming invasion. The new Supreme Commander replied it sounded good to him. 'It has the ring of importance,' he added jokingly. 'Something like a sultan.'

The feeling would not last long, now that Montgomery was on the home team planning the great endeavour which Eisenhower would call in his book on the subject a 'crusade'. For now Monty made himself the central figure among the London planners. They had been working on 'Operation Overlord', as the cross-Channel invasion was code-named, for two years without Monty's assistance. That didn't worry the little British general one bit. He demanded immediate changes. Perhaps the long-term planners felt some resentment at his suggestions. But Monty was at the height of his power. He was flushed with victory in Africa and had become a cult figure in both the UK, where he seemed to be mobbed every time he appeared in public, and also in the USA.

He certainly breathed new life into the old plan. Right at the beginning he made a decisive suggestion, which surprised some of the anti-British faction in the US Army. He ordered that his British Second Army and the US 1st Army (under Bradley's command), which would land on D-Day, would manage their combat zones separately. Although he would be in overall command of the Anglo–American land forces, Bradley would make his own decisions about the two US landing beaches code-named UTAH and OMAHA.

Perhaps Montgomery reasoned that he'd allow Bradley some leeway as a concession to the prestige of the US Army and American public opinion back home. But he knew that Bradley was, at the same time, no great military thinker and had little experience of command in combat save for those thirty days in Sicily. So Bradley, under his indirect control, was going to be given his head.

In a way Montgomery would make a bad mistake by leaving Bradley to carry out the low-level planning of the assault on the two American beaches. Freed from the yoke of Patton (still in exile), and seemingly allowed his head by the detested Britisher Montgomery, Bradley made several bad decisions. For OMAHA Beach he rejected the use of armour, offered by the British in the form of 'Churchill's Funnies',* and special beach clearing equipment. Further he declined to support the 4th US Infantry and 1st Infantry Divisions with heavy naval gunfire as had been shown necessary in MacArthur's island-hopping campaigns in the Pacific. In due course these failings, which would lead to the disastrous situation on D-Day at 'Bloody OMAHA' would add fuel to Bradley's resentments against Monty. When Bradley went to war that Tuesday 6 June, sitting on a rubber air cushion on account of his piles, he might well have thought that Monty had let him get into this initial mess because he wanted to see the Americans humiliated. For as the campaign in Europe progressed, the American generals would grow so suspicious of British motives, in particular Montgomery's, that one might think the former were fighting the British and not the Germans.

---

* General Hobart's 79th Armoured Division, called 'Churchill's Funnies' and which contained all kinds of specialised armour for crossing minefields, ditches, wet sand, etc.

1944

'Twas on a summer's day – the sixth of June.
I like to be particular in dates . . .
Not only of the age and year, but moon
They are a sort of post-house, where the Fates
Change horses, making history change its tune,
Then spur away o'er empires and o'er states.
                                    Byron, 'Don Juan'

CHAPTER XII
Where fate changes horses

On 17 February 1944 General 'Boy' Browning, the handsome commander of the British Airborne Corps, visited the headquarters of the 6th Airborne Division. With him he brought the plan for the airborne assault with which the invasion of Europe would commence. One British and two American divisions, the 'All American' (the 82nd) and the 'Screaming Eagles' (the 101st) would be involved. The British division, the Sixth, would seize the Caen Canal and the bridges across the Orne river to secure the left flank of the British land attack. Here the commandos and Montgomery's old 'Iron Division' would be coming in from the sea to link up with the airborne landing.

Two months later, in April 1944, the plan was altered slightly and the 13th Parachute Battalion was given the task of clearing the newly discovered German anti-glider defences. These would have to be removed so that the Sixth's glider component bringing in heavier equipment, such as jeeps, six-pounder guns, etc. could land in Normandy. Above all it was vital that the six-pounder, anti-tank guns reached the lightly armed paras before the German armour counter-attacked, as it was expected it would. For there were both the German 21st Panzer Division and the newly formed 12th SS Panzer Division, 'the Hitler Youth' in the area; and the Allied planners knew by now that the Germans were experts in the rapid counter-attack, once they had been alerted to the presence of an enemy.

So, that April the 13th Parachute Battalion toiled away day after day removing minefields, anti-tank defences and girders planted in the ground with wires stretched between them to prevent gliders from landing, working with plastic explosive and dangerous high explosives.

Thereafter, from 21 to 25 May the men of the Lancashire parachute battalion took part in a four-day exercise fighting the 'enemy' made up of the veterans of North Africa and Italian campaigns, the 1st British Airborne Division, and their comrades of the Polish Airborne Brigade.

It was to be their last exercise of the pre-invasion period and for far too many their last exercise altogether. For years now some of them had been taking part in one training scheme after another. But now the training was over. Soon they were going to experience the real thing.

On the afternoon of 25 May they moved into a heavily guarded camp at Brize Norton and were 'sealed in'. Here they'd stay cut off from the outside world until the time came for them to embark on their mission. Most of them were intensely possessive about the amazing variety of weapons they would take with them – tommy guns, stenguns, trench knives, daggers, brass knuckles and the like, plus the lucky charms that would surely protect them from all harm – rabbits' feet, St Christopher medals, silk stockings, etc. In due course, as paramedic James Byron would recall, they would parade in front of their aircraft, ready for take-off 'fantastically upholstered, our pockets bulging with drugs and bandages, with maps and money and escaping gadgets'. But that was still in the future.

As 1 June came and a heavy, dull mood seemed to settle over the country and the sealed off camps, with their thousands of young men waiting for 'it' to happen, Monty toured his soldiers on what he called 'the Public Hallowing of the Sword'. His aim in talking to his soldiers was to make them understand they were not fighting for their generals, but for their comrades and themselves, whatever their class and their politics.

The 'drill', as he named it, was always the same. They'd be drawn up in front of their tents. Their officers would report and Monty would order the men to stand at ease. Then he'd make his set speech. It was almost always the same. None of the old stuff that other generals in past times had sent their 'men' off to war with. Instead Monty mostly spoke of the Germans waiting for them on the other side of the Channel. He would say:

We don't want to forget that the German is a good soldier . . . a very good soldier indeed. But when I look round this morning [afternoon, evening] and see some of the magnificent soldiers here . . . Some of the finest soldiers I have seen in my lifetime, I have no doubt about the outcome. Now I have seen you, I know we will succeed.

Monty would look at them for one more moment, his head cocked to one side peering at them with those startlingly blue eyes of his, as if he was trying to etch each and every one of their faces on his mind and then he would be gone to repeat the performance elsewhere. Whatever the most bolshy of common soldiers thought about generals, Monty impressed them. For he gave them the feeling that he cared about them; that they weren't simply cannon fodder to be wasted on the battlefield to take some objective that meant little to them, especially if they were dead when it had been captured. 'No' they opined 'Monty was different.'

For many of the young men waiting for their call to action, the coming invasion of France had taken too long to arrive. There had been too many hard years of preparation. Would (*could*) the invasion succeed even now? On their black days the soldiers were plagued by doubts. And as southern

England basked in the bright June sunshine, the fine weather seemed only to heighten their feeling of spiritual and emotional emptiness. How would it all work out?

The Supreme Commander, General Eisenhower, also seemed to be affected by the general mood of uncertainty. He wrote: 'In this particular venture we are not merely risking a tactical defeat, we are putting the whole works on number one.' Brooke, Montgomery's long-time mentor and boss, was similarly affected. He wrote: 'At the best it will fall short of the expectations of the bulk of the people. At worst it may well be the most ghastly disaster of the whole war'.

On the other side of the Atlantic, the man who had created the 'special relationship' and brought these hundreds of thousands of young Americans and Britishers together ready for the common battle, President Roosevelt, seemed strangely uninterested.

Naturally FDR had been well briefed on the events now leading up to D-Day.

Daily reports from London and Portsmouth had informed the President of the state of the weather. He had learned how Eisenhower had been forced to postpone the assault from 5 June to the 6th because of storms. He had heard how Eisenhower had crunched back and forth down the cinder path outside his Portsmouth HQ, rubbing his coins for luck.

On that last weekend before the Tuesday cross-Channel attack, he stayed at the Charlotteville home of his military aide 'Pa' Watson and while he was there he had searched the Book of Common Prayer for a D-Day invocation. He found it, and on the evening of D-Day itself, he would go on national radio and ask for a benediction for 'our sons, the pride of our nation'. He asked God further to give him and his people, 'faith in our sons, faith in each other, faith in our united crusade'. But on the morning of the start of that 'crusade', FDR slept through the first news of the landing, as if it was not really very important.

The man who would lead that 'crusade' on the battlefield, Bernard Law Montgomery, appeared, however, to have no doubts, no second thoughts about the possible failure of the cross-Channel assault. On 5 June, the day on which Eisenhower had to postpone the attack because of bad weather, he met the four army chiefs who would be under his command for the next three months in France. They assembled for dinner at Monty's HQ at Southwick Park, where in characteristic fashion he had also parked the caravan from his desert days.

Patton, still waiting for the command of the US Third Army, was in a sense Montgomery's guest of honour. Tamed a little by his downfall in Sicily, he listened as the others, who would be in action the following day, talked about 'if all went as planned'. But he did not remark on the reference, though personally he thought: 'It never goes as planned.'

After the informal dinner, one of Montgomery's aides now produced the 'Master's' betting book. For despite his puritanical character, Monty was fond of a wager. Patton was now asked by Monty whether England would be at war or not ten years after the conclusion of World War II. As Patton recalled: 'Monty bet she would not, therefore to be a sport, I bet she would.' They laid a bet of £100 on the wager, which Patton would have collected. But by then Patton would have been dead for a decade.

The port was passed. Monty in his good humour indulged in a glass and toasted his army commanders. Patton rose to respond. He said:

> As the oldest Army Commander present, I would like to propose a toast to the health of General Montgomery and express our satisfaction at serving under him.

Later Patton recorded in his dairy: 'The Lightning didn't strike me.' But the toast pleased Monty. The next morning he said to Patton,' the old American general' he had first met in 1943 at his celebrated briefing: 'I had a good time and now we understand each other.'

They did and they didn't. They both knew they were vain, highly strung and egotistical. They knew, too, that they were very capable of leading men in battle and winning that battle, if they were given their heads. But Patton, the American, had the inborn notion that the British, in particular Montgomery, were slow and did not have the fire and dash of the Americans, naturally in the form of George S Patton. Montgomery, for his part, felt that the Americans were not professional enough, and did not know their jobs as they should as regular soldiers. Patton, he must have thought, was a dashing soldier, but one who never thought the military problem through to its logical conclusion. Perhaps it was, in essence, the difference in outlook of the cavalryman (Patton) and the infantryman (Montgomery), complicated by the fact that one was an American and the other an Englishman. For the time being they understood each other, but it wouldn't last.

The 1st Battalion of the South Lancashire Regiment of Montgomery's old 'Iron Division' had gone in with their comrades of the East Yorks. It had been just weeks short of four years since they had first begun their preparation for this bloody dawn. Together the two provincial infantry battalions were to clear the Normandy beaches to enable their comrades of Lord Lovat's commando brigade to push on and link up with the Sixth Airborne which had already been dropped along the line of the Caen canal and the Orne river. The result had been wholesale slaughter. Major Rouse of the South Lancs recalled:

> The noise seemed so continuous that it sounded like a siren. I have very little recollection of wading ashore. It was, however, apparent from the

beginning that it was by no means an unopposed landing. Mortar fire was coming down on the sands, an 88mm gun was firing along the line of the beach and there was continuous machine-gun fire. Immediately ahead of us a DD tank, its rear end enveloped in flames, unable to get off the beach, continued to fire its guns.

In planning the operation, the South Lancs' CC, Lt Colonel Richard Burbury, had tried to visualise some difficulties of command in the event of the battalion not being able to get off the beaches. He hit upon the idea of using a hand flag made in the battalion colours. The idea was that the flag, easily identifiable, would be a rallying point.

It was for the enemy snipers. The poor colonel was shot and killed by one of them even before he reached the beach wire. The second-in-command, Major Jack Stone, took over now. He didn't last long, as was the case with his fellow majors and company commanders of 'A' and 'C' Companies. They, too, were both killed.

'C' Company, which was in the rear of 'A' and 'B' companies, acting as support, soon lost all its officers, save for young Second-Lieutenant Bell-Walker. He reached their objective, a pillbox code-named 'Cod'. Going in alone, the young officer attacked the strongpoint with a hand grenade. He thrust the grenade through a slit and gave the pillbox a burst of stengun fire. Next moment he was cut down by a burst of German fire from another slit trench.

Now the way ahead was relatively free. There followed a period of 'confused fighting and many acts of heroism', as Rouse recalled later. But in the end the South Lancs and the East Yorks were through sword Beach and Lord Lovat's commandos could advance and attempt to make their link-up with the men of the Sixth Para.

But as Lord Lovat, with his piper playing bravely, started to move out to meet those other South Lancs, who now formed the 13th Parachute Battalion, they passed through a khaki carpet of dead and dying stretching from the water's edge to the other end of the beach. As one of Lovat's commandos recalled: '[they] were sprawled all over the beach, some with legs, arms and heads missing, the blood clotting the wet sand.' Another remembered 'running through piles of dead infantry who had been knocked down like ninepins'. A more cynical commando told himself they had died because they had failed to spread out, but they'd 'know better next time'. But there would be no next time for the dead of the 1st Battalion, the South Lancs.

Like their comrades of the South Lancs, the 13th had suffered casualties. But the 'win or die' men of the 13th Parachute Battalion were the elite and, green as they were, they had taken their objectives speedily and with no great loss. Indeed, by dawn they had taken Ranville, the first village to be captured in Normandy.

Naturally, the troops being British, the capture had to be celebrated in style. At two thirty on that morning of 6 June with the village's garrison of a company of German infantry wiped out by the paras, the letter 'L' for Lancashire and Luard was flashed to divisional HQ. This signalled Ranville had been taken. That was followed by Luard sounding 'gone away' on his hunting horn, announcing to anyone who heard the call that Ranville was now British.

Not that everyone believed it. For Lieutenant Pollak, the ex-Guardsman, his face covered in black camouflage paint, was still explaining in his schoolboy French to the elderly Comtesse de Rohan-Chabot at the local château that he really was an Englishman and not a German in British uniform trying to trap her. It was clear that not only had the German garrison of Ranville been taken by surprise, but the French had too.

While all this was going on, the paras' 'A' Company, under the command of Major Cramphorn, together with engineers, were clearing the fields around Ranville ready for the arrival of the gliders, carrying the Sixth Airborne's heavy equipment. This was, in particular, the jeep-drawn, anti-tank guns. They were urgently needed. For the 13th was already beating off the first German armoured counter-attack with only the primitive hand-held PIAT anti-tank weapon to knock out the German Panthers and Mark IV tanks.

Just as the first of the gliders started to fall out of the sky, charging down the field at 100mph, trailing huge clouds of dust and soil behind them, crashing into trees and overturning here and there, the skirl of Lovat's piper could be heard. Although Lord Lovat, the commander of the commando brigade had been badly wounded in the breakout from SWORD beach, his men had pushed on. Now they joined the hard-pressed paras. The link-up had been achieved. The men of the 13th Parachute Battalion had carried out their first mission with style, speed and precision.

But the cost had been high; and the fighting for the 13th was not over yet. Indeed, the elite paras served as frontline infantry until mid-August, before they were finally pulled out of the line and returned to Britain. In that time they suffered 358 casualties, in killed, wounded and captured. In the Battle of Normandy, the 13th lost over half its strength. But green as they were, they took all their objectives and retained them, despite the fact that they were facing fanatical SS troops of the 'Hitler Youth', most of them volunteers like the paras, who were equipped with armour far superior to the British tanks. All the same, it would be another four months before the 13th went into action again under circumstances that none of them could have visualised in their wildest dreams that summer of 1944.

But the landings under Montgomery's overall command had gone splendidly. There had been casualties of course, a total of 10,000 of the roughly 120,000 soldiers involved. 'Bloody Omaha' was the exception. For a while there had been some talk of evacuating the survivors of that terrible landing, commanded by Bradley, though US historians rarely mention the fact. There both of the assault regiments of the US 1st and 29th Divisions suffered a thousand casualties apiece, one third of their effectives. But slowly order was restored. At first it was the nameless heroes who attempted to sort out the chaos: the private who took command of a Sherman tank, while its commander skulked in fear in a nearby foxhole; the Sherman commander who regained his courage sufficiently to help the private attack; the captain, shot through both cheeks, who continued to fight and give orders to his men, the wounded medic who scuttled from one hit GI to the next sprinkling their wounds with sulpha powder and checking they had taken their wound pills, until he finally collapsed in the sand unconscious from loss of blood.

When order was restored, a Captain Stanley Bach, a liaison officer from the 1st attached to the 29th Division, scribbled a note to be dispatched to the Top Brass watching the battle at OMAHA Beach from their cruisers offshore. It read: 'Beach high tide, bodies floating. Many dead Americans on beach at HWM [high water mark]'.

How Bradley squatting on his rubber cushion on the USS *Augusta*, reacted to those words we don't know. But perhaps he reflected that his men had paid a high price on 'Bloody Omaha' for his disdain of 'Churchill's funnies' and his contempt for what he called 'British under-confidence and over-insurance.'

But now Monty's troubles commenced, causing another wave of 'Monty bashing' both among the anti-Montgomery faction at Eisenhower's headquarters and those American generals still under the 'Master's' command. Montgomery had promised he would capture the key city of Caen on D-Day. He failed to do so and, as the German defences solidified, Monty found himself fighting seven and a half German armoured divisions on his 2nd Army front. Half an armoured division opposed Bradley's 1st Army. Time and again he attempted to break out. Each time he failed with heavy losses. And the criticism mounted.

Eisenhower could have ordered Monty to get on with it. He didn't. Instead, he wrote to Marshall that 'the going is tough'. His deputy, Air Marshall Tedder, was not so sanguine. Tedder pressed Eisenhower to relieve Montgomery from ground command because Monty was too cautious. Now an angry Eisenhower wrote to Montgomery stating that 'we must use all possible energy to prevent a stalemate'. Monty didn't deign to reply. So Eisenhower turned to Churchill. He asked the PM to persuade Montgomery 'to get on his bicycle and start moving'.

When Brooke learned of the Eisenhower communication, he fell to rowing with Churchill. He felt that by conveying Ike's request to the British chiefs-of-staff, Churchill was belittling Monty. 'If he [Churchill] couldn't trust his generals for five minutes without belittling,' Brooke considered, it didn't say much for the PM's confidence in his soldiers. But the real object of Brooke's wrath was, as always, Eisenhower, whom Brooke felt was a pretty incompetent soldier. Brooke opined that going directly to Churchill as Ike had done was like the action of a 'sneaky schoolboy going to the headmaster' to blab on some fellow pupil.

In the end Caen was taken way behind schedule and the breakout commenced. But Monty's inability to take the now ruined French city, which had suffered ten thousand civilian casualties, had shaken his reputation. In particular, the American generals no longer respected the 'Victor of El Alamein', as they might once have done. Bradley referred to Monty as 'third rate'. Patton, who believed he had seen the problem of the beach-head breakout coming even before the invasion, requested Bradley's permission to 'drive the British into the sea for another Dunkirk'. The request was probably not serious, of course, but it left a nasty taste in the mouth. If this was the mood of the Anglo–American coalition at a time when they were about to jointly destroy the German Army in France and sweep on to the German border in less than a month, what would the feeling be like if that coalition faced a serious battlefield setback, as it would in exactly four months?

Now, even Eisenhower's attitude was beginning to change. The American, who had done so much to bring the coalition to life and make it work, felt he wasn't getting the support he deserved from the British when he had worked so hard in their interests. By now what he thought of as the Montgomery–Brooke coalition was definitely against him with only the PM, Churchill himself, trying valiantly to keep the peace and the coalition working. Besides, there were now two million troops in France and three quarters of them were American. The British were no longer the strongest military force as they had been since America had joined the war more than two years earlier.

Indeed, the British Army was now scraping the barrel for men. Monty signalled the War Office that summer that his Second Army 'is very strong'. But it had, in fact, reached its peak. 'It can get no stronger . . . In fact, it is getting far weaker as the manpower situation begins to hit us.'

Monty had to ask for divisions to be transferred from Italy to bolster up his front in France and would end the summer by cannibalising two of his infantry divisions to supply reinforcements of riflemen to other fighting divisions.

The casualties suffered in Normandy were also beginning to affect the morale of his remaining divisions, even veterans of North Africa such as the 51st Highland Division, known throughout the British Army as the 'Highway Decorators' for their habit of painting 'HD' (their divisional sign) on anything they captured. He signalled the War Office:

Regret to report that 51st Div. is at present Not repeat NOT battleworthy. It does not fight with determination and has failed in every operation it has been given to do. It cannot fight the Germans successfully.

Monty's remedy was to fire the divisional commander, a personal protégé of his. General Bullen-Smith relinquished his command with tears in his eyes. But Monty had no time for tears that summer. He was also having problems with the 3rd Canadian Infantry Division. Its fighting efficiency had slumped – and the Canadians were all volunteers. Monty blamed the divisional commander.

He [the commanding general] was obviously not standing up to the strain, and showed signs of fatigue and nervousness (one almost might say fright) which were patent to us all.

The Canadian General went too. It was a difficult time for the British commander. His resources were dwindling, his experienced divisions, such as the 51st and the famed 'Desert Rats', the 7th Armoured Division, were failing him and there were problems of ill-discipline and lack of morale among the newer formations which had spent years training in the UK. Bradley was facing similar problems, sacking divisional commanders at the drop of a hat. But Bradley was secure from the sort of criticism being levelled at Monty from – seemingly – all sides. Bradley had no great reputation to defend; but Monty had.

For the general public these worries and uncertainties were kept under wraps until the end of the war. So, despite his failings and critics at both Supreme HQ and among the ranks of the US 1st Army and the newly arrived 3rd US Army under Patton's command, Monty survived the summer. Now as September approached, the Germans were in full retreat, the problems of the breakout from the beaches were forgotten, and a mood of near euphoria swept through the ranks of the Allied armies. The Allied advance had turned into a victory march and even the hard pressed combat soldiers at the front started to believe the press pundits' promises that the 'boys will be home for Christmas'.

But despite the slackening of pressure on him, Monty's trials were just beginning. On 31 August 1944 Eisenhower called a major press conference. At it the Supreme Commander announced that 'as previously planned' (which it had been), he, Ike, was taking over total command of Allied ground forces. Overnight Monty, who was now compensated with the elevation in rank to field marshal, had lost command over Bradley's 12th Army Group, which consisted of Hodges' 1st Army, Patton's 3rd and Simpson's 9th US Army. Naturally some sections of the media thought this demotion was a result of Monty's slow progress after D-Day, especially his failure to capture the key city of Caen.

Eisenhower, always the good guy, tried to scotch this idea. He said:

Anyone who interprets this as a demotion for General Montgomery simply won't look facts in the face. He is not only my very close and warm friend, but the man with whom I have worked for two years and for whom I have a tremendous admiration, one of the greatest soldiers.

This statement incurred the wrath of his fellow US generals. In his opinion, Bradley told Ike's chief-of-staff Bedell Smith, Monty was 'a third-rate general and he had never done anything or won any battle that any other general could not have won as well or better'.

Patton, always eager for military honours, picked upon Monty's promotion to field marshal. 'The Field Marshal thing makes me sick,' he wrote and ever thereafter he would take Monty to task as 'the Field Marshal'. Bedell Smith, for his part, who tried to ape his boss Eisenhower and remain neutral, told a friend privately that Monty wouldn't have been worth a damn without Patton and that he, Patton, should be hauled over the coals for his 'intransigence and behind-the-scenes conniving to enhance his own prestige and obtain a major measure of command'.

In retrospect it is clear that the 1 September change-over of command marked a significant moment in British history and, in particular the WWII special relationship. Eisenhower, the only personality who could have solved the problem, and who had tried so hard to tame Monty and keep the military coalition alive, found his hand was being forced by his own generals and was at the same time being bitten by Monty.

His abortive 'Market Garden' operation to 'bounce the Rhine' at Arnhem didn't help either. It increased the ire of generals such as Bradley and Patton. The latter maintained – incorrectly – that fuel was being diverted from his Third Army to keep Monty's Second Army moving. As he snorted in that downright vulgar manner of his: 'Give me the gas and I'll go into Germany like shit through a goose!'

Naturally Eisenhower came in for a lot of criticism from his fellow Americans for allowing Monty to have his head over 'Market Garden'. But Monty showed little gratitude towards the Supreme Commander. At their first meeting on 10 September, after Monty had been relieved of land forces overall command, now taken over by Eisenhower himself, he was so insubordinate that Ike was forced to administer a mild rebuke. He put his hand on Monty's knee and said: 'You can't talk to me like that, Monty . . . I'm your boss.'

But Monty would never seem to realise that. Nor had Eisenhower really got the measure of his touchy British subordinate. The new field marshal might apologise for his conduct a few days after that September meeting. But in his heart he knew he was right and 'Ike' was wrong. Blinded by, to some extent, personal vanity, Montgomery felt the Americans, and the new overall commander, Eisenhower, were conducting the war in Europe in the wrong fashion. Only he, Montgomery, the Victor of El Alamein, it appeared to him, knew how the campaign should really be fought.

In terms of strategy, the conflict between Montgomery and Eisenhower rested on whether Germany should be attacked on a broad front (Eisenhower) or a narrow one (Montgomery). In advocating and implementing the broad-front strategy, Eisenhower believed that this would give every commander, particularly the Americans, the chance to involve his army in the final attack on the Reich. In order to do this, Eisenhower insisted that time should be given for his armies, facing Germany, ranging from the US 7th Army close to the Swiss border in Alsace to the US 9th Army, based on the Dutch border with Germany, to close up for the final assault. Naturally this strategy gained the approval of Eisenhower's US army commanders.

Monty, on the other hand, thought this approach wasteful. It would only prolong the war until all the troops were in place. In the meantime, Britain's manpower and resources would become ever weaker. That would mean that Britain's influence over the Americans, with their now superior manpower, would wane even more. Instead of the broad-front strategy, Montgomery wanted a powerful, pencil-slim attack of some forty divisions on the Reich, regardless of the danger to his flanks. The failure of the 'Market Garden' operation, based on a similar strategy, did not weaken his constant demands for the 'narrow-front' strategy. Naturally some of the US generals, who realised they'd be left out of this kind of attack or who hated the idea of being subordinated to Montgomery in his narrow-front assault, knew why Montgomery was pushing this strategy. It was simple. The commander of the narrow-front attack would be no less a person than Field Marshal Sir Bernard Law Montgomery.

As General Everett Hughes, an old crony of Eisenhower's, warned his old poker-playing partner that September, there was a need to play up the American side of the campaign and play down the British involvement now that Ike had finally got rid of Monty. 'I can't do that,' Eisenhower retorted.

'You'd better,' Hughes said. 'You're not going to live in Europe all your life.'

CHAPTER XIII
The happy hypothesis

In the same week that it was decided to remove Monty from his post as overall land commander, the last of the Sixth Airborne and the survivors of the 13th Parachute Battalion returned to the UK. Now the 13th could boast, as could the members of the other four para battalions of the Sixth, that after eighty-three days in the line they had become veterans.

In Normandy they had learned the lethal tricks of the trade. In their first twenty-four hours in combat they had found out if they didn't dig deep they died; that cover, even that offered by a wood, was no protection from the skilled German snipers and mortarmen; they discovered that the old Regular Army discipline of being a good marksman at distance was no good in Normandy. The trick was to get as close as possible and then let the enemy have a sustained burst of rapid fire. Even the notoriously unreliable stengun, produced at a cost of seven shillings and sixpence, proved to be an excellent weapon under such circumstances.

In Normandy they had found out that 'the most exclusive club in the world', as someone once called the frontline, had its own language, customs and rituals. There they had learned to eat what some wag called 'armoured pig' and 'armoured cow', i.e. Spam and tinned corned beef; they'd even stomached the worst can of food in the standard compo ration – the detested 'soya link'. This was a skinless, triangular sausage made of soya beans and embedded in fat with which to cook the horror. They had grown greedy for the boiled sweets and fruit cocktail which these compo ration boxes contained. Indeed sweet things, for some reason, were the most popular items in the compo after the seven ration 'fags' issued per man per day. Naturally every little Red Devil section would have some wag who would ask when the compo box was being wrenched open, 'and which tin has got the cunt in, Sarge?' It was a joke that would wear pretty thin as the days and weeks in that 'most exclusive club' passed by.

In Normandy their life had been simple, dangerous and, when they weren't fighting, boring. But it possessed a certain character that none of the survivors would ever forget. There they had 'stood to' at dawn because it was a British Army wisdom that 'old Jerry' always attacked at that time. All of them would be under arms then and ready in their slit trenches which smelled of fresh soil, sweat, shit and sometimes human misery. If nothing happened then, they 'brewed up' on their 'Tommy cookers': petrol fuelled portable cookers that lived up to their name all too often. For they routinely exploded and cooked their 'Tommy'. Some paras regarded them as worse than 'the bloody Jerry Mines'.

Thereafter, it was off to the 'thunderbox' or pit latrine to have 'a crap', or as the more polite of the paras put it, 'to take a shovel for a walk'. Then the latrine was usually a slit trench with a pole supported by two boxes suspended over it. But even as they squatted there in a row with 'army form blank' (khaki-coloured issue toilet paper) or more often a tuft of grass in their hand, they kept a wary gaze open for snipers. For the Germans were no respecters of their morning ablutions.

Then if they weren't actually fighting, they were kept busy, digging trenches, repairing wire, preparing for night patrols, even getting their hair cut by an amateur barber who charged 'fags' for his skills, clipping away the hair revealed under the rim of a cooking basin or the like, giving their comrades the traditional British 'back and sides'.

But even with all the harsh, brutal, violent life around them, these young men, who could die at any moment, developed a pride in themselves and their comrades, their 'mates' and 'muckers', that they would never experience again. For these young paras, the ones who had survived, had learned that they was an unbridgeable gap between their lives and those of the folks back home, even those of the 'base wallahs'. For the civvies and base wallahs could never have understood the way they existed even if they lived to be a hundred years old.

For, however much these young paras might moan about their lot, fighting 'for a frigging couple of bob a day', they had developed a pride in themselves, which was even greater than when they had received their wings at Ringway and had been rewarded for their courage and effort with the coveted red beret of the Parachute Regiment.

But the price had been high, not only for the 13th, but for the division as a whole – 145 officers and 2,500 other ranks killed, wounded or missing. That was over twenty-five percent of the Sixth Airborne Division. As one chronicler of the time wrote: 'In May they had left Bulford full of resolution; they returned there in September, tempered by the fire of achievement. Not only were they the liberators of Europe; they were the foremost of them.'

After the initial welcome was over and the terrible news came in of what had happened to their sister formation, the 1st Airborne, which had lost nearly seventy percent of their effectives, it was back to training and the difficulty of absorbing hundreds of newly fledged paras, some of them just 18.

Their training had to be accelerated too. For due to the manpower shortage in the British Army, the 13th, like the rest of the division, was on an eight-hour notice to return to the continent. And the veterans soon worked out that they were training hard again and absorbing so many green reinforcements because they were expected to be sent into battle again soon. This time, too, their training was different from that given them before D-Day.

They started to practise 'mouse-holing' in the bombed-out streets of Birmingham and the like. This consisted of working their way from house to house, often by burrowing through the wall separating one semi-detached house from another; hence the name. Then there was practice in the use of assault craft on stretches of the Thames. Why, the veterans asked themselves, would paras need to know the techniques of soldiers carried to battle by water instead of air? They concluded that there was no longer a need to cross the Channel by air or water. So they would attack over a river into some sort of large built-up area. But what river and in which country? That only a handful of staff officers and perhaps Colonel Luard, who still commanded 'Luard's Own', knew.

But as winter approached and it grew progressively colder – it would soon be the coldest winter in living memory – the thoughts of the 13th Para turned more to Christmas and leave. For they were sure they would receive leave before the Division would return to those East Lincolnshire airfields whence they would surely fly out to battle, as they had done before. They concentrated on saving their sweet ration for the festive season and winning the divisional cross-country championship, in which 1,000 paras, including men of the 13th, took part before the weather became too inclement. They 'bulled' their best battledress.

So the days and remaining weeks to the last Christmas of the war passed in hard work and boring routine, the bright spot of the week being a visit to the local pub for a pint and a game of darts. For a short while there was a flicker of excitement when intelligence discovered that nearly half a million German POWs in England were apparently going to rise up and be supported by German paratroopers landed in the country to assist in the coup.

Churchill was informed. He thought the German paradrop unlikely. All the same, the PM realised that the German POWs, all fit you young men, far outnumbered the remaining Anglo–American troops in the UK. The police and Home Guard were put on alert. All Christmas leave for POW guards was cancelled and in the end the paras were sent in to Devizes POW camp near Salisbury Plain to take out the ringleaders. In due course these confessed to the plot. They stated that the date of the abortive POW rising and mass breakout was to be Saturday 16 December 1944. Few if any realised then just how significant that date would become.

Behind his back his staff called him the 'hangman's dilemma'. The nickname was obvious when one looked at Brigadier Kenneth Strong, Eisenhower's tall Scottish chief-of-intelligence. For Strong had virtually no chin. It would have been very difficult for any potential hangman to put a noose around his neck and keep it in place long enough to hang him on a gallows.

'Ike' and 'Ken', as they called each other, had been together since 1943 when Eisenhower's previous British chief-of-intelligence had been sacked. Ken spoke fluent French, Italian and German and was indeed a prize. He had spent years in Germany as a junior officer in the Saar and later as military attaché in Berlin. As already noted, he knew many of the German generals now conducting the war on the other side and several Nazi bigshots, including Hitler. He'd even done a little bit of spying.

At the beginning of the war, instead of being posted to his regiment as he had expected, Ken became one of the three regular army officers sent to intelligence at the War Office. Here he was in charge of some very clever new personnel recruited from the universities and big business. Clever as they were, they looked up to Strong as the fount of all wisdom in matters of intelligence. One of them later described his boss looking 'like a beaver – an eager beaver – bursting out of his uniform, with dark hair, a fine forehead and clever shifty eyes'.

Perhaps the world 'shifty' wasn't quite fair. But one thing was certain. Strong did have an eye for the main chance. He knew, like all ambitious regular officers did, that if he wished to gain promotion and power he had to hitch his star to some important, up-and-coming senior officer. In Strong's case he attached himself to Ike and served him loyally right to the end, even when he knew that by doing so he had probably ruined his chances of gaining further promotion in the British Army, dominated in the post-war period by Montgomery and his supporters. Indeed, he was so close to Ike that there was talk of making him an American citizen so that he could continue his career in intelligence in the US Army or perhaps even the fledgling CIA.

But his loyalty to Ike and the Americans at Supreme Headquarters meant that he was regarded by the Brooke–Monty camp as one of those Britishers like Tedder who had gone over to the Americans and become anti-Monty. Indeed, by the winter of 1944 it could be said that Strong had adapted well to the US way of life in the great sprawling Versailles Supreme Headquarters with its huge staff that was probably the equivalent of a division and a half of infantry.

As one of his former subordinates, Major, soon to be Lt Colonel, Noel Annan noted that winter:

> I noticed that my old chief had changed. By now Strong had the sleek, well-fed look of a senior officer, who had adopted the life style of the American top brass . . . He responded to the informality and generosity of the Americans and had learned a lot about the in-fighting between one headquarters and another.

Studying Strong and his friend and boss Eisenhower and their roles in the functioning of the great Versailles HQ, Annan thought that Eisenhower was a leader who 'never originated anything', but presided over meetings which approved strategy drawn up by others. Strong's role was to make intelligence fit in with the new strategy; not the other way round.

As Annan saw it:

> Intelligence at SHAEF was governed by what one might call the 'Happy Hypothesis'. This was that the German Army had been shattered in Normandy and battered in Russia so that it was only a matter of two or three months before the war would end.

Annan recalled many years later:

> When I arrived at SHAEF, I formed the impression that the intelligence appreciations [made by Strong] were turned to justify Eisenhower's policy to attack all along the front. The policy required intelligence to report that the German Army was incapable of mounting an offensive.

Annan's analysis seems to be borne out by Strong's own post-war statement:

> Members of Intelligence were considered defeatist if they predicted anything but Allied successes; if they expressed doubts about the future they were accused of being out of touch with the realities of the war. Such accusations could only be countered by incontrovertible facts and figures.

Strong maintained that 'Intelligence is very seldom able to do so.'

But by mid-October the Anglo–American coalition's most senior intelligence officer, who was in a position to dominate and even overrule the forecasts of all other senior intelligence officers, British and American, received two former associates who now worked in the ULTRA operation in Britain's Bletchley Park. They were Wing Commander Jim Rose and Major Alan Pryce-Jones from Bletchley Park's famed Hut Three. We don't know now who sent the two officers to see Brigadier Strong, but despite their low rank and the fact that they were non-regulars, they were admitted to Strong's office immediately.

Pryce-Jones, a dapper soldier who was no great respecter of rank, perched himself on the edge of Strong's desk and without any preliminaries asked the latter why he thought the 'Huns' would collapse soon. After all, the 'Yanks' under Eisenhower's command had now been battering their heads against the German Westwall for two months and were getting nowhere. How did this stout defence of their western frontier against two US armies indicate that the enemy was about to throw in the towel?

Strong, apparently not offended by the young major's directness, answered that the Germans were near collapse because they were losing approximately a division a day. In the light of such losses, it seemed to him that Germany must collapse soon.

Pryce-Jones was not impressed by the brigadier's answer. Now he didn't pull his punches. He said straight out: 'Sir, if you believe that, you'll believe anything.' He went on to say that Bletchley was decoding German signals indicating that the enemy were replacing their losses rapidly. In fact they were forming a new reserve army in the north, which was supposed to be a million men strong.

Strong said he disagreed with Bletchley's assessment and analysis. But he didn't pull rank. He heard the two messengers from Bletchley Park out and when they had gone, he reported what they had told him to 'Beetle' Smith, Ike's chief-of-staff, who with his fiery red hair and flaming ulcers was noted for his equally fiery temper. Four days later, Smith reported to Ike what had transpired between the Britishers from intelligence. Smith stated that he thought the German Field Marshal von Rundstedt was gathering crack panzer troops (the German Sixth Panzer Army) for a lightning attack. But Smith's and Strong's predictions were not taken seriously and there the matter rested for the time being.

A month later, Strong's forebodings had evaporated and everything was seemingly back to normal. The Americans were still attacking along the Westwall and the German defenders were still losing large numbers of troops (at least Strong believed they were). The Germans would collapse at any moment now. But after a visit to London, when he told one of Monty's staff officers that 'the original plan for a lightning blow has lapsed', he returned to Versailles to be faced by a minor revolt among some of his intelligence staff officers, one American and three British.

The latter had worked out that the new divisions discovered by the ULTRA Bletchley operation were facing Middleton's US VIII Corps in the Ardennes. If one more German division was added to those already identified in the area, the rebels concluded, then a 'relieving attack', i.e. one to take off the pressure on the Westwall defenders, would be likely.

Strong now called a conference attended by Ike and Smith. But the chief-of-intelligence didn't stick his neck out. Instead he gave Ike and Smith three options. In other words he was playing safe, knowing that everyone at the Versailles HQ was supposed to think the Germans were finished. The last of the nine panzer and five infantry divisions now discovered in the general area of Middleton's VIII Corps, he stated as his third option, *might* attack Middleton.

In the end nothing came of Strong's half-hearted warning. Smith thought that Bradley ought to be warned. The latter said he knew of the danger and that he was taking 'a calculated risk' by allowing Middleton only four divisions to defend his quiet front of sixty miles in the Ardennes. As Ike wanted to keep the 'broad-front strategy' implemented, he couldn't spare any more troops for Middleton.

Bradley said further that he was already very short of riflemen for the score or so divisions under his command. Later, after the balloon went up, Bradley maintained that he and Ike had gone over the map together tracing the exact route the Germans would take in what became known as 'America's Gettysburg of the 20th Century'. Ike supported Bradley in December 1945 by telling the US Secretary of War Patterson that General Bradley had actually traced on the map many days before the German surprise attack the line to which he, Bradley, estimated the Germans would finally penetrate. But that was afterwards.

In essence, nothing came of Strong's rather weak attempts to alert Ike and his commanders to the potential dangers posed by the appearance of these new German formations on Middleton's front. However, there was another allied chief-of-intelligence working on the same scenario that winter, whose warnings seem to have been taken seriously. He was another 'retread', as the Americans called middle-aged regular officers who had been called out of retirement after Pearl Harbor to officer America's ever expanding new army (Corps Commander Middleton was another one).

He was Patton's intelligence chief, bespectacled Colonel Oscar Koch, who looked more like a professor than a soldier. On 9 December 1944, seven days before the German offensive in the west commenced, Koch told his chief Patton that a 'tricky situation' seemed to be developing on General Hodges' 1st US Army front to which VIII Corps belonged. Unknown to Hodges, Patton had an illegal secret intelligence unit commanded by a Captain Le Mars Barnes operating in Middleton's VIII Corps area. This was contrary to US Army policy but Patton wanted to know what went on on both his flanks, although he maintained that he never worried about the Third Army's flanks. Anyway, whatever Patton's reasons were, Koch tapping this source and others supplied by ULTRA, etc. informed Patton that:

> The enemy has an approximately two and a half division numerical advantage in the area.* The enemy build-up [has] been gradual and highly secret. A successful diversionary attack, even of a limited nature, would have a great psychological effect – a shot in the arm for Germany.

Patton took the warning seriously, though it seemed to concern another

* The area of Gen. Hodges' 1st US army.

army. He told Koch to look into the matter more deeply. To his staff he stated that the Third Army would have to make provision to break off the current attack in the Saar and move at least a corps north to aid Hodges in case of an emergency.

Thus Patton was in a position to move that corps northwards almost immediately when Eisenhower ordered him to go to the assistance of Hodges' First. Patton's surprise declaration at the Verdun Conference that on the morning of 19 December he would commence shifting a whole corps of three divisions and thousands of men over ice-bound roads on 22 December, has always been regarded by US military historians as one of 'Ole Blood an' Guts' outstanding achievements in WWII. Indeed Patton's breakthrough with this corps to the so-called 'Battered Bastards of Bastogne', the 101st Airborne supposedly surrounded in the Belgian town of that name (their commander incidentally always denied that his 101st had been surrounded by the Germans), made him the great hero of the coming Battle of the Bulge.

But on one seems to have ever explained why Patton would keep a secret intelligence unit in the territory of his neighbour, Hodge's 1st Army, and why he had prepared that move northwards *four* days before the Germans attacked and *ten* days before Eisenhower asked him to attack northwards. Added to these mysteries, which could indicate that the great German 'surprise' counter-offensive in the Ardennes wasn't such a surprise after all, there is the mystery of why Patton did not inform Bradley, his boss, of what he was capable of doing until 18 December. What did Patton know that was so important to him that he was prepared to break off his Saar Offensive and move north to aid Hodges, of whom he was so contemptuous? If it was so important, why wasn't Bradley party to it?

One explanation might be that if Bradley got himself in a hole by being caught by surprise – and he was – then Patton would capture the limelight, as he did at Verdun, by having the decisive and immediate rescue plan already prepared. If, however, he mentioned his plan to Bradley in advance, Bradley would receive the kudos of being prepared for the eventuality that Middleton's weak front might be attacked.

For the relationship between Patton's former subordinate, Bradley, and his now subordinate, Patton, had deteriorated badly. As Patton stated of Bradley: 'He is a man of great mediocrity . . . I do not wish any more of my ideas to be used without credit to me which is what happens when I give them orally to Bradley.' Whatever the reason for Patton's reluctance to reveal his plans to his army commander, and top level intelligence's stubborn refusal (perhaps under pressure from Eisenhower and his top brass) to see any danger from the Germans in the Eifel/Ardennes, we find the leaders who would fight the most significant Allied battle of 1944 in some kind of disarray.

We have Bradley, the US 12th Army Group commander, dull and unimaginative, suspicious of Monty and jealous of Patton, often ill with his piles, colds, bad teeth, etc. (his medical record was kept secret during the campaign as if it was of top-level intelligence value). Under him there is Patton, waiting in the wings for something that would restore his flagging reputation: a fighting soldier through and through, but one who was his own worst enemy.

Above them is Eisenhower, still valiantly trying to keep the peace between the Allies with the aid – sometimes limited* – of General Marshall in Washington. Marshall answered to a dying Roosevelt, who didn't know he was dying – no one save his secretive military doctors did – and who had his own plans for the future of the world once the military conflict, which didn't interest the President much, was resolved.

Then there was the junior partner Churchill, still loyal to the 'special relationship' and believing, despite contrary evidence, that FDR was also just as enthusiastic about this Anglo–American coalition. His foreign minister Eden had warned him about FDR's post-war intentions. Churchill himself had experienced the change in FDR's attitude when Roosevelt refused, after promising to do so, to use US shipping to ferry British troops to Greece when a political insurrection had taken place in Athens. It was the first indication that the US President was not going to support British ambitions in the Mediterranean, the sealink which was vitally important for the future of the British Empire.

Thus all of them (as on the other side of the Westwall, Hitler prepared for the great 'surprise' attack, which was aimed at temporarily breaking the Anglo–American military coalition in NW Europe) had their own plans and personal ambitions, many of which paid mere lip service to the 'special relationship'.

Yet none of them had taken into account the British soldier, who had long been listening to his own inner voices – Montgomery. Why should they? Just as Patton believed he had been hived off to a sideshow in the Saar, Monty could well have thought the same of his role and that of his Second Army stuck in the flat, featureless fields of a wet, cold Holland on the other flank of the great Allied front.

Monty had seen Eisenhower a meagre four times since the battle for Normandy had ended. Indeed he had not seen or talked to Ike by phone for the last month or so. He had promised not to bother Ike any more and Ike, taking him at his word, was certainly not bothering him, although the Supreme Commander had been doing the rounds of his army and corps commanders during the previous November.

Side-tracked as he was, Monty naturally was still capable of 'belly-

---

* According to President Truman, Marshall told him after the war that 'Eisenhower had to be led every step of the way' during it.

145

aching', as he liked to call it, about the Supreme Commander. And Monty, being Monty, felt that 'Eisenhower should himself take proper control of operations or he should appoint someone else to do it'. But Eisenhower seemed in no way inclined to do anything of the kind. In vain, Montgomery, stuck in his dreary village HQ at Zonhoven, Belgium, waited for the call. But it did not come. Eisenhower did not want any changes in command – at least not yet. The war had settled down nearly everywhere. The men were making preparations for Christmas 1944. Nobody, it appeared, needed him. The 'Victor of El Alamein' decided he'd take leave, his first since D-Day. He'd go home for Christmas Eve to see his son.

CHAPTER XIV

It could have been taken as a bad omen

On the morning of Sunday 17 December 1944, with only a few days to go before Montgomery was to return to England for Christmas, the surly locals of Zonhoven prepared for the spectacle of the little British field marshal, prayer book under arm, leading the men of his forward headquarters to the customary British Army church service. In the coming week, the pre-recorded Christmas carol service held in Zonhoven would be broadcast over the BBC. Now the locals wondered what kind of show would be presented to them this last Sunday before the feast of goodwill to all men.

Zonhoven had not been too pleased by the arrival of Monty and his small headquarters. For it had been decided that for the first time in the campaign the winter HQ would be placed under a proper roof. Not that 'Villa Mommsen' was any great shakes. Monty's own headquarters had only one bathroom, and the red-brick structure located on the main village street was shaken all the time by traffic heading for the front.

As former Member of Parliament and writer A P Herbert described it:

> Monty's room was full of the rumble of tanks and great guns and lorries. Doodle-bugs roared over now and again ... But the canaries and goldfish [Monty was fond of a variety of animals] were on parade as well; the canaries did their best.

But if the locals didn't like the English, who they felt only caused trouble with their immoral ways (on the first day there a 19-year-old British soldier had died from drinking wood alcohol), the British weren't fond of the locals with their privies, outside taps and great steaming manure piles beside their kitchen doors, the symbol of each peasant's wealth.

The day before Monty had relaxed. He had received a visit from Whiteley, one of those Britishers at Supreme Headquarters, whom the Monty faction felt had gone over to the 'Yanks'. He had been sent by Ike to solicit Monty's views on how the campaign should go in the future. The field marshal was not very encouraging. He told the assistant chief-of-staff that 'unless Ike could make his mind up quickly as to what he wanted to do and would issue some definite orders, we were quite likely to drift into an unfavourable situation vis-à-vis the enemy'. How unfavourable that would be, Monty would soon find out.

On the same day he flew across the border to play golf with Dai Rees, the professional golf champion who just 'happened' to be the driver of Air Marshal Harry Broadhurst. Here at Eindhoven in Holland, Monty had been informed that 'something is happening' on the front of the US First Army. Monty had flown back to Zonhoven, as he felt that this attack might be something to do with the newly discovered 6th SS Panzer Army, as it was now called, close to the 1st Army's front in the Eifel/Ardennes.

Now on Sunday Monty did not want to show the locals or his own rank-and-file that anything was amiss on the US front. He suspected that there were German spies among these Flemings who were so close to the German border. After all, many thousands of them, regarded by the Nazi creed as fellow Aryans, had joined the SS and the Wehrmacht. There were also German deserters and stragglers trying to get back to the Reich, wandering about the area, living in outlying farms. So at ten thirty that grey cold Sunday he started out for the church, as was his custom, carrying the Book of Common Prayer in his hands.

The military organist at the church, Sergeant Norman Kirby, who as a linguist helped with field security, recalled:

Monty was there as I was playing the organ for the early service . . . I stayed behind . . . but was called out in the middle of the recording to speak with the grief-stricken mother of a 4-year-old boy who had just been knocked down by one of our lorries and killed. It could have been taken as a bad omen.

The sergeant was right. It was on that day that the full fury of the 'surprise' German offensive broke through Middleton's VIII Corps front. Monty left quickly and got down to work in his gloomy red-brick villa HQ. That Sunday morning he was very much in the dark about what was going on at the American front. Ike had not contacted him. Nor had Bradley, who was still at Ike's Versailles HQ celebrating Congress's award of Ike's fifth star, making him the equivalent of a British field marshal. Why should they? Monty, they thought, didn't count for much any more. Soon they would realise just how badly mistaken they were; and in due course Monty would rub their noses in the dirt in revenge for that oversight.

After he had returned to his HQ and had eaten his usual frugal lunch, Monty went back to work. At this time the British 2nd Army had withdrawn several of its divisions back to Holland and Belgium to prepare them for the New Year drive into Germany. So he had at least five divisions or more readily available, especially Horrocks' XXX Corps which would spearhead the New Year attack.

The first thing a worried Monty, still very much in the dark, did was to put his best infantry division, the veteran 43rd Infantry, under the command of 'Butcher' Thomas, and the 1st Guards Armoured Division, which boasted an eye divisional patch which was supposed to wink when it saw a virgin on the Continent (the Guardsmen maintained it had never winked yet), on six-hour alert ready to move into action.

At the same time he ordered his 'eyes and ears', as Monty called them, his battle-experienced British, American and Canadian liaison officers, to set out to discover what was going on. Six of them, three British, two American, and one Canadian, set off hot foot to find out the situation at Hodges' 1st Army front, where the German breakthrough had taken place. Nothing was coming from Hodges' HQ at the Belgian resort town of Spa. For the land lines that connected the Headquarters with Versailles and Bradley's HQ at Luxembourg City at the far end of the US line seemed to have been cut.

Thereafter, at five o'clock that grey dark winter's evening, he signalled Brooke at the War Office: 'The Americans are definitely tactically unbalanced and the First Army at 1700 hrs had no idea as to how they could deal with the problem.'

How right he was, Monty little realised. One of Hodges' divisions, the green 106th Infantry, 'The Golden Lions', was in the process of getting itself surrounded and its neighbour, the 28th Infantry 'the Bloody Bucket', had had its centre broken through with its 110th Infantry Regiment shattered and in full retreat – what was left of it.

Monty's message added: 'I am taking certain measures myself to ensure adequate security in my southern flank. 'Naturally Monty couldn't refrain from gloating a little over the Americans' discomfiture. 'It looks now,' he signalled, 'as if we may have to pay the price for the policy of drift and lack of proper control of the operations which has been a marked feature of the last three months.'

But if all was gloom at the US front, at Monty's HQ, despite their depressing surroundings at Zonhoven, the mood rose. As one of Monty's 'eyes and ears', Major Carol Mather, ex-SAS and escaped POW remembered fifty years on: 'At this point the atmosphere [at Zonhoven] changed completely, the gloom disappeared. Things were happening. We were in business again.' The reason was obvious to Monty's long-suffering Chief-of-Staff, Freddie de Guingand, who had flown in hastily from a fog-bound England. What was now happening was just 'Monty's cup of tea'. It certainly was and Monty was going to enjoy that cup of tea to the very last drop.

That same evening of the 17th, Bradley finally reached his Headquarters in the centre of the old city of Luxembourg, the Hotel Alfa, opposite the station. By this time he had known of the German counter-attack for nearly thirty hours since Strong's deputy General Betts had told Ike and Brad during what was supposedly a conference on the shortage of riflemen, but which was in all probability the start of Ike's fifth star celebrations.

During this period Ike had alerted the US 7th Armored Division in the north and the US 10th Armored in the south to move towards the area of the breakthrough. Bradley himself had done very little. On the morning of that Sunday he had departed Versailles, taken a leisurely lunch at the Paris Ritz and then, totally out of touch with his own HQ or anyone else's for that matter, he had motored back to Luxembourg.

He seemed strangely unworried. Naturally he didn't know his main land lines had been cut between Versailles, Luxembourg and Spa. But it didn't seem to worry him to have learned from Strong that his front was being attacked by the elements of nineteen German divisions and that he, Bradley, had very little idea of what those enemy divisions were aiming for. Was this simply a German spoiling attack? Was it a major thrust? Was it an attempt to outflank and unbalance Hodge's own attack in the Eifel launched on the 15th?

In the light of what was to come and the bitter quarrels between the British and American top brass, it might be opportune to point out that on the evening of 7 December Bradley was best placed to do something about the as yet confused situation in the Eifel/Ardennes. The 1st Army under Hodges was his responsibility and his Luxembourg HQ could reach Hodges in Spa in an hour by car and both HQs had US Army landing strips close by which could shorten that journey considerably. Thus, even if the land lines were cut, Bradley could have reached his commander in the field or have him come to Luxembourg without difficulty.

On that evening the German penetration of Middleton's corps was not deep enough to cause any kind of split between the 1st Army and its neighbours, Simpson's 9th to the north and Patton's 3rd to the south. Middleton's corps had been penetrated, but not as deeply as to make necessary the formation of southern and northern defensive 'shoulders', as they were called in military parlance.

In essence Bradley was still in the most favourable position to take over control at Hodges' level, or at least give encouragement to the hard-pressed ex-infantryman, who now found himself in a very tricky position.

But Bradley didn't take over, or at least, give Hodges more direct couragement at his HQ in Spa. To all extents and purposes, he did nothing that Sunday evening that might contribute to the defeat of the German attack, save to maintain proudly that he would never move his present HQ. As he wrote later:

> I will never move backwards with a headquarters. There is too much prestige at stake. To retreat would be a sure sign of weakness – to the

Germans, the Luxembourgers and my own troops. A panic would ensue.

It was not a good move. It would ensure that Bradley, the commander of three American armies in the area, would be cut off from two of them, with only the 3rd Army directly under his control. And as we know, the 3rd US Army was commanded by General George Patton, determined to make a name for himself in the coming battle. It was going to be the worst kind of move for Bradley, a case of the tail wagging the dog. In effect, Bradley would end up commanding no one save his own headquarters staff. As we shall see, Monty would be in charge of the bulk of the US troops in what would be called the 'Battle of the Bulge', while an angry, frustrated Bradley would be on the sidelines – a mere spectator of his subordinate Patton gaining all the glory of the epic relief of Bastogne, ensuring himself that place in US military history that would never be Bradley's.

For on the morning of Monday 18 December, when Patton, together with his driver, the sole representatives of the Third Army to enter the new battle, arrived in the Hotel Alfa to take up residence there for the remainder of the battle, it was already clear that Patton's and Bradley's roles were being reversed.

Bradley said to his subordinate: 'You won't like what I'm going to do but I fear it is necessary.' Thereupon, in Bradley's words: 'I briefed him on the extent of the German penetration. I outlined my strategy. We had to break off our attacks eastward, turn Hodges' army south and Patton's army north.'

Then Bradley asked what Patton could do to help Middleton's hard-pressed VIII Corps. 'His answer astounded me. Patton said he could have three divisions – the 4th Armored, 80th and 26th Infantry moving northwards in about twenty-four hours.'

In effect, Patton had already decided his own strategy. As we have seen, his staff had been planning it ever since 9 December. Bradley's 'strategy', if he had ever really had one, as he so confidently maintains in post-war memoirs, meant nothing to Patton. Patton was out for glory – on his own terms. Now Bradley would be relegated to the status of an observer and in the end he would blame Montgomery for this role – erroneously. If anyone placed Bradley in that position it was his erstwhile subordinate, Patton, who would write in his diary two days later: 'Destiny sent for me in a hurry when things got tight. Perhaps God saved me for this effort.'

On the morning of that Monday, Monty must have been animated by a feeling somewhat akin to Patton's, though probably he would have kept 'Divine Providence' out of the matter. After three months of being the shunned outsider, whose usefulness was militarily limited, he now had another chance to prove himself as a great captain. Naturally he had not received the call from Ike which would summon him to repair the damage of the Supreme Commander's neglect of what he, Monty, saw as the correct strategy to win the war. But he must have felt that summons would soon come.

It had to. The German attack had shown the weakness of Ike's command and strategy. Now, with Middleton's front pierced, once the Germans broke through his eggshell-thin line completely, there was nothing much to stop them ranging far and wide. In Belgium and Luxembourg there were practically no reserves save for supply troops and reinforcement holding units and no natural defensive lines once the Ardennes woods were cleared, save the Meuse river. If that was crossed, the Belgian capital Brussels and the great supply port of Antwerp were wide open. How were the Americans going to get themselves out of the mess that, due to their foolishness and inability to listen to advice, they had gotten themselves into?

Freddie de Guingand, recovered from the 'peasouper' over the Channel and his hairy flight to Eindhoven, found the 'master' at the top of his form and really enjoying himself. 'I never admired my Chief more than on occasions like that.' Despite the really bad news coming in, directly or indirectly from Hodges' HQ, Monty was optimistic, ready to tackle the problems which were beginning to mount up rapidly.

That morning General 'Lightning Joe' Collins, who had gained his reputation in the Pacific and was Monty's favourite US Corps Commander, paid a visit to Hodges' HQ at Spa. He found Hodges trying to ignore the confusion all about him. Outside the great hotel, where Field Marshal von Hindenburg had forced the Kaiser to surrender Imperial Germany in 1918, US trucks were already lined up, their drivers gunning their engines nervously, as HQ staff threw their gear out of the windows to them, impatient to escape before the 'Krauts' came down the hill into the Belgian resort town.

Hodges welcomed the corps commander with:

Nice to use you, Joe. Big Simp [General Simpson, commander of the US 9th Army to which Collins' 7th Corps belonged] is letting me borrow you until we've straightened this mess here.

Just at that moment, a pale-faced colonel popped his head round the door, came across and leaned against Hodges' skinny shoulder, saying urgently: 'General, if you don't want to be captured, you'd better get out of here. The Germans are only a mile away' [they weren't].

'Later . . . later!' Hodges exclaimed.

'But General,' Colonel 'Monk' Dickson, Hodges' Chief-of-Intelligence, who three days before had predicted the Germans would attack in 1st Army's sector, interjected swiftly, 'there is no time to lose.'

Hodges, trying to keep cool even under pressure from his closest staff officers, said to Collins: 'Yes, you're going to be my strategic reserve.'

Collins' reply is not recorded. It didn't really matter. He wasn't going to be Hodges' 'strategic reserve' for long. Soon he'd be under the command of Montgomery. For at the Spa Headquarters of the US 1st Army things were moving far too fast for any kind of forward planning.

Colonel Bigland, the first of Monty's 'eyes and ears' to arrive at Spa, saw immediately that disaster loomed. Bigland was very pro-American and had served some time at Bradley's HQ. But he was a realist and felt 'they [Hodges' staff and officers] were not too happy about their own position and were certainly not planning far enough ahead . . . [such as] a reserve corps under General Collins.'

Bigland was very sympathetic. He believed he knew what the Yanks thought of the British; that they were too cautious because they had had a lot of good people killed and had been fighting since 1940. All the same, that typical vaunted Yankee 'get up and go' was lacking this Monday morning at Spa. To him Hodges looked a 'tired old man – and I think a frightened one'.

At his own headquarters at Zonhoven, Monty was everything else but tired. He rose to meet the challenge with the energy of a man half his age. While his chief-of-intelligence, Brigadier Williams, faced up to the 'flap' and later panic at Versailles – 'they kept calling us until we thought we would go crazy. Strong . . . got hysterical over the Ardennes,' Monty called the 'useless' Whiteley at the Versailles HQ and told him what was really happening.

The latter's responses is not recorded. But later Monty signalled Brooke:

The Germans can reach the Meuse at Namur without opposition . . . I have told Whiteley that Ike ought to put me in operational charge of all troops on the northern half of the front. I consider he should be given a direct order by someone to do so. This situation needs to be handled very firmly and with a tight grip.

Again Monty was pushing his own case with absolutely no sense of personal modesty. He wanted the northern command, which would place him in charge of most of Bradley's troops, plus his own 1st Canadian and 2nd British Armies. But when that was said about the supreme egoist Montgomery, what was the alternative?

It was clear that Hodges, despite the later cover-up, was a broken man. At his headquarters, staff officers were burning secret plans in panic, and weren't making a very good job of it. Hodges had been advised he should fly to his rear HQ at Chaudfontaine on the Meuse river before the German armoured columns came barrelling down the steep hill that led into the resort town. In fact, 1st Army's rough-and-ready appreciation of German intentions was wrong. The Germans, primarily 'Battle Group Peiper' of the 1st SS Division, had turned south-west instead of heading north in the direction of Spa. But his staff officers convinced their chief and naturally themselves that this was the German intention. Thus, by ten o'clock that Monday night, the headquarters of the 1st US Army had, to all intents and purposes, been abandoned.

Worried that he was not receiving any information from Eisenhower, Hodges or Bradley, Monty sent out his whole force of liaison officers to discover what was going on. He didn't believe that two of Hodges' divisions, the 106th and 28th, could just disappear, so he dispatched his 'eyes and ears' even down to the level of US Corps commanders to find out the truth.

One of his men reported back from Bradley's HQ in Luxembourg City that 12th Army Group headquarters was particularly alarmed. But by the time the message reached Monty, that situation had changed. At the little Belgian town of Aywaille, soldiers manning a road block at the bridge had stopped a US jeep and discovered it contained Germans of SS Obersturmbannführer Otto Skorzeny's* commandos dressed in US uniform. These men had confessed that while they had been in training in Bavaria, they had heard a rumour that some of their English-speaking comrades had been specially picked to assassinate Eisenhower, Montgomery and other high-ranking Allied officers.

This caused something akin to a panic, not only in Ike's HQ, where the Supreme Commander was placed in what amounted to 'protective custody' for over a week, but also in Bradley's Luxembourg headquarters. Bradley immediately had the stars removed from his helmet and the vehicles in which he drove. When the Luxembourg manager of the Hotel Alfa told him that a sniper over the square in front of the city's railway station could shoot him easily from that building, Bradley took to leaving the hotel by the back entrance in a side-street and every night he slept in a different bedroom in the rambling, turn-of-the-century hotel.

Monty, who was also warned of the threat through Bletchley, seemed to have ignored it, though in his pre-war Rolls Royce adorned with a large Union Jack, which he used through most of the Battle of the Bulge, he presented an easily identifiable target. He concentrated not only on preparing to protect his right flank, but also to go a major step further to defend the last natural barrier in the path of the advancing Germans, the Meuse river. Well might Bradley's Chief-of-Staff snort when he heard what Monty was up to: 'What the devil do they state we're doing ... starting back for the beaches?' But a cocky Montgomery had no intention

*Skorzeny, the man who rescued Mussolini from his Italian captors, was now running Germany's equivalent of the SAS.

of doing any such thing. For as signalled cheekily to Brooke: 'We can't come out through Dunkirk this time . . . the Germans still hold the place.'

On that night of the 18th, while Monty was working a little later than normal, planning his moves (Montgomery was a stickler for a routine, always going to bed promptly at ten after his glass of hot milk), Patton was returning from his visit to Bradley's HQ and heading for his own headquarters in Nancy in France. He didn't like travelling at night even at the best of times. He was scared that one of those 'crazy truck drivers' might run him down. Now however, he had another worry. He had just heard that German paratroopers had landed in force behind US lines and that Skorzeny's 'killers' were on the rampage, looking for top brass to assassinate. But he finally reached his HQ safely after some delay, for the French and the American military police had put up roadblocks and checkpoints everywhere on the dead straight road that led from Verdun to Nancy, sixty-nine kilometres away.

There he was informed, even before he had taken off his pistol belt and celebrated lacquered helmet with its outsize gold stars, that General Bradley wanted him urgently on the scrambler phone. When Patton got to the phone, Bradley wasn't there. His chief-of-staff instead told the 3rd Army commander that the orders Bradley had given Patton earlier were cancelled. Instead of beginning the relief operation within twenty-four hours, he was to start moving his best armoured division, the Fourth, towards Longwy on the French border with Belgium–Luxembourg at once.

Some time later, at eight o'clock, Patton called Bradley and was informed by a now serious and alarmed Army Group Commander that 'the situation is much worse than when I talked to you, George'. Bradley added, surprising Patton a little at the sudden change in plan: 'You and a staff officer are to meet me at Verdun for a conference with General Eisenhower tomorrow morning at eleven.'

We don't know much about Patton's reaction to that eight o'clock phone call of Monday 18 December 1944. We know that he had his plans already worked out. But what Patton didn't know that night was that he was on the verge of becoming the great American hero of the Battle of the Bulge, next to the GIs who would fight it.

At the conference of the morrow held in the 19th-century French *caserne*, named after the giant who had lost a leg at the battles fought on the height beyond, André Maginot, and created France's great white elephant which bore his name, the Maginot Line, Patton would receive his call to greatness; be given that chance to achieve his destiny. It would be George S Patton's finest hour.

CHAPTER XV

Every sign of an evacuation in a hurry

Just after midnight on the morning of Tuesday, a young duty officer of the 29th British Armoured Brigade, which belonged to the 11th Armoured Division, was awakened from his uneasy doze by the incessant ringing of his phone. Sleepily he picked it up and then awoke completely, shocked into instant awareness. For he was speaking to no less a person than Monty's Chief-of-Staff, Major General Freddie de Guingand!

Hurriedly the young captain seized his writing pad and started scribbling down the order that de Guingand dictated to him. 'The Brigade will move as quickly as possible . . . The brigadier will start at once . . . for Army Group headquarters-rear . . . to receive detailed instructions . . .'

That brought to an end all thought of sleep for the four regiments which made up the 11th Armoured Brigade. It was not as days of yore for the cavalry regiment to be ordered into battle by the notes of a bugle; they had been summoned by telephone. But where were their armoured steeds?

Not where they should have been, attached to their riding masters, the four regiments. For the cavalry regiments of the 11th Armoured (the 1st Royal Tanks, 23rd Hussars, the 2nd Fife and Forfar Yeomanry and the lorried infantry of the 8th Battalion, the Rifle Brigade) had just been withdrawn from the line and had handed in their battle-weary old tanks. They were going to be replaced by newer and better models, ready for Monty's coming attack over the German border. Now all the Brigade possessed in the way of armour were a couple of dozen clapped-out tanks, to face (unknown as yet to the tankers) elements of five German panzer divisions heading for the Meuse river.

The brigadier was soon located, however. He had had a couple of days off, the first since the 11th Armoured's 29th Brigade had first gone into action in Normandy. He was away shooting as brigadiers do; this time at birds and not human beings. He protested over the phone that dawn: 'But I haven't got any bloody tanks.' Then the 45-year-old brigadier realised that this wasn't some kind of pre-Christmas joke, intended to ruin his holiday. This was the real thing. He was ordered harshly: 'Get your old ones back, those that are runners.' With these battle-worn 'runners' he was to proceed *immediately* to Dinant on the Meuse 'to block the passage of at least two Panzer armies'.

Brigadier Roscoe Harvey, the 29th Armoured Brigade's commander, did not know whether to laugh or cry. All the same, four hours later the first of his 3,000-man force was heading across a fogbound Belgium towards the new battle to come.

All that morning all available staff officers in Zonhoven and Brussels worked flat out to alert troops, patch up the holes in the defences of northern Belgium, ready to back up the Meuse defence line that Monty aimed to create with whatever ad hoc formations that could be found.

In charge of the operation was a handsome, young major-general, David Belchem, located at Montgomery's Brussels rear headquarters. He had been told by the 'Master', as Monty's staff officers called him irreverently behind his back, that his first priority was to secure the main bridges across the Meuse, five in all. They had to be secured while other and larger formations were brought up ready for battle in case the Germans attempted an assault crossing as they had done back in 1940.

Monty's guess was that the Germans would attempt to do so at Namur. Monty was wrong. The German objective was the bridge at Huy which Obersturmbannführer Peiper had been told to capture and hold even if he had just one tank left. Already one of Skorzeny's Jeep teams had recced the Huy bridge and found it defended apparently by an anti-aircraft unit on the other side of the river and a handful of infantry on the eastern bank. As they reported back to their headquarters by radio, the Huy Bridge was ready for the taking.

But the Germans had reckoned without Belchem. He had already told Monty that the Namur bridge was being defended by five lonely, 'and probably shit-scared', GIs.

Monty had laughed and had said in his 'quiet, reassuring way': 'Put road-blocks around Brussels. If any German armoured cars do get into the city, get yourself a Boyes anti-tank rifle [an antiquated weapon which had gone out of fashion back in 1940] and stalk them with any of your chaps whom you can muster.' With that he hung up and let Belchem get on with the business of the Meuse bridges.

Despite Monty's throwaway comment, the situation in the Belgian capital was becoming worrisome. Its citizens, panicking already at the approach of the Germans (Eisenhower had ordered a news blackout; still the locals could scent there was trouble coming their way) now started severing all contacts with British soldiers. The portraits of Roosevelt and Churchill, together with the flags of Britain and the USA which had adorned virtually every citizen's windows since the Liberation, had been hastily removed overnight. Even black market contacts between Belgian racketeers and the armed services virtually ceased. Already the previous November there had almost been a rising of left-wing Belgians in the capital and Monty had been forced to discreetly surround it with the 11th Armoured Division. Now with the communist guerrilla revolt in Athens, which was taking 80,000 British troops to contain, Belchem could fear similar trouble here in Brussels – and there were no fighting troops in the city.

Still Belchem, the organiser, started hurriedly to round up troops wherever he could find them. Clerks, cooks, drivers, men who hadn't fired a rifle in years, were handed weapons, still in their original grease, and hurried out into the countryside and made to form roadblocks on the roads leading from the east into the north Belgian plain. (It was said that at that time that even the Canadian medics manning the underground green cross VD centre in the Boulevard Max were taken away from their irrigation tubes and contraceptive bags to help succor any potential wounded in the battle apparently soon to come.)

Belchen heard, for example, that there was an anti-tank regiment ready to embark at the Belgian port of Zeebrugge to return home to the UK. A whole regiment of anti-tank gunners would be really useful against the advancing panzers. He grabbed the phone and tried to contact them. But their CO was already on board ship. He switched to the port's British movements officer. From him he heard that the gunners' ship was already in Zeebrugge's lock, waiting for the water to rise to the requisite height so that the craft could pass into the North Sea. The movements officer reported that there were exactly fifty minutes to go before that happened. Belchem didn't hesitate. He didn't know how such things were done, but he bellowed down the bad line: 'Everybody off!' Half an hour later, the time-expired gunners, grumbling that they were going to miss Christmas at home, as would so many others this year, were rolling eastwards. They reached Namur that night.

Patton had planned the move of his three divisions from the Saar to Luxembourg several days before, but as yet had not done so (though his feat would go down in US military history). Meanwhile a handful of British staff officers were moving everything from a small, secret unit called the 'R-Engineers', who would blow the bridges across the Meuse if necessary, to one armoured and two infantry divisions, within a matter of hours.

But Monty wanted even more strength on the Meuse. The situation in the Ardennes was getting steadily worse by the hour and the first of the German armour was expected to make its appearance on the river's eastern bank soon on this Tuesday. But where was it to come from? The British manpower barrel was about scraped clean. Ike, faced with the same problem, had alerted the last two US combat divisions in the UK, which were ready for action, though both were totally green and would suffer accordingly in the fighting soon to come – the 11th Armored and the ill-fated 17th US Airborne Division.

Now Monty did the same. He called upon the only combat-ready and combat-experienced division in the British Army left in Home Command: the now reinforced 6th Airborne Division.

The sudden move for the 'Red Devils' came as a complete surprise. The 13th Battalion now up to full strength once more, was no exception. Because of the news blackout that Ike had immediately slapped on the Bulge battlefield, the fighting units of the 6th Airborne knew little of what was happening at the front and just how grave the situation was in the Eifel/Ardennes. For example, on that morning of Tuesday 19 December the London *Daily Mail*'s headline read: 'TWENTY-FIVE MILE GAP IN ALLIED LINE. But the news allowed through by SHAEF censors minimised the penetration. It stated that the Germans 'in a small force' were still stalled around the Belgian border town of Stavelot and had not yet reached Bastogne. In fact, the leading German armoured units had bypassed the key Belgian road junction and were on their way to the Meuse.

So Major Keane of the Sixth Division's 7th Paras, for example, was surprised when he was informed that the divisional commander, Major-General Bols, had called an immediate conference of all staff officers. He wondered why, as many did that day. He told himself that they didn't need a conference to plan for 'Operation Christmas Leave' – the mass exodus of the division for home, scheduled for forty-eight hours before Christmas Day. It had already been long worked out by the men of the parachute battalions eager to spend some time with their families once again. In fact, the men of the Sixth wouldn't celebrate Xmas '44 in England, nor Christmas '45 or '46 for that matter. Indeed, many of the young Red Devils would never celebrate another Christmas; they'd be dead.

Now surprised paras, coming back from a pint in the local pubs around Salisbury Plain, or the lucky few who had got their 'feet under the table' in some willing female's kitchen, or even managed to 'cock their leg over' in a winter-chilled bedroom, were told to get packing; they were moving out. Hastily they were briefed that the Germans had really broken through in strength and were heading for the bridges across the Meuse. There was no time to plan a para-drop; the weather was lousy for flying anyway, and many airfields in Britain and the Allied-held continent were socked in. They'd go to war this time on wheels, embarking on ferries at Dover and Tilbury and the like. There they'd be given some 'hot grub'. They were; fried sausages and beans with fried bread! It wasn't much for cold, hungry young men with healthy appetites. But later they were glad of the 'bangers and beans' – this would be the only hot meal they'd get in the next three days as they rolled towards the bridge at Dinant. From now on the only real food the Red Devils would receive, as they crawled through the snowbound countryside at twenty miles an hour, 'was apples and other fruits and chunks of bread handed us by the civilians who lined the road and cheered the Red Devils on their way to meet the enemy'.

'Twas ever thus. When had the British Army ever spoiled its soldiers? But Monty knew his men. The average British soldier might grumble a lot, but in the final analysis, he accepted his humble, hard lot. Not for King and Country, as some of the hurrah patriots believed, but for his regiment and his mates.

But even if Monty had had time to consider the hardships inflicted on his long-suffering 'Tommies' by this sudden move that had not allowed for planning any luxuries such as hot food, he couldn't have done much about it. Now he was moving large-scale forces, not just battalions of infantry, squadrons of engineers and SAS men. General Horrocks, who had watched Brooke weep on Monty's shoulder at Dunkirk, now four years later commander of the five division-strong British XXX Corps, had been alerted by Brussels. He later recalled:

> Then the incredible happened. The telephone rang and the voice of a senior staff officer at General Dempsey's 2nd Army HQ said, 'The Germans have smashed through the American front on the Ardennes and the situation is extremely confused'.

Horrocks, who would be soon following up the 29th Armoured Brigade to the Meuse with his two key infantry divisions, the 51st Highland and the 53rd Welsh Divisions, could not have imagined how confused the situation was even in his wildest dreams. The lead brigade was battling not only terrible weather on their journey to the river, but also panic everywhere. As one of its officers, Noel Bell, noted as his troops passed through Brussels:

> Signs of the alarm and despondency ... were already evident. Reinforcement holding units were all standing to, manning road blocks. In the city itself the 'Whitehall Warriors' were packing their bags and preparing to evacuate themselves and probably their girlfriends, too, to safer climes.

As the four regiments of the 29th Armoured Brigade got closer to the new front, they found US 'soft traffic' streaming back across the bridges, eager to put as much space as possible between themselves and the advancing Germans. At Givet, the 23rd Hussars of the 29th discovered that a reinforcement holding unit, including men of the 101st Airborne, had made no attempt to defend the bridge. No slit trenches or defensive positions had been prepared. It seemed that the local 'Screaming Eagles' had no ambitions to become members of the 'Battered Bastards of Bastogne' just up the road.

But those were not the only problems the 29th faced. The 23rd Hussars discovered that their Shermans had really deteriorated while they had been in the depots waiting to be exchanged for newer vehicles. 'Mice had got into the abandoned Shermans,' one of them wrote later. 'Some had no wireless sets or sets that did not work, or machine guns that were missing.' All the way to Givet the advancing Hussars were plagued, not only by the terrible icy weather, the fleeing Americans and the shortage of food, but also by tanks dropping out at regular intervals to be repaired at the roadside under harsh conditions. Yet still they were getting there followed by their comrades of the 51st, 53rd and the seasick Red Devils, who were taking twenty-four stomach-churning hours to cross the Channel.

As Patton, Eisenhower, Bradley and the rest of the top brass set out for the great conference at Verdun, three of Monty's 'eyes and ears' were rolling into Hodges' HQ at Spa, wondering at the quietness and eerie atmosphere of the resort town. The handful of civilians they encountered as they drove down the long, straight, tree-lined road that led to Hodges' HQ looked the other way when they saw the young officers. They told themselves that something was definitely wrong. Where had all the Yanks gone?

They finally came across two Yanks. They looked as puzzled as Monty's 'eyes and ears'. As one of the officers recalled: '[They] had just been to bed with two women and were hanging around the deserted street wondering what to do next.'

A little later the team came across a German civilian. That was not surprising. There were plenty of Germans in the area, some friendly, some not. This one was friendly. He told the surprised Britishers a tale they could hardly believe. All the 'Amis' had pulled out of Spa at three the previous day. Even the *Ami* general in charge had fled. Where they had all gone he did not know.

Finally they reached the big headquarters in the centre of this strange ghost city. In spite of the cold, many of its windows were wide open and the lights were still blazing, though not a sound came from within the former hotel. They entered and discovered the place'[was] completely deserted, with Christmas lunch laid out and every sign of evacuation in a hurry', as Major Carol Mather of the SAS recalled many years later.

Colonel Bigland, just as bemused as Mather, remembered as they stood perplexed in the big room, '. . . the Christmas tree was decorated in the dining room, telephones were all in the offices, papers were all over the place'. (An hour or so later two staff officer of the US 7th Armored Division, hurrying to the Bulge battle, even found top-secret maps pinned to the walls of the HQ and were kept busy ripping them down before the place became too much for them and they themselves fled.)

Later, in his account of that strange day, Mather wrote: 'It was though we had come upon the *Marie Celeste* floating upon an empty sea.' Slowly the truth started to dawn on the three young officers.

The German attack was more serious than we thought, for the evacuation of the headquarters showed every sign of panic. We could find no American troops or civilian helpers to explain the mystery . . . Running through the offices, equipped with the usual paraphernalia, we collected some classified papers to prove that we had actually been in the place in case we were met with disbelief on our return.

Now while Colonel Bigland set off from Bradley's HQ in Luxembourg, the two other 'eyes and ears', Majors Mather and Harden, prepared to return to Zonhoven. On their way they'd pass through Chaudfontaine, Hodges' rear headquarters, where they hoped to find out what had happened to Hodges and his Spa headquarters staff.

With the sound to the east of the guns rolling back and forth like thunder, the two young officers drove through strangely deserted countryside and villages, shuttered-up and locked-door, though they had the impression that frightened people were hiding behind those closed wooden shutters listening tensely to every sound, their hearts beating like trip-hammers.

Finally they came out of the hills down to the wet sports field where Hodges had his rear HQ. Here they found the quiet, middle-aged officer, who looked more like a moderately successful businessman than a general. They had never met Hodges before, but they were shocked by the appearance of this man who commanded nearly as many US divisions as the 'Master' himself. He appeared 'considerably shaken' and could give 'no coherent account of what had happened'.

So they set off once more to report to Monty. They wondered how he would take the news they brought with them. They need not have worried. Monty, who had boasted to Freddie de Guingand that this situation was 'just his cup of tea', would turn even the flight of an army commander and his headquarters to his advantage.

Mather reached Zonhoven after dark. Monty allowed him time to have a cup of tea. Later Mather thought he deserved something stronger. But Monty had no time for that sort of thing. He wanted Mather's report immediately. Monty reacted sharply to Mather's news. The young major of the Welsh Guards, who had joined the SAS and escaped from an Italian POW camp, was to return to Chaudfontaine at once. 'Tell Hodges,' Monty ordered, 'tell Hodges he must block the Meuse bridges. He must hold them till my troops arrive.'

Mather objected. 'But how am I to give him these orders when he is not under your command, sir?'

Monty didn't bat an eyelid. 'Just tell him,' he rasped. 'The Liège crossing, in particular, must be defended at all costs. Call up L-in-C troops. Use any obstacle he can find . . . including farm carts.'

For a moment Mather thought that Monty was making a joke, but the

'Master's' face remained very solemn and the young officer knew he wasn't.

'He must hold all bridges all day tomorrow and make sure that officers supervise each operation. You can tell him that from me.' Just before Mather left, Monty added, as the former recorded, 'there would be 90 jeep officer patrols from Phantom [Phantom Recce with direct wireless links to Monty's HQ] on the other side of the River Meuse to do a recce of the German point. They'd be followed by the defences troops of Horrocks' XXX Corps'. Monty's last words were: 'Wake me up at half past five if you're back.'

Those last words indicated to Mather just how serious the situation was. Never since he had joined Monty's headquarters had anything been allowed to disturb the 'Master's' routine, especially his sleeping habits. Muffled in his duffle coat and hurrying through the thick, damp fog to his jeep, the young SAS officer realised the full impact of the 'Master's' instructions. Monty was sending him to give orders to an American army commander, who wasn't under his, Monty's, command. Without Ike's permission – or the London War Office's for that matter – Montgomery, in essence, was taking over a large US army numbering half a million men or more. As Mather was to write in his old age: 'A drama was being played out which had in it the seeds of certain imponderable events to come.' How right he was Mather could not even guess as he set out on his key mission that fog-bound night in December sixty years ago. For it was to start the end of that special relationship which Churchill had worked so hard to bring about four years earlier.

The top brass met at Casern Maginot beneath the blood-soaked heights of Verdun where, back in the 'old war', a certain Corporal Hitler had been wounded and that 'damned Joan of Arc' (as FDR called de Gaulle contemptuously) had been captured. All around the environs of the French city on the Meuse were scattered the eighty-two cemeteries filled with the dead of the two-year battle. It was certainly not a place to inspire confidence in the American generals this grey December morning, especially with the point of the German attack over the border in Luxembourg only fifty miles or less away.

The surroundings of the French barracks, set by a little cobbled side road, did little to cheer up the brass. They met on the second floor, which was spartan, smelly and cold, heated by a solitary, pot-bellied stove and most of them kept their coats on. Now Ike arrived. He had come from Versailles in an armour-plated Packard, escorted by tommy-gun toting suspicious-eyed MPs. He looked 'grave' and 'almost ashen', as one eye-witness recalled, and he was chain-smoking more than ever – sixty a day now.

He had reason to. Hodges appeared to be a broken reed; his front was virtually split in two and the 1st Army commander was seemingly doing little about it. As General Betts, Strong's deputy, would soon report from Chaudfontaine:

I found the place a terrible mess. They just [didn't] know what was going on. As far as fighting [was] concerned, the First Army . . . seemed to have no plan for meeting this attack and I couldn't see any orders going forth.

When Smith, Ike's chief-of-staff, heard this, he recommended Hodges' relief. In the end, the prestige of the US Army demanded that Hodges' breakdown had to be concealed – the official war historian of the Department of Defense stated that Hodges was 'in bed for two days with a viral infection' which was a patent lie, and the 1st Army commander retained his job until the end of the war.

After criticising Strong and his staff for being ten minutes late, Ike started the key conference, letting Strong do his briefing, during which he pulled his punches as he always did. He told the generals what they wanted to hear, encouraging Bradley and naturally Patton (as he wrote himself to the author) in their belief that they 'would welcome an attack when it came'.

For his part Bradley said little during the two-hour 'historic conference', as US historians always call it. Indeed, he was ignored by Ike, who in the end turned to Patton who, in the absence of Montgomery, was now obviously the principal player in the whole tense situation.* We all know how Patton then dominated the show, telling Ike he was prepared to turn his already briefed and prepared XXX Corps north to attack into the Bulge, before turning to Bradley and snarling, cigar in hand: 'Brad, the Kraut's stuck his head in the meat grinder.' He turned his fist in a grinding motion. 'And this time I've got hold of the handle.'

Patton fielded a few questions. For he had already rehearsed his answers to the questions that would likely come from Eisenhower. All in all, it was a bravura performance and his aide, Colonel Codman, wrote later:

Within an hour everything had been thrashed out – the divisions to be employed, objectives, new Army boundaries, the amount of front to be taken over by 6th Army Group . . . and virtually all of them settled on Gen. Patton's terms.

Eisenhower's reaction to Patton's dramatic announcement that he was prepared to send a corps into battle within three days is not properly

---

* All the details of this 'historic conference', it must be remembered, are from the memoirs of eye-witnesses who had some shortcoming or other to hide or protect.

recorded. After all, for the next week he would become a virtual prisoner of his own security men. Despite Patton's partisans, such as Martin Blumenson, stating that Patton's announcement that he was moving north to battle was 'the sublime moment of the operation that only a master could think of executing', Mongtomery already knew of it and was, as we have seen, already moving three divisions of his own to the south to be followed by two more if necessary.

But it is clear from subsequent events this Tuesday/Wednesday 19/20 December 1944, that Eisenhower was not entirely satisfied that Patton's help would suffice. Bradley's VIII Corps had been broken, with two divisions shattered and Middleton's other two separated from each other. Now what the Americans called 'shoulders' were developing: one in the south under Bradley's command (and Bradley had really only the three Patton divisions at his disposal), the other in the north under Hodges' command – and as we have seen Hodges appeared to be a broken man who could not exercise control. Could a failed general in the north and a militarily impotent one in the south restore the situation in time?

What was Eisenhower to do? For, in the final analysis, he would be held to account for any real debacle in the Ardennes. Who should he turn to? Who would advise him reliably – *and swiftly*? Should it be the Commander-in-Chief of the US Army, FDR, personally? That was out of the question. FDR was enjoying his first Christmas at home with his family since 1932. Besides, FDR seemed little concerned by the military events in Europe. Should he go through channels then and approach his next superior, Marshall? Could the latter advise him swiftly enough and dare he admit to Marshall that he had made a mess of the overall land command in north-west Europe? What about Churchill? The old boy knew a lot about war and had always backed him in his military decisions. But Churchill was, after all, a half-limey. That wouldn't go down well with the Great American Public.

For Eisenhower it must have been a day of agonising and doubt. It seemed that Patton and Bradley felt they had the situation well in hand, at least on the southern 'shoulder'. Yet Eisenhower knew that Bradley, so far, had made no attempt to direct the 'northern' one. He had not even flown to see the broken reed Hodges, although he had promised on the 18th he would. Now, when America was suffering its greatest military setback since that 'Day of Infamy' four years before, he was taking a tremendous risk by backing the self-appointed American team of 'Brad and George'. What if they didn't stop the rot? Who would be blamed? Naturally, he, Eisenhower, would. *What was he to do?*

In the event, others would make the decision for him. There would be his trusted senior staff officers, Smith, Strong and Whiteley. The other was Monty. With his typical single-mindedness and blind egocentricity, he didn't consider there was still a problem about who should take over and fight the Battle of the Bulge. He knew already who should command – Bernard Law Montgomery.

CHAPTER XVI

Talking like a damned British Staff Officer

General Strong, stiff, weary and cold from the long journey from Verdun to Paris, returned to his Versailles HQ to find the situation had worsened dramatically. His staff hurried back and forth bringing ever more tales of woe. More and more German assault formations had been identified and they were some of the best the Wehrmacht still possessed – the 3rd and 5th Parachute Divisions, the 12th SS-Hitler Youth, the Führerbegleitbrigade. From all sides came alarming rumours of German paratroopers and saboteurs being dropped behind Allied lines, even as far as the French Riviera. German agents were attempting to bribe Belgian dockers in Antwerp to strike, just as they were doing with French communist railway workers. From England came alarming tales of a mass rising of German POWs planned for this very week. The POWs would break out of their camps and either march across to Yorkshire, where they would be picked up by a German fleet of small craft, or march on London itself. Trigger-happy GIs were manning roadblocks all over the Allied zone, asking each other stupid questions about movie stars and baseball giants in order to check if the other person was a genuine American or not. It was said that a US general who answered a question wrongly had been thrown into jail by his own MPs for several hours; that six American blacks had been shot by mistake at a bridge near Liège; and that even Field Marshal Montgomery had had the tyres of his Rolls Royce blasted by an over zealous GI at such a roadblock.

Chaos reigned everywhere and everywhere broken US formations were fleeing to the rear, leaving behind their equipment, even their artillery, while pockets of brave GIs from already shattered units were putting up last-ditch stands without a hope of surviving.

Now Strong, who had wrongly guided Eisenhower on the intelligence situation back in the second week of December,* decided he must inform his boss of the true picture at the front and make that overwhelming

---

*General Strong told the author that it was not until a quarter of a century after the event that he had learned that the US Army had carried out a secret inquiry into pre-Bulge intelligence, including his own role in the matter.

suggestion, which would bring with it all sorts of imponderables, including his own future. It was now that he contacted Whiteley, no partisan of Monty's and a man the latter thought 'quite useless'. The big general, nicknamed 'Jock', had already been in contact with Monty again. The latter had suggested in his usual immodest manner that he, Monty, should be given command of all US troops on the northern 'shoulder'. Strong concurred and the two of them decided to put this proposition to Smith.

Smith had risen from enlisted man to major-general. He had achieved this rank by hard work, clever staff reports and a temper as fiery as his red hair. He was no respecter of persons, male or female. He was a womaniser who kept a WAC mistress, though his comment that 'A WAC is a female GI with a built-in foxhole' seems to show he didn't think much of her either. Although reputedly anti-British, he kept his views to himself because he knew Ike would not tolerate any such attitudes among his key staff. But that didn't make Smith *pro*-British. He was a long-time regular US officer and naturally he thought that American interests should come first.

Predictably Smith flew off the handle when Whiteley suggested Monty should take over the northern shoulder. He said he had always counted on Whiteley to maintain a 'completely Allied outlook'. Now here he was 'talking like a damned British Staff Officer'. It was obvious that cracks were beginning to appear right at the top in the much vaunted 'special relationship'. Still, Smith called Ike and relayed his message to Strong and Whiteley, saying that 'General Eisenhower says we can decide the matter after our staff meeting tomorrow morning'.

No panic here. No problem with urgency. Ike, it appeared, had the situation well in hand. The two British staff officers were simply just 'nervous nellies', as such officers, especially if they were in intelligence, often were. Indeed, as the official US war historian Hugh Cole recorded the event in his massive tome on the Battle of the Bulge (commissioned originally by Eisenhower incidentally), Bedell Smith . . . brought up the matter in the Supreme Commander's usual meeting with his staff (i.e. at 0800 hrs on 20 December). Eisenhower, in his turn, telephoned Bradley who agreed to the division of the command. In other words, the events of that night and morning of 19/20 December were all sweetness and light: a perfect example of harmony and co-operation at a moment of great crisis.

The truth was totally different. In fact a quarrel broke out between the two British staff officers and the hot-tempered Bedell Smith, who before the month was out was threatening to sock Juin, the French commander, 'on the jaw'. Smith told the two Britishers:

> . . . our proposal [as Strong called it] would be completely unacceptable to the Americans . . . and that because of the view we had taken of the

situation, neither Whiteley nor I could any longer be acceptable as staff officers to General Eisenhower. The next day [the 20th] instructions would be issued relieving us of our appointments and returning us to the United Kingdom. This looked like a sad ending.

At three o'clock that wintry day, with thousands of men fighting for their lives in the bitter darkness of the front, totally unaware of the feuding staff officers in their warm, cosy offices, Strong and Whiteley had effectively been sacked. Monty had not received the command he had coveted so greedily. His right flank was virtually wide open and the Germans were still racing through minimal opposition to that eggshell-thin defensive screen on Belgium's last natural barrier, the Meuse river.

Smith, however, had been shocked by the revelation of the two officers and their suggestion which had caused him to fire them. That was natural. After all, he was a general in an American army. Now, after they had departed, he started to think the suggestion over in a more rational manner. He decided to telephone Bradley in Luxembourg and see what he thought of the two Britishers' proposal. According to the first account of that call made by Bradley in 1948 (in his memoir *A Soldier's Story*), Smith said:

> Ike thinks it may be a good idea to turn over to Monty your two armies on the north and let him run that side of the Bulge from the 21st Army Group. It may save us a great deal of trouble.

According to Bradley's 1948 account, he queried whether such a changeover was necessary. He claimed that Smith then said it was 'the logical thing to do'.

In his later memoir, a rehash of the first one, most of it written by a ghost writer after Bradley was dead and his young wife was trying to cash in on his fame, Bradley lashed out at Smith and Whiteley, stating that he had been 'completely dumbfounded and shocked' by Smith's phone call, which he said had 'an Alice in Wonderland air'.

In this second account, the ghost writer concluded on behalf of the dead general of the army:

> I made one of the biggest mistakes of the war . . . instead of standing up to Smith, telling him SHAEF was losing its head, that I had things under control and reassuring him that Hodges was performing magnificently under the circumstances . . . [I] knuckled under.

Of course, as we have seen, Hodges was not 'performing magnificently'. Indeed, by the time Monty's 'eyes and ears' reached his Chaudfontaine HQ for the second time, he had gone downhill even further. Mather and

Harden were shown into the bedroom of Hodges' chief-of-staff, Major General Kean. He sat on his bed in his pyjamas, with a thick, brown blanket around his shoulders. He confirmed Monty's handwriting on the message they had brought from the 'master' and then continued talking.

Finally the American laid down the phone and took them to Hodges' quarters. He was fast asleep with an ADC in the other room. They roused him and the four of them draped a blanket round his skinny shoulders. Then Hodges put on his spectacles and read Monty's message. Just out of earshot, he and his chief-of-staff engaged in conversation. Mather strained his ears and heard some talk of 'consulting Brad and Ike'.

But nothing came of it and Hodges, whose 'reactions were slow', reread the Monty letter. It was, thought Marden, as if the 1st Army Commander couldn't believe the evidence of his own eyes.

Now Mather and Harden, as was their duty, started asking questions. Hodges told them that there were three gaps in his line, where the situation was fluid, but as Mather wrote later, Hodges had nothing to say 'on the important question of the Meuse Crossings'. He implied that they weren't important and anyway they'd be looked after in due course.

Kean, more aware of the problem, chimed in here and maintained that nothing would threaten the bridges of Liège, Huy and Namur for at least twenty-four hours, despite the fact that Skorzeny's jeep teams had already recced the last two crossings. And that was that.

As Mather later summed up his feelings:

It was evident that the Army Commander was completely out of touch. His chief of staff was more completely informed, but cagey or out of date. Neither of them seemed to be aware of the urgency of the situation and all that might imply to the Allied foothold in Europe.

Naturally Ike didn't know all this. But he did feel that things were not as they had seemed at that Verdun conference of the day before. In fact a solution had *not* been achieved there, despite Patton's promises and bold words. There were too many imponderables, in particular, how was Bradley going to control and defend the northern shoulder? He was refusing to move his HQ from the extreme end of the southern shoulder in Luxembourg; he was not really in touch with Hodges in the north; and, it appeared, his assessment of Hodges' fighting capability was incorrect. In essence Bradley had nothing to control save Patton's three divisions coming from the Saar; and well as he, Eisenhower, knew George Patton, he didn't think that Bradley could really control that particular maverick.

On that morning of the 20th Smith called the two crestfallen British officers, Strong and Whiteley, whom he had sacked during the night, to his office and told them he would put their suggestion about Montgomery to Eisenhower as his own suggestion, and one which was coming from an American and not a Britisher. During the eight o'clock staff conference, Smith raised the point that Bradley was in no position to control the battle from his HQ in Luxembourg. He said firmly that it was 'an open-and-shut case'.

Now he raised the question of a reorganisation of the command structure. He recommended that the control of the Ardennes should be split into two and that Bradley should retain control of the southern shoulder and that Monty should be ordered to take over the northern one and be given *temporary* command of the two US armies there, namely Simpson's Ninth and Hodges' First.

Ike had no alternative but to accept. The front was already effectively cut in two and Bradley had been out of touch with Hodges and probably Simpson, too, for over forty-eight hours. He needed Monty. Later that day Smith apologised to Strong and Whiteley, saying: 'What made me really mad was that I knew you were right. But my American feelings got the better of me.'

The reference to his 'American feelings' was indicative of the way things were going in the Anglo–American alliance. The US top brass realised that they were now the senior partner in the coalition and that they had to promote America's position within it.

Bradley reflected this growing feeling among the more anglophobe US generals. After the Monty decision had been made, Eisenhower immediately phoned the 12th Army Group commander to inform him of it. Strong, who was close by, heard some of the conversation. Bradley was loud and angry in his protests, crying: 'By God, Ike, I cannot be responsible to the American people if you do this. I resign.'

Eisenhower was not impressed by the threat. He pointed out that he and not Bradley was the one responsible to the American people. He added curtly, knowing that he could not afford to have the scandal of a Bradley resignation at this crucial stage of the battle: 'Your resignation, therefore, means absolutely nothing.'

Bradley continued to protest vehemently. But Eisenhower had had enough. He cut him off with a harsh, 'Well, Brad, those are my orders.' That was that. But Eisenhower took one major precaution to protect the prestige of the senior partner and its army in Europe. He ordered a news blackout on the new appointment. The world and the Great American Public were not to know that for the rest of the Battle of the Bulge, indeed from 20 December 1944 until 5 January 1945, the bulk of the US troops fighting in north-west Europe were commanded by a foreigner, the man George Patton customarily referred to as 'that little limey fart, Monty'.

Now in the days leading up to that black Christmas of 1944, Montgomery, rejoicing in his command, was here, there and everywhere. Riding in his pre-war Rolls with a large Union Jack on the bonnet and accompanied by outriders in mud-splattered jeeps and motorbikes, he toured the front cajoling, encouraging, praising, even inspiring, some thought, the hard-pressed GIs trying to hold the Germans. Unlike Ike or Bradley, who never even went close to the front this crucial week, he knew the value of a commander being seen by his ordinary soldiers, especially at a time of crisis.

The Americans had all heard of Monty, and from divisional commander downwards they seemed to feel that now they were getting some sort of direction and purposeful leadership. Major Harden recalled Monty visiting the troops of the US 7th Armored Division, attempting to defend the road-and-rail centre of St Vith, which was much more important than Bastogne really. There he found an atmosphere bordering on panic. An officer told him: 'We're cut off.' Monty replied: 'That's funny. We just drove in.' Later Monty would order, against US wishes, that Brigadier-General Bruce Clark, the defenders' commander, should abandon St Vith to save his command which numbered 22,000 men. Afterwards both General Hasbrouck, the Seventh Armored's commander, and Bruce Clark would be grateful to Monty for saving their division.

They weren't the only ones. Although Monty treated Hodges quite shabbily at times, he and his fellow army commander, General Simpson of the 9th US Army thought highly of the man Simpson always called 'the Marshal'. The latter wrote to his namesake at the War Office, General 'Simbo' Simpson:

> You see from the start I got clear and definite orders what I had to do. From Bradley and my own people I never got any orders that made it clear to me what I had to do.

After his first visit to Hodges at his rear HQ, arriving there like 'Jesus come to cleanse the temple', as one US officer commented bitterly, Hodges told Ike he found Monty a bit pompous, but:

> I and my army are operating smoothly under the command of the Field Marshal. The most cordial relations and very high spirit of cooperation have been established between him and myself personally.

US Corps Commander 'Lightning Joe' Collins, whom Monty admired, was given the task by Monty of building up a reserve attack force on the shoulder. Monty left it to Collins and his divisional commanders to get on with the job, while he 'tied up' the rest of the shattered US front, and though Collins might have chaffed at Monty's deliberate pace, he obeyed loyally enough and became another qualified admirer of the 'little limey fart'.

But while he directed the Americans on the northern shoulder, at the same time he was also concerned about building up his own British force on the Meuse. For the Germans were advancing and the Americans were still 'bugging out' for the rear, whenever their command structure broke down. In the case of the badly hit 28th Infantry Division, for example, which would soon shoot the only US soldier for desertion to be executed on that charge since the American Civil War, the divisional staff and commanding general fled the HQ town of Wiltz. Behind them they left their wounded in a sorry state. The latter were tended to by a volunteer team of dentists, lawyers and the like, all of whom were captured later.

Now Monty was slotting his units 'like clothespegs' into the Meuse line. Already some of his formations, British and Belgian SAS, elements of the 61st Reconnaissance Regiment, and individual tank outfits were over the Meuse, scouting for the German point, while the 51st, 53rd and 6th Airborne divisions hurried to the great river.

These 'odds and sods', as they were called at the time, some 1,000 men or more, were not only to find the German point, but also to attempt to make a link-up with what was left of Middleton's VIII Corps in the general area of Bastogne. But it was difficult. What they met, especially the SAS troopers, were American stragglers and dubious strangers who were in uniform and existing in the snow-bound no-man's land between the Meuse river and Bastogne. They were, of course, deserters who maintained when questioned that they were trying to reach Givet and 'get back into combat'. That was very far from true. Once the SAS were satisfied that they were not Germans in US uniform, they left the deserters to it. They'd probably never reach 'Gay Paree', which was obviously their objective, and the whores of 'Pig Alley' (Place Pigalle) in the hope they could make a living on the French black market as so many thousands of their comrades were already doing. (Soon Eisenhower would have sentenced to death officers and men of a service company who were hijacking by the million cigarettes intended for the front.)

It was not only lowly GIs and junior officers who were 'bugging out'. A young ex-lawyer, now a corporal and deputy provost marshal in that same Givet, was shocked at the way the deserters were streaming through the city heading for Paris. He was even more shocked when he was present while his chief, Colonel Hardie, a veteran of WWI who had lost his son at 'Bloody Omaha', cross-examined a major general who didn't have a movement order.

He was General Alan Jones, the ex-commander of the ill-fated 106th Infantry Division, whose son was now a German POW after the surrender of two regiments of that division. Hardie looked at the plump-faced Major General Jones with his Don Ameche moustache, who only a week before had sworn to his son that 'they'll never take me alive' and snapped, 'General, where are your men?'

175

Jones, who according to the official history had suffered a heart attack at St Vith and had been sent to the rear in an ambulance, looked at the colonel, while he patted his pistol holster, and answered, pointing to the driver of his jeep: 'He's the only one I know of.'

Hardie didn't like the answer. He snarled:

General, we're losing because we're running. I called ETOUSA [Headquarters] this afternoon and they gave me full discretion as to whether to stay or to pull out. I am staying and I will shoot the first man who runs.

Jones was allowed to pass and, after a quarter of a century in the US Army and five days in combat, to retire, a footnote in the history of the Battle of the Bulge. But the acting provost marshal at the age of 26 was pleased by his boss's hard line with these 'bug-outs'. 'I felt a great elation and feeling that a steel spring had come into my spine,' he recorded many years later.

But Corporal Bill Burdett's feeling of elation didn't last long. A few days later Hardie introduced him to a captain of the 11th US Armored Division, a completely green outfit straight from England to the new battlefield – well almost. For he was lost. He had been sent up from France to find the fighting. He paced up and down in agitation, saying to Hardie in a plaintive manner:

Colonel can you tell us where the enemy is? We've been ordered to the front but we don't know where the front is. We can't get no information and we don't want to put our heads in the noose.

Hardie didn't know either. So he took the officer and Burdett to newly arrived Brigadier Harvey, who was 45 but didn't look to an impressed Corporal Burdett 'a day older than twenty-five'. Seated at a table, 'he was sipping wine while he studied the map'.

The lost officer started blurting out questions. Harvey parried them and talked about the USA of which he seemed to know a great deal. Then:

. . . after about fifteen minutes, the Brigadier turned the map board over and drawn on the overlay there were the positions of three panzer divisions, their strengths, their armament and the names of their commanders.

Both Burdett and the lost captain were impressed. So the 11th Armored man went on his way to the bloody battle it would soon face, leaving Burdett to wonder at the British. That night, however, his wonder turned to respect. He was fast asleep in his billet in Givet when he heard the stamp of steel-clad boots. His first thought was 'My God, the German infantry have broken through'. Swiftly he woke his comrades and told them to get out of the back door and head for the cover of the nearest woods. He, however, 'couldn't resist the temptation to take one last look at our formidable enemy'.

Barefoot he crept to the unblacked-out window. In the light of an icy full moon he saw them: 'British Tommies – no better fighting men. They were marching in close order, in step, arms swinging, veteran troops. British Infantry.'

Monty's divisions were arriving on the Meuse front. Then after they started to cross the bridge at Givet, heading for the unknown, they yelled out to Colonel Hardie's security company they were leaving behind: 'Don't worry, Yanks . . . we'll take care of them fer yer.' Then they were gone.

1945

I think the less one says about this battle the better, for I fancy whatever I do say will most certainly be resented.

FM B L Montgomery

CHAPTER XVII

They have given the Americans
a bloody nose

Back in June 1940, when Montgomery had re-assembled his 'Iron Division' as the only combat-ready division in the whole of the British Isles, Dwight D Eisenhower was an obscure lieutenant-colonel some five thousand miles away attempting to train a raw battalion of infantry. He still had ambitions. But Ike didn't think there was a chance in hell that he would become a general unless that war everyone was talking about came soon, very soon. For his age was against him. All he really could look forward to was a slippered retirement in some warmer part of the USA where the living was cheap enough to allow him to play a game of golf every now and again.

Now on this New Year's Day, 1945, his career had changed dramatically. He was the only five-star general since old 'Black Jack' Pershing in WWI. He had a mistress, talked as an equal with heads of state, and commanded a huge Allied army which numbered nearly five million men. That transformation hadn't been easy, of course. He had been forced to weather many a storm. In North Africa he had lost the confidence of Britishers such as Brooke, and in the Mediterranean Monty had followed. He had never regained these experienced combat officers' confidence in him: a general who had never heard a shot fired in anger. But they now no longer mattered. Britain had become the junior partner in the Allied coalition. It was America in the shape of Dwight D Eisenhower which gave the orders now.

His health had suffered. He kept breaking out in boils, his skin looked awful and there were deep bags under his eyes. Besides, due to his consumption of sixty cigarettes a day, his circulation and heart were not of the best. Still he knew he would survive. For he had new ambitions. Secretly he had already been approached about a presidential nomination. He had turned the Republican offer down. But he knew the wheelers and dealers would be back, once the war was won. Hadn't that happened to Grant after his victory in the Civil War? But there was a fly in the ointment this New Year's Day, several of them in fact.

There was the problem of his two commanders of the northern and

181

southern shoulders. Both were prima donnas. In particular Bradley, who now seemed convinced that Ike was party to the plot to take his troops away from him. But Ike felt he could deal with the man he had convinced the press to call 'the GI's General', though Bradley was everything but a friend of the ordinary footsloggers. Indeed Churchill, who had once called Bradley a 'sour, stubborn bugger', had probably visited more Allied troops at the front than Bradley ever had.

Monty was at this moment the paramount problem, especially now that he was in command of the bulk of the Allied divisions in NW Europe. Just before the New Year, he had ventured out of his 'protective custody' to visit Monty at Hasselt. Three days later he received a letter from Monty couched in language bordering on insulting arrogance. Again Monty demanded a single command. He wrote that 'any loosely worded statement [on the post-Bulge command structure] will be quite useless and that if you [Ike] merely use the word "co-operation" it will not work'.

With that really impertinent letter from his subordinate, Ike had also received word that Monty had postponed Collins' attack into the Bulge: something that Ike had been wanting for days. For although Patton had finally broke through to Bastogne, the fighting in that area had actually intensified, and it was imperative that Patton should receive support to link up with the northern shoulder and cut through the 'Bulge'. Besides, the Great American Public wanted a victory after two weeks of fighting in the Ardennes.

If that was not enough, Ike had also received a letter from Marshall, in which the austere man noted that the British press had been urging the appointment of a single *British* commander for all the Allied ground forces. In the letter Marshall instructed his protégé that 'under no circumstances' was he 'to make any concessions of any kind'.

Ike understood. But he was more worried by the fact that sooner or later the secret would be disclosed that Monty was commanding the bulk of the US troops fighting in the Ardennes. The hundreds of correspondents sniffing around his and Bradley's headquarters couldn't be kept in the dark for ever. What if some British newspaper revealed the secret prematurely before the battle was won? How would that affect his reputation back home? Was it not time to get rid of Monty now?

Thirty years after the events of that December/January 1944/45, General Bruce Clark, now a four star general himself and an adviser to Presidents Kennedy and Johnson, made a startling statement about the command decisions of that black Christmas. Clark, who after St Vith had a profound respect for Montgomery and a hearty dislike of Hodges and, to some extent, Bradley, wrote in 1976:

Since the war, it has been reported to me that some of the people on Eisenhower's staff were concerned because of the adverse publicity that had resulted from the complete surprise achieved by the Germans in their initial breakthrough on December 16.

These staff people believed steps should be taken to insure that if a second breakthrough occurred, it would not reflect adversely on the American command.

Clark went on to state:

The step decided upon was to relieve Bradley, the American commander, of the responsibility for the threatened sector and place that sector under Montgomery and the British 21st Army Group.

It is a startling theory. If the Germans did break through, cross the Meuse and head for their objectives, which would be a major defeat for the Allies, it would mean that Monty and not Bradley or Ike would be blamed.

In a private letter from Bradley which Clark had received two years before on 19 December 1976, the former 12th Army Group Commander tried to explain in detail what had really transpired on 20 December 1944 when Smith had phoned to inform him of the Monty appointment to the command of the northern shoulder. As Bradley explained it to Clark in this up-to-then unpublished letter:

I asked if the changeover [the transfer of the northern shoulder to Montgomery] was to be a temporary one. Bedell agreed it was and it would last only as long as the Bulge.

With this assurance, my only other objection revolved around the question of face. For unless the changeover were clearly explained by SHAEF, it could be explained as a loss of confidence by Eisenhower in me – more significantly in the American command . . . If this action was taken to mean repudiation of the American command, if it were inferred that we were bailed out by the British, the damage could be irreparable to our future role in the war.

It might seem on the basis of these Clark revelations that Smith, who had fired the proposers of the changeover only five hours before, suddenly had a completely, irrational change of heart at that eight o'clock conference on Wednesday 20 December; and that he was fitting Monty up to be the fall guy if the situation in the Ardennes got worse.

Be that as it may, it appears that now, in this new year of 1945, Ike felt the time had come to deal with Monty. With the willing help of Tedder, Ike dictated a letter to Marshall, which to all intents and purposes was a call to him to engineer Monty's dismissal. He used as his excuse Monty's insubordinate behaviour as evidenced recently at their December meeting in Hasselt.

It was a big step for Eisenhower to take. It really signified the end of his role as Allied co-ordinator, the peacemaker between the British, Americans and quite recently the French too in the shape of de Gaulle, that other prima donna. As Ike of the ear-to-ear grin, the glad-hander who shook the hands of common GIs, he was now 'tired of the whole business'. Nobody was going to push him around any more.

In the case of Monty, he knew that he was risking Churchill's wrath. For Churchill realised that however insufferable Monty could be, the little field marshal commanded a great following among ordinary British men and women, and he had the support of the British press too. Churchill would probably fight any attempt to get Monty to resign and he, Ike, might lose a political ally, who had a direct line to FDR that could even circumvent General Marshall.

In the event that particular scenario was avoided – at least for the time being. On that same New Year's Eve, when Montgomery wrote to his friend Grigg, the War Minister:

> Dear Friend, all is well and the Germans will now not get what they wanted . . . But they have given the Americans a colossal bloody nose and mucked up all our plans; however as we have not got a plan, I suppose they will say, it does not matter.

Freddie de Guingand happened to be at Versailles. Here he heard what Tedder and Eisenhower were about from the small pro-Monty faction at Supreme HQ.

Hurriedly he flew back to Eindhoven to explain what was afoot. Monty was 'amazed', according to de Guingand. He flashed a humbling, apologetic signal to Eisenhower. It read: 'Very distressed that my letter [the one of a few days before] may have upset you and I would ask you to tear it up.' The signal was signed: 'Your very devoted subordinate, Monty'.

The signal sufficed. Monty was off the hook. But Ike knew he still had to proceed with caution if he were to fulfil his as yet vague post-war plans. Back in Washington he was facing criticism, still muted, but criticism all the same. There, FDR asked to comment on the dying Battle of the Bulge, described it as a 'setback'. He praised the gallantry of the fighting GI, but remained restrained about Eisenhower. Indeed he damned him with faint praise, pointing out that Ike retained his 'complete confidence' and 'faced this period of trial with admirable calm and resolution'. Marshall forwarded the full text of FDR's message to Ike by 'direction of the President'. Otherwise he made no comment.

Stimson, the aged US Secretary of War, did, however. The old man wasn't particularly anglophobe, but he was convinced that Churchill was fighting the war to protect British national interests, in particular to retain control of the British Empire. This was something that wasn't acceptable to him. He felt that Eisenhower, on the other side of the Atlantic, was too busy playing the international statesman, dealing with Churchill, de Gaulle and now Stalin. (Ike had just sent Tedder to Moscow to urge the Russian dictator to bring forward the date of his January offensive to take the pressure off the Anglo–American force in the Bulge.) In his diary Stimson noted that although Ike was being 'extraordinarily successful . . . in keeping the composite command' together, 'he had lost sight of the necessity of supporting sufficiently our national views where they are at variance with the British'. America had other interests than Europe, namely the Pacific.

Marshall was more outspoken on this question of national interests and policies when Eisenhower asked for ten more divisions for the European Theatre of Operations. He told Stimson he was 'flatly opposed to talk of raising 10 more divisions for the ETO'. It had come to a point, as he told Stimson, that he would rather resign than do so. He asked Stimson to tell the President this.

Eisenhower, who had many contacts in Washington, must have learned of this new attitude towards him and the way he commanded in Europe. The time would soon come when he would be *forced* to clip the wings of troublesome European Allies, especially the British, and play the American card. But first on this first day of the New Year, he realised that the Battle of the Bulge had to be won – and won swiftly.

Monty knew it, too. But for other reasons. The war was dragging on too long for a virtually exhausted Britain. Already Churchill was being forced to call up a quarter of a million 45-year-olds to make up for the British losses. Monty didn't want the war to go on much longer. For that might mean the country wouldn't have enough men to take control of a regained Empire.

Thus it was that his order went out to divisions on the Meuse. It was brief and brutal. Shocking, too, for a man who abhorred the mass slaughter of the trenches in WWI and always tried to conserve the lives of the men fighting under his command. It read: 'The 53rd (div) is to be put into battle until it is exhausted, when I will pull it out immediately and replace it by the 51st Highland.'

Currie's 29th Brigade had had its first minor casualties in clashes with the enemy in the last week of December 1944. After a Christmas dinner of cheese 'wads' and tinned soup, some of his units had begun crossing the Meuse and probing the advance units of the German panzer divisions of the German Fifth Panzer Army.

One of the first of these little skirmishes and clashes with the enemy had taken place near the famous Belgian landmark of Rocher Boyard. Here a Sergeant Baldwin of the 8th Battalion, the Rifle Brigade, a veteran formation, had set up a roadblock where the road narrows there. The men of the 8th RB had strengthened their little position by dragging a chain of mines across the road.

On this particular afternoon, Baldwin was taken by surprise by an American jeep going all out down the riverside road heading straight for his position – and the mines. Frantically he jumped out into the middle of the road, waving for the jeep to stop. Too late. The jeep struck the mines. It erupted. Next instant it slammed down again, smoke pouring from its ruptured engines, its tyres burst.

With a sinking feeling of guilt and compassion, Sergeant Baldwin rushed to help. Already he was imagining that he'd be court-martialled for this. But there would be no court-martial. He hadn't killed three Americans, his allies. For the jeep's occupants were dead Germans, Skorzeny's spies and saboteurs clad in US uniforms.

It was the first warning for the 29th Armored that the Germans were not far off.

Two days later the enemy struck in what turned out to be a curious three-sided battle, involving not only the British and the Germans, but also the Americans of General Harmon's 2nd Armored Division, 'the Hell on Wheels'. On Christmas Day, the Germans of the famed 2nd Panzer 'Vienna' Division, a formation of the former Austrian Army, attacked at Foy-Notre Dame five miles east of Dinant. Here the Germans walked into a trap, with the British Churchills waiting for them in a hulldown position. In swift succession, the British knocked out four of their tanks and several halftracks filled with panzer-grenadiers.

Then came a lull in the fighting and the troopers ate bully beef wads in the freezing hulls of their tanks, waiting for the enemy to come again. One of them, Lt Noel Bell remembers: 'It all seemed peaceful. Then men in large numbers started to run about.' From his position, the young British officer couldn't make out what they were. 'Some said they were Germans, some Americans.'

A few minutes later the confusion increased when two large tanks appeared on the skyline. A furious debate broke out among the tankers. Were they Jerries or Yankee tank destroyers? For the American TDs were larger than the German tanks. The debate ended abruptly when an easily recognised six-wheel German armoured car made its appearance chasing the fleeing members of the British machine-gun platoon. They were Jerries all right.

Next moment twin-boomed Lightning fighter-bombers fell out of the sky. White tracer zipped through the air. The American pilots went to work with a will, machine-gunning the German panzer-grenadiers. A ding-dong bloody battle commenced.

All the same Noel Bell was enchanted by the spectacle of murder and mayhem on this day of peace and goodwill to all men. He recounted later:

It was a really wonderful spectacle and compensated for our Christmas lunch. After the last wave of planes had disappeared, from our left came a perfectly deployed formation of fifty Shermans in drill movement with their machine guns blazing.

The Yanks of the 'Hell on Wheels' division had arrived. The Germans fled.

Unfortunately the Germans were not the only casualties that day. Colonel Merriam of the 2nd Division's 82nd Recon Battalion was talking to a British officer of the supporting 3 Royal Tank Regiment when an American anti-tank gun opened up. A white blur stabbed the grey afternoon gloom. It was the flight of an armour-piercing shell. Unfortunately its target was not a German panzer.

The hollow boom of steel striking steel followed. A British tank reeled back on its bogies. Smoke suddenly poured from the tank's turret. Merriam looked at the victim of 'friendly fire' aghast. But the British tank officer took it with typical stiff-upper-lip control. Quietly he said: 'I say one of your chaps just browned off one of my boys.'

Now, however, infantry were going in and as New Year's day closed, the tankers who were to support them were kept busy in the bitterly cold weather turning over their tank engines every half hour to stop them freezing up, and smearing the sights of their guns with a special arctic grease so that they would be able to use them when the firing commenced.

The plan was for the sappers to build a bridge at Chanley on the Leese river, fifteen miles east of Givet. The 29th Brigade's 2nd Fife and Forfarshire Yeomanry, plus some Rifleman and Belgian SAS, would cover the crossing while the 6th Airborne massed and prepared an attack by their 5 Para Brigade.

This attack by the 7th and 13th Parachute Battalions would have as its initial objectives the hillside villages of Wavreille and Bure, six miles to the east, dominated by the 2,000-foot high Chapel Hill.

Once the villages and Chapel Hill were taken, the 6th would advance, as would the 51st and 53rd Divisions in an attempt to link up with the reformed US XXII Corps under Middleton below Bastogne. If these objectives were realised, the Germans would be trapped in a pocket, with the US 1st and 9th Armies on the northern shoulder, Patton on the southern, and the British of Horrocks' XXX Corps at its base. In other words, the Germans would be unable to expand their salient to their flanks, nor press forward over the Meuse and on to their initial objectives.

It wasn't a particularly imaginative plan, but it was the best that Monty could come up with under the circumstances. After all, he was directing two American armies, and one British trying to co-ordinate their attacks with another army under Patton, with Bradley as his supposed chief, in weather that was the worst that Europe had experienced in a quarter of a century. All in all it was not going to be easy.

It was Wednesday 3 January 1945. This time the men of the 6th Airborne Division were going into battle on foot. To support them there would be the tanks of the 29th Armoured Brigade. Already some of the tankers had crossed the start line and were attempting to locate the point of the German armour, which backed up the defenders. For here the farthest German penetration had been reached and, although the German commanders on the spot wanted to withdraw, the Führer didn't allow it. Although it was clear that the Wehrmacht couldn't win the Battle of the Bulge, Adolf Hitler still wanted to hold on to his gains. As Corporal Hitler in 1918 he had witnessed the withdrawal of the old Imperial German Army and the subsequent breakdown and collapse of morale and discipline. Any withdrawal, Hitler reasoned, might cause a similar breakdown. The Germans would hold their positions. *Ende!*

The going was hell for the tankers in their rubber-shod, narrow-tracked Shermans. Unlike the Germans who, after their experiences during the Russian winters, had introduced broad steel tracks to their tanks so that they didn't slide and skid so much, the American-made Shermans designed originally for desert warfare had not yet been modified. The consequence was that the British armoured advance ran into difficulties almost immediately.

That Wednesday, the weather in the Ardennes had become positively savage. Spasmodic blizzards reduced visibility to a matter of yards. The cold was bone-chilling and the ice and deep snow made the roads, what there were of them in that rugged hilly region, treacherous. The Shermans of the Fife and Forfar Yeomanry slithered and skidded from side to side, sometimes threatening to go over the side of the mountain trails, with the tankers soaked to the skin as they worked to free their tanks from snow drifts. Behind them they towed supply vehicles, which when they reached 'thus-far-and-no farther', as the point was named, would be left to the exhausted troops to manhandle up to where they would be needed. Progress was terribly slow and already the tanks were coming under long-range shellfire. The Germans knew they were coming. They knew, too, that in this kind of terrain, tanks would never attack without infantry. Soon the footslogging 'Tommies' would be arriving to do battle and they, the 'stubble hoppers', as the German infantry called themselves, would be waiting.

'The condemned man ate a hearty breakfast', the men of 'Luard's Own' quipped as they tucked into mess tins filled with 'canned Canadian bacon, baked "cowboy" beans and hunks of bread' and naturally 'char': hot sweet tea brought up in buckets and enriched, if they were lucky, by cans of evaporated milk so that it now became that most prized of liquids – 'sergeant-major's char'.

Thereafter they broke the ice from whatever source of water was available – in one case a horse trough – and washed and shaved and

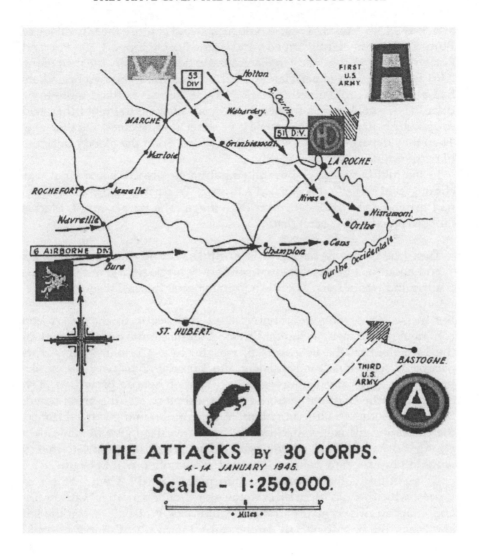

THE ATTACKS BY 30 CORPS.
4-14 JANUARY 1945.
Scale - 1:250,000.

brushed their teeth for the first time in three days. As always the British soldier went into battle washed and shaved. It was ever thus.

Not far away, Brigadier Nigel Poett, the dome-headed commander of the Sixth's 5th Parachute Brigade, gave his final orders to his commanding officers. The three colonels were all old friends: Pine Coffin (a name that always caused a reaction of some kind or another) of the 7th Para; Peter Luard of the 13th; and Ken Darling, who had just taken over Luard's rival battalion, the 12th Para (Yorkshire).

Poett, looking his usual toothy self, told his commanders that the 5th Brigade's main objective was the large village of Grupont. To support this attack, the 13th 'Luard's Own' would attack and capture the hill village of Bure. To give the lightly armed paras some heavy support, the Fife and Forfars, which were already in place, would be relieved by the men of the 23rd Hussars of Brigadier Harvey's 29th Armoured. The two brigadiers had already co-ordinated the attack. Now there was nothing more to be done. They shook hands formally, as they had done the night they had dropped on Ranville in Normandy in what now seemed another age. Then they departed to their waiting battalions. Soon the bloody business of battle would commence again.

In the hilltop village of Bure the inhabitants already knew what was coming. Since the Americans had left on 23 December and the Germans had arrived, calm had settled on the village. The parish priest, Marius Hubert, noted in his secret diary:

> They [the Germans] have two Tiger tanks . . . and other smaller tanks and about one or two hundred soldiers, who begin the mining of the surroundings of Bure. There is nothing special this last week.

But in the last seventy-two hours, things had begun to change. A jeep containing three men, including Private Claude Comte de Villermont, of the 1st Squadron the Belgian SAS, was hit by a German shell. All its occupants were killed immediately. On Tuesday 2 January the parish priest was called out to bury a British soldier 'whose body had been dropped by the Germans in front of the presbytery'. As the priest noted: 'The Germans asked me to bury him.' With guns booming in the distance, the priest and his helpers tackled the frozen earth to give the unknown young Briton his final resting place. The priest told himself that it wouldn't be long now before the battle for the hilltop would begin.

At eight-thirty that Wednesday morning 'Luard's Own' set off in lorries, which would carry them to the start line. There they'd dismount and attack in two-company strength, Major Jack Watson's 'A' on the left and Major Bill Grantham's 'B' on the right. Luard's 'C' Company would be in reserve. The attack would go in from the heights above the village. Poett, the Brigadier Commander, who had already been awarded the US Order of Merit and the Silver Star by Bradley back in July 1944, felt being on the height would give his paras a slight advantage over the defenders. But when he had worked out his plan he had not reckoned on the heavy snowfall of that day. Now it made going hellish for the tanks which would support his attack on Bure.

The Shermans were slithering and sliding their way up Chapel Hill, the key feature, and, as Poett thought, the bastion vital to the success of the 13th's attack. The going was terrible. As one tanker recalled: 'With snow showers howling through the trees, not a solidly built house anywhere in sight, the country was at its mid-winter worst.' Then at some two hundred yards from the village, the lead tank hit a mine. Its track snapped and rolled behind it like a broken limb, as the enemy alerted by the noise started shelling. Hurriedly the remainder of the troop found another approach. Still their progress was terribly slow, with great vomits of earth and snow from exploding shells leaping up on either side.

Around one o'clock that afternoon, the men of the 13th Para debussed and approached their start line. Perhaps only half of the 700-strong 'Win or Die' battalion were veterans of the fighting in Normandy the previous summer. But all of them were imbued with the spirit of the Parachute Regiment. The red beret, the blue wings on the shoulder of their camouflaged smocks, the knowledge that they were all volunteers gave them a sense of comradeship which was perhaps more strongly developed than that of Monty's other formations. But like all other British soldiers commanded by the little field marshal, they came from all walks of life, sharing the same rewards and hazards: proud, right into old age – those who survived – that they had once been members of a British Army that had fought and won after six years of war.

Now this afternoon, the veteran and the new boy, 'still wet behind the lugs', were going into action once more. Already six of their fourteen sister battalions had been wiped out in 1943/44. Was it the turn of 'Luard's Own' now?

They didn't know. Nor have any of the survivors recorded their thoughts that midday, as the minutes ticked away to 1.30 when they would cross the start line and the battle would commence in earnest. But we can guess them. With the snow falling heavily now and the guns bellowing their dark chorus of death, they prepared themselves for the order to move. Some fiddled with their equipment, others checked to see if the magazines of their weapons were firmly attached, others urinated more than once, their urine steaming in the freezing cold and turning the snow yellow – a sure sign of nervousness. Some might have prayed. We don't know. All we know so long afterwards is that one third of the men preparing 'to go in' that Wednesday would never come back.

CHAPTER XVIII

The condemned man ate a hearty breakfast

While the 13th Parachute Regiment crossed the start line that day, Churchill was on his way from Versailles to Monty's HQ at the remote Belgian township of Zonhoven. He had just returned from Athens, trying to make some sense of the Greek rising there, once it had been liberated, and trying to appease de Gaulle. The latter had threatened to withdraw support for the Allied infrastructure in France if the Americans evacuated the Alsace city of Strasbourg in the face of renewed German pressure. Churchill had helped to soothe de Gaulle's nerves and to get Eisenhower to continue to hold Strasbourg.

At Versailles Churchill had discussed Ike's problems with Monty. Now he was on his way to Zonhoven, a troubled man again, because he knew the London tabloids were chafing under the eighteen days of censorship which Ike had imposed upon them since the start of the Battle of the Bulge and were demanding that Monty should be given greater command in the West. Perhaps, Churchill must have thought, they had guessed that Monty had already been given a greater role in the Ardennes and wanted the scoop of being able to publish the news that Monty commanded more US divisions than any American commander did. That, he knew, would cause bad blood in Washington; and FDR, consummate politician that he was, was always eager to hear and follow the wishes of 'Joe Public'. That is how he won elections.

Perhaps by now Churchill had realised that his high hopes for a 'special relationship' between Britain, where he had been born, and America where his mother had first seen the light of day, were diminishing. By now he knew that Britain was the junior partner at the military level. At the diplomatic level, he was still one of the 'Big Three'. But while he still ate at the top table with FDR and 'Uncle Joe', he no longer had the clout to do much contrary to the wishes of Roosevelt and Stalin. Indeed, at times, he must have thought that it was between the Russian dictator and the American President that the real 'special relationship' existed.

But had Monty appreciated the change? General Fred Morgan, who had planned D-Day and was now at SHAEF, had understood it after working closely with the 'Yanks' for years. He summed up the new relationship thus:

> I was well placed to watch the distressing drift apart, the growing impatience on the American part with British bombast and bland assumption of superiority in so many fields. While on the British side there appeared all the evidence of a growing inferiority complex, jealousy of lavish American resources of all kinds and reluctance to acknowledge the scale of American achievement.

Churchill knew this. But he would not accept the fact that the British Lion was very old and very tired. Her killing skills were weakening. The ferocity of her youth had vanished. Soon the lion-baiting would commence. Why? Because the lion was toothless and could no longer bite. In ten years Prime Minister Eden, who had warned Churchill about the Yanks, would see the lion die, slain in a sordid little skirmish by a petty Egyptian adventurer of peasant stock, who back in WWII had been in the pay of the Germans.

But had Monty accepted the basic fact that he could no longer determine how the military coalition should be run? Churchill suspected he hadn't. Now as he journeyed to Zonhoven to lecture Monty, he sketched out the draft of the cablegram he would send to FDR. Using his big cigar like a spear as he emphasised his points, he wrote that he was worried by the reports in both the US and UK press that there was a conflict between the Supreme Commander and Montgomery. That was not the case, Churchill insisted:

> He and Monty are closely knit and also Bradley and Patton – and it would be a disaster if it broke up the combination which has in 1944 yielded results beyond the dreams of military avarice.

But Churchill protested in vain. The newspaper correspondents in the Ardennes had seen the breakdown of the command structure. They had witnessed the resultant chaos and, although most of them didn't know of Monty's secret appointment to command the US 9th and 1st Armies, they had seen how he had taken over the northern shoulder. Patriotic as newspapermen were in those days, they felt the time had come to reward Monty, who back in 1943 had brought Britain a first properly big victory at El Alamein.

What Monty really said to Churchill when they met is hard to discover. We have only Churchill's statements to go on and naturally he was not about to write down anything, especially when it was addressed to FDR, which might indicate that Monty was taking an anti-Eisenhower stance. As Churchill wrote to the President: 'Montgomery said to me today that the [German] break-through would have been most serious to the whole front but for the solidarity of the Anglo–American Army.' Even Churchill, desperate to keep the special relationship intact, must have known that was a patent lie.

One thing is clear, however. From that meeting came Monty's request to be allowed to make a statement. As Churchill saw it, it was occasioned by an earnest desire on Monty's part to counter the current media demand in the UK for a command change in Europe which was due to Eisenhower's inability to do the job properly. Monty, so Churchill told it, wanted to set the record straight. The PM agreed. In due course Monty set the ball rolling. He would talk to a group of select correspondents, some of whom he had known for years. Churchill little realised what he had done. Monty's decision to talk to the press was going to prove a recipe for disaster. That same night, the editor of the London *Daily Mail* prepared his front page headline of the morrow. It would read: MONTGOMERY: FULL STORY . . . BRITISH HALTED DRIVE TO MEUSE. It was a headline that would anger Washington and Versailles, too, for that matter. As for the exhausted men of 'Luard's Own' that same night of 3 January, they must have felt they had halted nothing. The boot was on the other foot. It was they who had halted.

The 13th Para came under heavy shelling and mortar fire almost as soon as they crossed the start line that snowy afternoon. Coming out of the woods, they headed to the south-west of Bure and were spotted at once. Major Jack Watson, commanding 'A' Company for the first time as a company commander, recalled: 'As soon as we broke cover we came under heavy fire.' To his front he spotted a German MG 42, black against the snow, scything the line of advancing men furiously and saw 'the trees above me being shattered by machine gun fire and mortar bomb splinters'. At the briefing by Colonel Luard he had been told the Germans were in the process of retreating. Now he realised to his dismay that they were going to make a fight of it.

The troopers of the Fife and Forfars, supporting the paras, soon realised that too. Two hundred yards short of the village, their lead tank hit a mine. For a few minutes 'C' troop were stymied. Then they followed a new route into Bure. Another tank was hit and another. In the end, before the troopers of the Yeomanry gave up for the day, all three tanks inside the village had been 'brewed up'.

Meanwhile Jack Watson's company was taking more and more casualties. The German machine-guns firing on fixed lines dominated the approach to Bure, while the enemies' skilled mortar crews were pouring down a lethal metal rain onto the hard-pressed 'Red Devils'. Even the well-camouflaged snipers covering the company's advance were being hit.

As Colonel Luard would one day write to the parents of one of them, Private Anselm Snelham, the youngest of nine children born to a Liverpool Catholic family, who perished that afternoon:

Your son, always cheerful, was cracking jokes as they went forward, he with his other snipers, to cover the attack. I have never ever seen him in better spirits. If ever there was a man who regarded not fear, it was him. He was very near to my heart.

That was the kind of farewell letter of condolence that Luard would be writing to the next-of-kin of his dead troopers all too often in the days to come. For the casualties were mounting ever more rapidly.

Old soldier Major Alfred Clarke, who had risen from the ranks and would one day take holy orders, was one of the first to enter the village. As he recorded after he had been wounded and partially blinded: 'The enemy could see us perfectly on the snow. We were deployed over half the village, but we couldn't do much with our light equipment against their tanks.' As the village priest noted that day, there were two 60-ton Tigers and three self-propelled guns hidden there, and all the British had to fight them off was the hand-held, spring-loaded PIATs. By the time Clarke would be evacuated from Bure seriously wounded and dripping blood, he would have helped to repell six German tank attacks.

Major Watson and his 'A' Company were still, however, trying to get inside the cover of the village houses. 'I got a grip of my company,' he remembered, 'and gave the order to advance again, whatever happened, we had to get into that village as quickly as possible.' It was the same old delusion that has always dogged young, hot-blooded soldiers in combat: the total overwhelming importance of taking a field, a chunk of hillside, a concrete pillbox, which in a few hours' time will have no significance whatsoever, so that in the years to come a visitor chancing on the same spot will ask in wonder: 'Why?' Why were so many young men's lives spent just to capture *that*?

Once again the terrible chant of death commenced: the hiss of the machine-guns; that strange unreal whispering of bullets cutting the air; the hollow clang of metal hitting the ground; the stomach-churning howl and thud of mortar fire. Then the agonised screams, the pleas, the obscene curses of those who would die, and those fighting death off to live and fight another day.

Again the men of 'A' Company suffered. One of Major Watson's soldiers – his batman – was struck by an incendiary bullet. It was a terrible wound. It would kill the young soldier – but not immediately. As he writhed in the scuffed, bloody snow, the man pleaded with his officer to shoot him. Watson wouldn't – couldn't. The batman died later, 'still screaming for someone to shoot him'.

At last they hit the dirty-white 19th-century cottages of the village. Carried away by the mad, unreasoning fury of battle, the paras of 'Luard's Own' rushed them at bayonet point. Grenades flew through the air. Doors splintered. Men shrieked. The Germans tried to pick off the officers and NCOs in the growing gloom of that terrible January day. Pick off the senior ranks, the Germans reasoned, and the attack would go to pieces. The enemy were wrong. The paras' blood was up. Nothing was going to stop the 'Tommies' now. But already there was the rumble of tanks approaching. The Germans were counter-attacking with their armour.

Watson halted. His company needed re-organising. 'B' Company, which had taken even worse casualties, was moving again. Right on the start line, 'B' had come under fire from artillery and German tanks. Its commander, Major Bill Graham, had been killed immediately. With him fell a platoon commander, Lt Tim Winser, and the backbone of the company, CSM Moss. Now they were pushing on. But now 'B' Company's second-in-command was knocked out by wounds. One of the two surviving platoon officers fell too. By the time darkness descended upon the village, 'B' was commanded by Lt Alf Largeren, who pushed on relentlessly, leaving behind a trail of slumped bodies in the snow. But the brave young officer didn't last much longer. Trying to clear a house in the village, he took a burst of machine-gun fire and died on the spot.

Major Clarke, the old soldier, was out looking for German tanks and his wounded. With him came the stretcher-bearers who would treat the wounded and carry them back to House Number 42 in the main street where the hard-pressed doctor worked on the growing number of casualties. There the Germans were so close and the fire so intense that 'the stretcher-bearers were forced to throw morphine and dressings ballasted with a cartridge because they couldn't cross the street,' as Major Clarke remembered long afterwards.

But despite the cost in human life, Clarke, the future clergyman and Military Knight in an order (Knights of Malta) formed in 1348, was proud of his soldiers.

The Battle of Bure was hard but we behaved well . . . The British fought courageously, attacking tanks with grenades. German grenadiers and British paras were later found skewered in each other, frozen in the position in which they had died.

Now the 39-year-old Major was about to do a little 'tank-busting' of his own. A Tiger tank had infiltrated the British positions, while the house next to Clarke's was full of German panzer-grenadiers, who were 'making a nuisance of themselves'. Clarke wanted to deal with these Germans, but the Tiger was protecting them. Still Clarke had moved into the street together with his 'stretcher-bearers' to deal with a wounded para. Despite the German fire they were attending to the man, when a German recce tank drove around the house. 'He stopped one metre from me, in front of the door. My stretcher-bearers were just in front of him. I was ready to drop my grenades when the turret hatch opened.'

A surprised Clarke, who had been just been about to kill the German commander, thought him a 'very brave man and [he] had evidently lived in England because he said in perfect English, "Listen, old chap, I'll let you go this time, but don't come back, otherwise I'll have to shoot you down."'

Clarke's stretcher-bearers were stunned at the German's little speech and 'cleared off with the wounded. And I couldn't throw my grenade onto the tank. This German was a gentleman and I let him go . . . The hatch closed and the tank moved backwards till behind the corner.' Clarke thought it was wiser to do the same. He retreated to the house he and the other paras shared with 'old Father Noel', a brave Belgian, who would share his bread and raw potatoes with the hungry soldiers that night, as all about them the first day of the Battle of Bure ended. There Clarke and the others waited by the light of a flickering candle for what was to come, listening to the arrival of 'C' Company of the Sixth's Oxfordshire and Buckinghamshire Light Infantry which would be reduced to platoon size by dawn; the hollow boom of steel striking steel as the German Tigers started to knock out the five Shermans left in the village by the Fife and Forfar Yeomanry. Soon they knew the Germans would counter-attack in strength.

A handful of miles away, another of Montgomery's divisions in the Ardennes was taking a similar hammering to that of the Sixth Airborne. Indeed the British 53rd Division, pushing northwards in an attempt to link up with Middleton's re-formed corps of the 11th US armoured and 17th Airborne, both suffering severe casualties too, would need 4,000 reinforcements before it would be able to go into its next battle.

In the lead was another Lancashire regiment, the 1st East Lancs. They had set out at first light, marching a mile through deep snow to their startline. The weather was so bad that it was virtually impossible for their support tanks of the East Riding Yeomanry to keep up with them. As the latter's regimental historian recorded:

> The river [the Ourthe] on their left flank was in flood and blocks of ice flowed down at a great rate. Packed ice on the roads caused tanks to slither around uncontrollably. A tank would frequently block a road for some time, but on the camber of the road, two men could slide a tank, all forty tons of it, sideways, merely by pushing it.

But all that pushing didn't help the tankers to keep up with the infantry, luckily for them. Thus the East Riding Yeomanry escaped a blood-letting similar to the one the East Yorkshiremen had suffered at the hilltop village of Cassel in Flanders back in 1940, when they had been virtually wiped out helping the BEF to escape at Dunkirk.

Now the East Lancs started to climb a wooded height, blinded by the driving snow. Among the snow-heavy trees they were soon divided into little groups, even individuals, each man concentrating on the back-breaking climb, loaded down as they were with their equipment. Suddenly, startlingly, a German machine-gun opened up right in their midst. In the snowstorm they had blundered into the position of the 'Greyhounds', the panzer-grenadiers of the veteran 116 Panzer Division.

But the 'Greyhounds' were just as surprised as the Lancashire men. A wild, confused fight broke out. Swiftly it deteriorated into a crazy melee. For some of the East Lancs it seemed to last for an eternity. Others thought it lasted a few minutes only. For several it was the last dramatic moment of their young lives. Finally, however, the panting, sweating infantrymen reached the ridge line and flung themselves into the foxholes dug by the Germans.

For a while the East Lancs and the 'Greyhounds' took a breather as the snowstorm continued to rage. Huddled in their freezing pits, with the snowflakes flying and the wind howling through the bullet-scarred pines, they were dying for a smoke. But they were not allowed to do so; they might have given their positions away. Now their stomachs started to rumble and they began to think of food, even the dreaded 'soya links'.

Back at their base camp at the village of Verdenne, the cooks worked all out to prepare hot rations for their freezing comrades in the line. Now the first convoy of Bren gun carriers set off through the dangerous forest to take the food containers to the forward companies of the East Lancs. It was Hansel and Gretel country. But this wasn't a fairy tale where everything ended happily. Here men lost in the snowbound firs froze to death. It was reported by the 51st Reconnaissance of the 51st Highland Division that two of their men who slept on the roadside that night woke to find their heads frozen to the cobbles by their hair.

Time and time again the carriers slipped a track on the forest trails. This meant that the rest of the convoy had to wait while the freezing, cursing crews repaired the track. They had to spread the track out, grind it forward over the bogies and then hammer home the pin that held the two pieces of broken track together with a sledgehammer. Every blow sounded to the waiting men like a signal of impending doom; for the Germans were all around in the snowy gloom. In the end, Quartermaster Sergeant John Moore gave up on the tracked vehicles. He asked for volunteers to carry the containers forward. In a British Army not given to volunteering, he got them too.

Together the senior NCO and his volunteers manhandled the heavy dixies and hayboxes up the steep incline to the hungry riflemen.

Lukewarm 'meat and veg stew' was not the most exciting dish for a frozen soldier, living – soon perhaps dying – in a hole in the ground. But even the stew had attractions at midnight in temperatures of twenty below zero.

Moore wasn't finished yet. As the regimental history of the East Lancs records:

> Soon afterwards John Moore struggled up again with a warming cargo of rum which he had personally carried all the way from Verdenne like some great St Bernard dog.

An hour later the slit trenches of the East Lancs were swamped with heavy artillery fire and tree bursts. The battle had commenced once again.

That same morning the brave men of the 13th Para took on five more German tank-led counter-attacks. Frantically the surviving officers called for artillery support. A future high court judge, with his pyjamas over his uniform to give some extra warmth, stationed to the rear, speedily obliged. Suddenly that grey morning was made hideous by the sound of 5.5 inch shells ripping through the sky like the sound of express trains through a deserted station. Great steaming brown holes appeared as if by magic.

A tank or SP was hit. It shuddered to a stop, trembling like a living thing. What looked like a giant smoke ring slowly emerged from its turret. None of the crew got out. Still the young panzer-grenadiers of the 'Greyhound' Division continued their attack. In a kind of crazy despair they pelted in and out of the houses firing as they ran. In some cases, the paras were in the ground floors of the cottages with the Germans above them; in others the situation was reversed. It was the worst kind of close-order combat. The soldiers, German and British, needed a great deal of discipline, skill and bravery to fight that kind of action.

For a while it seemed the decimated company of the Ox and Bucks would fall back. But in the nick of time they rallied and held their positions. Now Major Clarke was hit and blinded. His batman was hit too and died a few days later still 'fighting the good fight'. As he was carried away from the battle, Clarke swore that if he ever recovered, and regained his sight, he would devote his life to God. He did and by the time the war was over and the Sixth Airborne had been posted to troubled Palestine, he had become the chaplain to the same division in which he had fought the bloody battles of 1944/45.

Now the Germans were bringing up reinforcements from the next village of Tiranrue. The British did the same. The Fife and Forfar Yeomanry sent up more tanks to replace those of their 'C' Troop which had already been knocked out. The new Shermans didn't fare much better either. Almost immediately one of the British tanks was knocked out as the new boys attempted to outflank the embattled village. In the end 'C'

Squadron of the Fife and Forfars would have lost two-thirds of its tanks before it was pulled out of Bure to make way for the 23rd Hussars to take over the attack with the 13th Para.

Captain Steel Brownie, who was to be awarded the Military Cross, being decorated personally by Montgomery for his bravery at Bure, recalled long afterwards that final day at the hillside village, while they awaited relief by the Hussars.

> There was no wind, no more snow. But it grew colder and colder. The ground was too hard for digging so we slept in the tank . . . *Sleep!* Within ten minutes the icy cold of the metal had seeped through your clothing and the breath froze on your lips . . . We had been suddenly wrenched out of the comforts of Ypres [they had been waiting there for their new tanks] at such short notice that some of the troops went in gym shoes, having no time to get their boots never mind their bedding.

It was not surprising that sentries on both sides froze to death under such terrible conditions, especially as they had no kind of winter clothing whatsoever.

'My abiding memory,' Brownie wrote years later, 'is of the tiny black figures labouring in the white landscape, while we did our best to support them.' But as the Fife and Forfars prepared to leave, having lost sixteen Shermans, the 13th's 'A' and 'C' Companies sent fighting patrols into the unoccupied parts of the village. The Germans were quieter now after the paras had broken up the five German counter-attacks of the morning. But here and there they were still attempting to infiltrate the positions they had lost as both sides poured in heavy artillery fire and a lone Tiger prowled about, making mopping up extremely dangerous and difficult.

From time to time the paras encountered young civilians who had crept out of the cellars of the local school (the paras called it the 'castle') in order to scavenge for food, risking death at the hands of both sides – German and British alike had become, of necessity, very trigger happy. These brave young Belgians shared what they could with the paras, especially raw potatoes, which were plentiful; for both the paras and the Belgians were short of food.

But the paras were unable to hold the unoccupied part of Bure, especially as their tank support was diminishing rapidly and the 23rd Hussars were finding their approach march hellishly difficult and dangerous.

Major Ted Harte's 'A' Squadron of the Hussars found their top-heavy Shermans skating and slithering across the icy roads 'like a stampede of drunken elephants'. Trouble commenced immediately as soon as they got close to the village. A Sergeant Huthwaite's tank went over a mine. A few minutes later, Sergeant Roberts' Sherman was hit by a lone panzer-grenadier firing his bazooka at close range. Roberts died instantly and two of his crew were wounded. By the time they'd reached the Fife and Forfars waiting anxiously for the relief to arrive, the Hussars would have lost four more tanks, all their crews killed. And the trouble didn't stop there. Once they were within the environs of the village, the main street littered with German and British bodies, a Tiger started trying to pick off the much inferior British tanks.

As the new boys came across the first survivor of the Fife and Forfars, whom they knew, they barely recognised him. The tanker in question 'seemed to have shrunk in size, half his normal height, face black and blue, encrusted with dirty icicles and beard'.

But there was no time for commiserations. A Tiger came rumbling up. Its mighty 88mm cannon blasted flame and smoke. The shell passed through the tank of the troop leader, knocking it out, coming from the rear engine doors and blasting all hell out of the following tank. The Hussars were off to a bad start.

Still the British fought on. Somehow that 4 January 1945, when death stalked the streets of the remote hilltop village, Sergeant Harry Watkins of the 13th managed to enter the place, 'miraculously arriving out of the blue', as Major Watson recalled, 'with a hot meal! How the hell he found us, I do not know because we were still scattered among the houses along the main road of the village'.

Watkins dished out the rations of stew, as men, crouched low, dashed from their cover to dip their tins in the congealing mess before rushing back to take part in the battle once more, knowing the cheap, primitive meal might well cost them their lives. But after a diet during the last two days of stale bread and raw potatoes, they were prepared to take that risk.

But now casualties on both sides were mounting rapidly and both German and British commanders were going to have to make hard decisions as 4 January gave way to the 5th. Just as their comrades of the 1st East Lancs somewhere to their right were losing men all the time, as they battled the 'Greyhounds' of the 116th Panzer Division (who were suffering similar casualties as they tried to hold the British so that the elite SS divisions of the 6th SS Panzer Division could be withdrawn and thrust into a new offensive against the Russians in Hungary), the 13th Battalion were incurring almost unbearable losses. And no one from Luard up to Montgomery wanted another 'Arnhem', which had seen the 1st Airbourne Division virtually wiped out.

By now the 700-odd string Battalion had lost nearly two hundred men in killed and wounded (seven officers and eighty-two other ranks), plus those of the Ox and Bucks who had come to their assistance. That meant 'Luard's Own' had lost nearly a third of its strength (as would their fellow Lancashire men of the 1st South Lancs). Something would have to be done. A decision would need to be made.

CHAPTER XIX
Straight from the horse's mouth

On the night of 4 January 1945 SHAEF finally lifted its nearly three-week old censorship ban. In particular, the information was released that, since 20 December 1944, Field Marshal Sir Bernard Law Montgomery had been commanding the bulk of the US troops in NW Europe. The censorship hadn't been voluntarily relaxed, it had been done under pressure, namely from the British media.

For days now those in the know in the London press world had been agitating for the ban to be removed. Some Fleet Street papers had tried to get round the restrictions in the customary manner adopted by smart editors during WWII. They quoted alleged sources in neutral capitals, and even in enemy Berlin. It was an old dodge. But it hadn't sufficed. London editors wanted it straight from the horse's mouth, namely from SHAEF's press spokesman. Now they got it with the Versailles man announcing that the change in command had come about by 'instant agreement of all concerned', and that it had been due mainly to the breakdown of communications between Bradley's headquarters in Luxembourg City and the two commanders in the field. The changeover in command 'had absolutely nothing to do with any failure on the part of the three American generals'.

As the London editors now knew from their correspondents in the field what had really happened that Christmas, they were appalled by the blatant whitewash job. They wanted more detail – *and now!* While Bradley, who had played virtually no role in the Battle of the Bulge, raged that the SHAEF announcement hadn't mentioned that the change in command was only temporary, and that the gleeful British press was celebrating 'a Roman holiday', i.e. was having a sadistic feast at his expense, the London editors went to town.

The *Daily Telegraph*'s report was decidedly one-sided and patriotic:

British troops, it was revealed tonight, played a vital part in foiling Rundstedt's bold bid for the Meuse crossings. On December 17th [sic] the day after the German offensive opened, Field Marshal Montgomery was appointed to command all Allied armies on the northern flank of the breakthrough. Immediately a dramatic race developed between British armour and the panzer spearheads for the main bridges over the Meuse between Namur and Givet. The British won. Now British tanks and infantry are engaged in a counter-offensive mounted by Field Marshal Montgomery on a twenty mile front between Marche and Abrefontaine.

It was the sting in the tail of the *Telegraph*'s report which angered the Bradley faction in Luxembourg the most:

His new command includes the US First and Ninth Armies, as well as the British Second and the Canadian First. Lt General Bradley commands the Allied troops on the southern flank of the Ardennes battle.

The statement was perfectly true, but such detailing of Monty's command compared to the lack of detail of the troops under Bradley's leadership in the Ardennes (Patton's corps and the re-formed one under Middleton's command to be exact) made Hansen, Ingersoll and naturally Bradley himself fume with rage.

The equally conservative, but brasher *Daily Mail* laid it straight on the line. Under the headline MONTGOMERY:FULL STORY, the paper stated:

British halted drive to the Meuse Line. This is the crucial part of the Western Front since General Rundstedt started to push, and the knowledge that Marshal Montgomery is now in control there will be received with relief in this country.

But it wasn't only the British press which angered Bradley and his faction and caused concern in Washington. Even the US Army newspaper, printed in Europe for the troops, picked it up and headlined it. The *Stars and Stripes*, under the headline MONTY TAKES THE NORTHERN FRONT, announced the changeover in command. For the first time there was mention of British troops taking part *in strength* in the fighting in the Ardennes. After twenty-two days of fighting in the Ardennes, mostly under British command, the *Stripes* informed its GI readers that their British C-in-C had led them in an advance of three miles along a twenty-one-mile front.

Backed by British tanks, the US 1st Army has driven into the town of Abrefontaine, some seven miles south-east of Stavelot ... The heaviest fighting of the day is reported south of Rochefort at the western tip of the salient where British troops have been making a bloody and bitterly fought yard-by-yard advance against the enemy's 2nd Panzer Division.

The news was out, but would be soon smothered in order not to cause any more offence to Bradley and his faction. But the damage had been done. Bradley and his staff had just received the daily summaries of the US press. They didn't make good reading. Hanson Baldwin, the respected military commentator of the *New York Times* wrote: 'If such a move [Monty's appointment] has been made ... it will mark up another political–psychological asset for the Nazis as a result of the Offensive.' Other US writers were even more outspoken. They referred to 'slap at General Bradley' and 'justification for the Anglophobe school of thought in our country'.

Perhaps that was a reference to the *Daily Mail*'s Washington correspondent's complaint the week before: 'This Xmas the slogan in some quarters seems to be:"War on earth and ill-will towards men, particularly Englishmen".' This caused some protest among anglophile Americans. But there had been worse from British papers. Just after Christmas the *Economist* leader-writer stated:

> It is not reasonable to suppress legitimate British interests because they offend American sensibilities . . . And if the Americans find this attitude too cynical or suspicious they should draw the conclusion that they have twisted the lion's tail too often.

Even the *Yorkshire Post*, the provincial paper over which the Foreign Secretary, Anthony Eden exercised some influence, criticised America for looking to its own advantage politically as well as militarily, stating:

> It appears that America will only do this [take part in future European military security] if she thinks fit in her own interests and if in the meantime we have behaved well according to her ideas.

Eden, who we have seen had already warned Churchill of a future in which America was the dominant power, was perhaps using this regional paper for expressing his concerns about the future, the current situation in the Ardennes being a convenient excuse.

Major Hansen and Major Ralph Ingersoll, the ex-journalist, who seem to have been the prime movers at Bradley's HQ in the new battle, not against the Germans, but against the erstwhile ally, Montgomery, recorded that Friday:

> Now the First Army of Hodges has suddenly lost its identity and Monty emerges as the commander. In all press releases the troops are referred to as Monty's troops in a palavering gibberish that indicates a slavish devotion on the part of the British press.

Hansen went even further. He attacked Montgomery directly. He wrote:

> Monty is the symbol of the British effort on the western front. He is regarded as such by the British press and by the quasi-official BBC and London *Times* . . . He is the symbol of success, the highly overrated and normally distorted picture of the British effort on our front.

There was nothing much to distort about the stark, bloody facts of the British advance into the bottom of the German salient that Friday 5 January 1945. Lt Colonel Lindsay, CO of the 1st Gordons of the 51st Highland Division, noted that a Welsh battalion of the 53rd Division, which the Highlanders were relieving, was unexpectedly attacked by 'a couple of hundred young Nazis full of brandy. The battalion had three companies overrun and one hundred and sixty casualties.'

The 1/5th Welsh Regiment, another Welsh unit, lost its CO and second-in-command within two hours of attacking. Major Bill Owen took over, feeling 'like a jinx as this was the third CO who had been wounded at my side'. In that same battalion a Major Lewis noted:

> One private soldier [Pte J Strawbridge] after being hit was seen carrying back wounded on five occasions before being hit again and mortally wounded. A lance corporal with his lower arm blown off continued to lead his section into attack until the objective was taken. How could the enemy withstand such courage?

That same night, Colonel Lindsay was shown the casualties for his own First Gordons since D-Day. He later wrote:

> They are really appalling. Their combined officer strength is 20; their casualties have been 9 killed and 30 wounded. Their combined Other Ranks' strength is 500; their casualties have been 149 killed and 351 wounded, a total of exactly 500.

As for that other Lancashire regiment, the 1st East Lancs of the 53rd Division, it had lost eleven officers and 232 men in combat in a handful of days. As they were pulled out, only their CO Colonel Hill was still on his feet at battalion headquarters. All the rest of his officers and men were dead or wounded.

The 13 Para were still fighting that day. All morning they had beaten off attacks. Now Major Watson decided the time had come to clear out the rest of the Germans who were now subjecting the paras to heavy shelling. With his survivors, 'C' Company and those men still on their feet of Major Granville's company, they advanced to complete the job of capturing Bure.

It was not going to be that easy, although the paras now had the support of two artillery regiments. Hardly had the paras started their advance, than two Tigers rumbled into view, with behind them German panzer-grenadiers formed into what the Germans called 'Trauben' (bunches of grapes), taking advantage of the massive cover offered by the huge tank. A fierce fire fight followed. But the paras beat the Germans off and suddenly, as if someone had thrown some gigantic power switch and cut off the supply of electricity, the thunder of the guns and brittle snap-and-crackle of small arms fire died away. The Germans were still there, the paras were sure of that, but as they pressed deeper and deeper into the other half of the village, it seemed to them that the heart had gone out of the defenders. Soon they'd find out why.

Major Watson recalled:

By 2100 hours that night we had finally taken the whole village, with my company overcoming the last enemy position. We established ourselves in defensive positions. Nothing happened however. We later discovered that the 7th Parachute Battalion had made an approach from a different direction and meeting little opposition, had taken Grupont. As a result we ourselves did not have to go any farther.

For the 13th Parachute Battalion the Battle of Bure was over (though the follow-up battalion of the Sixth Airborne, the so-called 'Red Devons' had a nasty little encounter with a Tiger tank and German infantry before the village was finally subdued). Now for the men of 'Luard's Own', the time had come to pick up the pieces, as the orders came through that night that they were to leave Bure at first light on the next day, Saturday.

The Battalion's medical officer, Captain Tibbs, who had been working flat out for the last forty-eight hours tending the steady stream of casualties and who had twice narrowly escaped being shot himself, went out with the lightly wounded, while the chaplain, Captain Foy, remained behind to tend to the severely wounded and bury the dead until the 'Red Devons' arrived. He and a couple of sergeants volunteered for this unpleasant task which entailed burying the bodies of sixty-eight men, half of them from Watson's 'A' Company which had frozen hard so that they could be handled almost as if they were boards of wood. Watson, for his part, assembled 'his very tired and very wet' survivors and they withdrew to the nearby village of Tellin.

In all the men of 'Luard's Own' had suffered losses which amounted to about a third of the battalion in a matter of forty-eight hours, namely seven officers and one hundred and eighty-two soldiers killed and wounded. The former South Lancs, raised in the Americas nearly two centuries before, had come a long way since 1939. Then the South Lancs' territorial battalions from which they stemmed had been 'odds and sods', switched from one part of Britain to the other: soldiers for the day of no particular importance in the scheme of things.

They had gone on 'booze-ups' and 'got pissed'. They had gotten girls 'in the family way', with 'a bun in the oven'. Now and again some of them had infringed military discipline and been 'put on jankers'. They had 'bulled up' with the best of them, as if they had been regular guardsmen. Occasionally it had all been too much and they had 'gone on the trot', until finally and inevitably the 'redcaps' had picked them up and they had been sentenced to the 'glasshouse' if they were unlucky.

Suddenly in 1942, however, they had been transformed from soldiers who one day might walk into battle on some disputed beach in France, to an elite, sporting a red beret, camouflaged smock and those blue-and-white wings, who flew into combat: men who knew instinctively that Fate had a special role in store for them in the battles to come, from which they guessed – also instinctively – they had a good chance of not returning.

And it had happened as they had guessed it would. They'd fight again, of course – and die – but the survivors would always remember that battle in the snowbound hills of Belgium. They'd be alone in doing so. Behind them in the Ardennes they'd leave little sign of their passing, save graves.* So it would remain in the future, right up to the present day. Even the grandkids of those Belgian civilians, who also suffered in the battle that terrible winter, are mostly unaware of the British sacrifice at Bure. The politics of the 'special relationship' ensured that the bloody sacrifice of the 13th Parachute Battalion had to be forgotten, as indeed had the whole British involvement in the Battle of the Bulge. As Montgomery would write in his memoirs:

'I think the less one says about this battle, the better.'

But in that first week of January 1945, with the Battle of the Bulge almost won (though Patton had proclaimed in despair on 4 January 'we can still lose this war'), Monty was determined to have his say, cost what it may.

Once in August 1944 Montgomery had cried out in despair:

Give me forty divisions. Give me a force so strong as to fear nothing and I will drive through to the heart – Berlin – and so end the German war.

But he hadn't been given that force and would never get it. After Caen and Arnhem, the Victor of El Alamein's fame had started to wane, with the

*Researching this book, I asked a local shopkeeper in Hotton, Belgium, where the British War Cemetery was. He didn't know. It was only half a mile away, approached by a rough dirt road. Here rest 665 dead of the battle. They ranged from a 54-year-old brigadier of the 53rd Welsh Division to one of those 18-year-old troopers of the 61st Reconnaissance Regt.

American armies now stealing the limelight. Rightly so because they were fielding three times the number of men that Britain could field.

Montgomery took little account of that difference in numbers. He wanted the campaign in Europe to consolidate his reputation as a great commander: the Wellington of the 20th century. But that ambition could only be achieved if he had the numbers to carry out that massive thrust on a narrow front he dreamed about. But Eisenhower wouldn't allow that. Time and time again Monty harassed a very patient Eisenhower with his demands to be given control of the majority of the Allied ground forces, which would mean hundreds of thousands of Americans coming under his command.

Once in the presence of one of his 'eyes and ears', Major Dawney, Montgomery again made his demands to Eisenhower. As Dawney recorded:

In the end Monty's relentless arguments reduced Ike to a condition of speechlessness and he said he was ready for bed. I got him a whisky and soda, escorted him to his room and then came downstairs again. Monty immediately said: 'Get this message sent to the C.I.G.S.' I wrote it down at his dictation and was astonished to discover that he was claiming that Ike had agreed in general with his single-thrust strategy. I read the message back and asked if it was correct. He assented. I said, 'May I say something sir?' 'Yes certainly.' 'Ike does *not* agree, sir.' His only comment was 'Send that message, Kit.' And so I did. But Ike had not agreed.

Eisenhower had always been very courteous to Monty, despite the constant harassment (and one must say that Monty really liked Eisenhower as a person, though he disliked his strategy intensely). It was only people such as Bedell Smith who could attempt to cut Monty down to size and make him realise he was no longer the power he had once been, before and immediately after the D-Day invasion.

Once one of the planners of that great operation, General Frederick Morgan now at SHAEF HQ, was summoned to Smith's office where the American chief-of-staff, 'white with passion', handed him the phone and rasped, 'Look boy. That's your bloody Marshal on the phone. I can't talk to him any more. Now you go on.' Morgan, who was no admirer of Montgomery, listened as the 'bloody Marshal' ranted on about the great thrust to Berlin, and then seizing a pause in the monologue, told Montgomery what Bedell Smith had just ordered him to do. If he didn't, Bedell Smith would cut off the supplies to Montgomery's 21st Army Group.

But still Montgomery wouldn't give up, especially as he knew that he had the support of his chief and mentor, Field Marshal Brooke. The latter didn't think much of Eisenhower as a soldier, nor did he support Eisenhower's broad-front strategy.

Throughout the campaign, Brooke and Montgomery corresponded, with Brooke making the same point about Eisenhower and his American staff that he expressed in a signal to Monty on 21 December just after he had taken over the command of the northern shoulder. Then he felt that the changeover might well bring great opportunities with it: 'If I felt the American commanders and staff were more efficient than they are.'

Throughout that December and over that black Christmas of 1944, Brooke had given Monty his support. He had warned Monty against 'rubbing the Americans' nose in it 'over their failure to predict the coming German offensive and stop the German counter-stroke. At the same time, he had encouraged Monty to make official representations. This support from Brooke was probably decisive, because Brooke was one of the few soldiers whom Montgomery respected both professionally and personally.

Now this first week of January, Montgomery was in a position of power. He had saved the Americans' bacon (as he saw it); he had proved the broad-front strategy of Eisenhower didn't work; and he was still actively commanding two whole American armies. It was the right time, Monty reasoned, to show the world just what he had done during the Bulge. By doing that he probably would convince the Americans to give him the command of enough US troops to make that 'pencil-like thrust' to Berlin which he had been advocating for months now.

Later he would say he was wrong. In his memoirs he wrote: 'So great was the feeling against me on the part of the American generals that whatever I said was bound to be wrong.'

But if Monty already knew that at the time, why did he do what he did? Churchill had already seen, as he wrote later, that:

When Monty was given back the [US] Army after the Germans had broken through in the Ardennes, he made such a cock-a-doodle about it all that the Americans said their troops would never again be put under an English general.

Still Monty persisted in giving his disastrous briefing to the press on Sunday 7 January 1945. Why? Was he such an innocent?

By now, Monty had been working with the Yanks for two years. He knew just how touchy they were about national pride and the prestige of the US Army, which, as Bradley phrased it pompously, 'never gave up ground bought with American blood'. British people didn't talk like that. They didn't wear their hearts on their sleeves. But Americans did and Monty must have already known that when he planned his briefing at the Villa Momsen that Saturday.

Or was there something else that motivated him? He had Brookie's support and Churchill had sanctioned his briefing. As Monty might have reasoned, his remarks, therefore, condescending and caustic in presentation as they were, would represent not only a personal (his) position, but also an official one, supported by Brooke, Britain's most senior soldier, and Churchill, the Prime Minister and the creator of the special relationship between Britain and America. But when all that is said and done, what Monty would do this weekend was of his own creation. Neither Brooke nor Churchill had any direct part in it. The only people who might have stopped his doing what he would do were his own staff and they were lesser mortals, whom Monty could dismiss and send back to the UK in disgrace, their army careers ruined, at the drop of a hat. No, Monty and Monty alone had to take full responsibility for the events of this coming Sunday.

Later some would halfway apologise for him, maintaining that he did not really understand just how much of an anathema he had become for the American top brass. Blinded by his own vanity and feeling of self-importance, he had been carried away by his own achievements during the Battle of the Bulge. He had blown his own trumpet too much and had forgotten who had really done the fighting, or the bulk of it, *the poor old GI.*

Other apologists would maintain his actions had come at just the wrong time. He shouldn't have given his briefing that weekend when, despite the US protestations that they could have cleaned up the salient much earlier if their new commander, Monty, had given them the go-ahead, the Patton counter-attack had run into serious difficulties and was slowing down: a costly, weary grind, in which ground gained could be gained in yards. Indeed both a divisional and a corps commander had protested that the Patton attack should be postponed, while those two green divisions, the 11th Armoured and 17th Airborne were suffering tremendous casualties. Under such pressure and stress, the anti-Montgomery faction of Patton and Bradley would not take kindly to 'the little limey fart' telling them how he had won the Battle of the Bulge.

But was Montgomery so blinded by his own vanity that he could not see the problems and the anti-British feeling that his remarks would occasion? He stated himself later that whatever he said, the Americans would misconstrue his words and make 'a dog's dinner' of them. So why did he speak out in the first place?

Could it be that Monty knew all along that what he was going to say would set the cat among the pigeons? Right from the start was it his intention to speak out for British interests – his own, too, naturally? Montgomery knew only too well from personal experience as British Army commander just how stretched the Army and Britain were.

Since the campaign in Europe had begun, he had been forced to cannibalise two of his divisions to provide reinforcements for his other divisions. He had asked for divisions from the Italian front to be sent up to NW Europe for the same reason and he, the advocate of massed artillery bombardments, was in the process of turning artillerymen into infantry.

However, through their carelessness and lack of viable strategy, as Monty saw it, the American failure in the Ardennes had landed poor, down-and-out Britain with perhaps another year of war. The USA could afford to fight into 1946; she'd find the necessary soldiers if she had to. Britain couldn't. It might well mean the end of the Empire. If the war lasted much longer, Monty knew Britain would end it, broke, short of troops for her many Empire commitments and in no position to play the full role she had earned in post-war affairs. The USA would then be the dominant power, as she had already become the dominant partner in the military alliance.

Could Monty have reasoned that Saturday, as he prepared his expose of the following day, that the time had come to show America and the Americans what had transpired in the Ardennes due to the faults, false hopes and foolish strategies of their generals? To the cost of Britain, the war had been prolonged. Now he, Field Marshal Montgomery, who had attempted to stop the rot for months with no success, would tell them the truth. Monty would speak for Britain!

CHAPTER XX
I ruffled people's feathers

That Saturday on the other side of the world, President Roosevelt had his eleventh 'State of the Union' address delivered to Congress. In the parlance of the time, 'it touched all bases'. Indeed it seemed to some of those who listened to it, bored and yawning, that it was like that of a book-keeper who was about to lose his job. For not only did Roosevelt's speech deal with the current problems, but it also referred to the achievements of his 'New Deal'. Mostly his comments were bland, the kind of statements that politicians make on grand occasions, which have more sound than substance.

However FDR did make reference to the current problems in Greece and Poland. In the former, Churchill appeared to have carved himself a sphere of influence; in the latter, Stalin was taking over. Here the President made his appeal for the right of small nations to self-determination. His speech read:

> We and our allies have declared that it is our purpose to respect the right of all peoples to choose the form of government under which they will live and to see sovereign rights and self-determination restored to those who have been forcibly deprived of them.

It was a speech well received by the US press. But not by Churchill and some of his cabinet, especially Foreign Secretary Eden. For those references to 'peoples' right to choose the form of government under which they will live' did not only apply to Greece and Poland; for the British that also meant those parts of the British Empire currently under Japanese control.

Indeed FDR's only real reference to the war concerned the Japanese and the battles in the Far East. It was as if the ailing head of state regarded the war in Europe as virtually over. If Churchill, who had just asked for a vote of confidence from the House of Commons, stating 'Poor old England...we have to assume the burden of most thankless tasks and undertakings, then to be scoffed and opposed from every quarter', still took an intense interest in the European War, FDR didn't.

Of course he was a very sick man. He appeared to be possessed of a disastrous lassitude, so much so that his long-suffering wife became impatient with the President. His appearance seemed to be getting worse by the day. His hands trembled. His lips were blue. His clothes looked a size too large for him. The wheelchair, which in his eleven years in the White House had sped along its corridors, was now propelled laboriously by a bent, gasping FDR. That winter, passing the White House with a friend, Vice-President Harry Truman, the snappy little ex-haberdasher was told by the former: 'Someday soon, you will be walking through the doors of that place.' Truman looked at the front door and answered: 'I hope not.' The man who would bring the 'special relationship' to an end before 1945 was out added after a pause, however: 'But I think you're right.'

Thus the dying President (for he was dying, though FDR didn't know it himself; his real state of health was guarded like a state secret), perhaps the most powerful man in the world, was not overly interested in what was happening in Western Europe, where Germany still had to be beaten. Now and then he went into the White House map room and watched young staff officers stick blue and red pins on large-scale maps of the battle areas. That was about it. The nasty business of the battle, blood and the frightful butcher's bill paid by America's youth over there seemed no concern of his. He left all that to his generals in Europe, who were guided by his brown eminence, General Marshall.

Naturally there was always Churchill in London, who loved the military side of this great conflict. He was always prepared to interfere, as he had just done in the case of de Gaulle and the proposed evacuation of Strasbourg in Alsace. But even Churchill, who would fight his cause to the last under normal circumstances, was beginning to realise that his influence over the US generals was starting to wane. Churchill still had a good relationship with Ike, his favourite American, the commander he had supported right from the start back in 1942. But the PM had also realised that Ike, who had grown tremendously in stature over the last year or so, was primarily an American, who had now in this new year of 1945 to represent American interests.

Thus it was against this background, an uninterested US president, a changed Eisenhower, conscious of his own post-war future and ambitions, and a coterie of US generals, grouped around Patton and Bradley, still smarting from the field marshal's take-over of so many US troops on 20 December 1944, that Monty put the final touches to the briefing he would give to a select crew of war correspondents on Sunday 7 January in Zonhoven.

'I ruffled people's feathers; Freddie smoothed them,' Monty often quipped. But Freddie de Guingand, Monty's long-time adviser, was away ill again that Saturday at Zonhoven. So there was no one present at

Monty's forward HQ to advise him that on the morrow he was going to ruffle a great number of feathers, and then some.

It seems that Monty was happy that day. He wasn't particularly pleased with the progress of Hodges' 1st Army, and his own XXX Corps in the Ardennes was still engaged in heavy fighting, while Patton, over whom he had no control, had been fought to a standstill. Still he was happy with his lot. Hadn't he just won one of his constant wagers on when the war would end with his friend, the Minister of War, Sir James Grigg? He wrote to Grigg: 'Cheque for two pounds received. Thank you. The bet was a sitter for me.'

He went on to tell the Minister and old crony that he was winning the Battle of the Bulge, adding to Grigg who had often warned Monty against 'shooting off his mouth at the Yanks' that the 'real trouble with the Yanks is that they are completely ignorant as to the rules of the game we are playing with the Germans. You play so much better when you know the rules.' Unfortunately for Monty (and Britain, too, in the long run), he didn't know the rules as far as the Yanks, the new senior coalition partner, were concerned.

Monty had invited a good cross section of the Allied press corps to his briefing scheduled for Sunday. Some were admirers and old acquaintances going back to his time in the desert, such as Alan Moorehead, the Australian journalist, who had seen more action than many a soldier since 1940 and would be Monty's first professional biographer. Then there was Chester Wilmot, another 'colonial' and great admirer of the field marshal. He, too, would write an excellent early book on the campaign in Europe in which he was a strong advocate of Monty's strategy. The Anglo–Irishman, Cornelius Ryan, was the 24-year-old correspondent of the *Daily Telegraph*. There were Yanks, too, such as Jack Belden, who had covered the Ardennes battle extensively. It was said that Ernest Hemingway, the future winner of the Nobel Prize for Literature, might also attend. But that wasn't to be. He was still in Luxembourg, sick and drunk and embroiled in a drunken quarrel with his wife, Martha Gellhorn, another war correspondent.

Monty was making sure that his remarks would get the wildest possible coverage, though he didn't know then just how widely his speech would be reported. Now he was concerned about how he should appear before these tough, cynical newspapermen, who had been everywhere and seen everything. They wouldn't be easily taken in by the customary bullshit tendered by the top brass. He had to appear different from the usual heavy-set, bullish British officer, red-faced from years of passing the port at mess dinners.

Monty had never been noted for his sartorial splendour. Indeed, for a regular officer, commissioned before WWI, he was decidedly sloppy in his appearance. He had been the first divisional general to wear the unbecoming new British Army battledress in 1940. In the desert he had worn more civilian outfits than uniform. At times he even sported a 'gamp' in the style of the Duke of Wellington, together with corduroy trousers. The King-Emperor himself had once reprimanded him for being 'improperly dressed'.

Now Monty decided he would appear in his 'airborne togs'. He had just been made the colonel of the parachute regiment, the same unit that had been decimated at Bure, and given the honour of wearing its maroon-red beret. He decided to wear that beret, complete with two badges, plus airborne wings, to which he wasn't entitled, together with a camouflaged smock. If Patton could get away with uniforms of his own design, so could he.

The outfit, quite contrary to the Army's 'King's Regulations', didn't go down well with his senior staff. Brigadier Bill Williams, nicknamed at the HQ 'Gee One Eye' (GI-Intelligence), recalled later:

> Monty appeared in a new Airborne Corps beret with a double badge on it and sort of said, 'How do you like my new hat?' so to speak – and the whole sort of business of preening made one feel uncomfortable.

The senior intelligence officer was going to feel decidedly more uncomfortable before this January weekend was out.

Monty was not listening. Soon his big moment was to come. He would tell the world through the correspondents just how he had won the Battle of the Bulge – well almost won it. In vain Williams pleaded with the 'Master': 'Please don't give this conference.'

Monty didn't react. Desperately the bespectacled ex-Oxford don played his last card. He remembered there was only one man who could talk any sense into Monty. He was Brooke, the Chief of the Imperial General Staff. As Williams recollected, 'He [Montgomery] was really afraid of him', and 'held Brookie in enormous respect. Now Brookie was our last hope.'

In due course Williams got in touch with the War Office that Saturday and asked if the speech to the correspondents had been cleared with 'Brookie'. To his surprise and chagrin he was told that it had. There was nothing more that Williams could do. 'I can still remember this sort of feeling,' 'Gee One Eye' remembered many years later, 'as though hitting one's head against a rubber wall.' He told himself that 'this is going to be awful'. It was.

The room in which Monty spoke that Sunday was crowded, that we know. There was not an inch of space between the correspondents in their khaki duffle coats, drab raincoats or US jeep coats. Those who held little for the military kept on their battered caps with their semi-military looking badges. Others smoked (for a while, after all this was Monty who was going to address them), chatted, consulted their notebooks. Meanwhile at the back of the room, the photographers waited with their big awkward cameras, waiting for permission to snap the field marshal when he entered.

Did the Army Commander make them wait before stepping briskly up to the podium, fixing them with that hard blue gaze of his, before barking 'Cigarettes out. You can cough for exactly thirty seconds now.'? How often had he done that in the past? Even Ike had been told to stop smoking in his presence. But perhaps by now he knew correspondents and their cynical ways and didn't go through the usual procedure.

We don't know. All we have of that celebrated briefing is the text and the first horrified statements from his supporters and the immediate steps taken by his loyal Chief-of-Staff, Freddie de Guingand, to contain the damage before it got any worse. Unfortunately for the future of the Anglo–American special relationship, it didn't quite work.

Obviously Monty was in a buoyant mood now. Everyone there who mentioned the 'Master's' manner notes that. It was understandable. Monty felt he had pulled the chestnuts out of the fire for the Americans in the Ardennes. He overplayed the role of the British Army admittedly, but that was to be expected of a successful British general who had managed the corps he had employed on the Meuse Line in a very skilled manner, ensuring none of the men involved would suffer the lack of leadership that several of the US divisions and corps had in the initial stages of the Battle of the Bulge.

He launched into his account of the battle with gusto. Since 16 December 1944, he lectured the correspondents, 'von Rundstedt' had 'driven a deep wedge into the centre of the United States' 1st Army and the split might have been become awkward . . . ' That 'awkward' was typical English understatement. What Monty said wasn't; it was boastful and self-congratulatory. 'As soon as I saw what was happening, I took certain steps myself to ensure that, if the Germans got to the Meuse, they certainly would not get over that river.'

Naturally that was all very true, as we have seen. However, Montgomery's manner of presentation – as one American described it, 'St George come to slay the dragon' – grated on US ears and would continue to do so in one way or another until the end of the war.

It implied, too, that Montgomery's 21st Army Group had had to save the Americans. Monty continued with the events of 20 December, stating:

General Eisenhower placed me in command of the whole northern front. I employed the whole available power of the British group of armies. You have this picture of British troops fighting on both sides of American forces who have suffered a hard blow. This is a fine Allied picture.

217

That, of course, was only partially true. For Monty certainly didn't employ 'the whole available power of the British group of armies'. Instead, in the actual fighting, he used two infantry division, one parachute, two armoured brigades and several ad hoc formations such as the SAS and the men of the 61st Reconnaisance Regiment and the Household Cavalry – perhaps some 70,000 men, just 10,000 larger than US General Middleton's XIII Corps, which had been shattered in the initial battles of the Bulge.

Now Monty, acting perhaps in response to Churchill's suggestions, proceeded, as he would have it, 'to butter up' his American allies. He praised the average GI. He stated that he 'never wanted to fight alongside better soldiers', and singled out the GI's 'herioc stands' at the Elsenborn Ridge, St Vith and Bastogne for special praise. Then it was the turn of the Supreme Commander. Monty said he was 'absolutely devoted' to Ike. It grieved Monty when he saw uncomplimentary remarks about him in the press. Ike 'bore a great burden' and 'needed our fullest support'. Indeed Ike had a *right* to expect it. 'I would ask all of you to lend a hand to stop that sort of thing. Let's rally around the captain of the team and so help to win the match.'

But the presentation was already beginning to rub his audience up the wrong way. Monty claimed he had put his army into the Battle of the Bulge 'with a bang', which he hadn't. Then there was the condescending 'A very interesting little battle' and the GIs had been 'jolly brave'. Such expressions might well have gone down fairly well with British listeners who knew Monty's typical formulations, often with their references to British-type sports and pastimes, such as cricket and horse racing. But they didn't with this mixed bunch of cynical international war correspondents.

As 'Gee One Eye', i.e. Brigadier Bill Williams, recollected many years later:

The presentation was quite appalling . . . It was meant to be a tribute to the American troops, that was what he had meant it to be. But it came across . . . as if he had rescued the Americans . . . Of course they were jolly brave and so on and so forth, but he used that powerful phrase 'a very interesting little battle', or words to that effect.

In total Brigadier Williams thought Monty's briefing was 'innocuous', but that 'the presentation was appalling'.

He was not the only one present that Sunday, who felt that way. Alan Moorehead, who had been Mentioned in Dispatches for rescuing wounded under fire and who was head of the 'war correspondents' committee' summed the presentation up more succinctly and with typical 'Aussie' vigour. He exclaimed: 'God it's bloody awful', rounding on Williams, 'How could *you* let him do it?'

But there was no answer to that overwhelming question. Monty would probably not have listened to a warning even from God himself at this, his moment of triumph.

According to Montgomery's biographer, Nigel Hamilton: 'The first reports of Monty's Press Conference on 7 January 1945 were good – the American newspapermen, in particular quoting Monty's generous tribute to the fighting performance of US troops in the salient.' Mr Hamilton quotes the *New York Times* for 9 January as stating: 'No handsomer tribute was ever paid to the American soldier than that of Field Marshal Montgomery in the midst of combat.'

But the facts do not seem to gell as Mr Hamilton thinks.

Freddie de Guingand, who was not present at the briefing, learned quickly that his boss had been 'naughty' and had been 'human enough to adopt the 'what a good boy am I' approach. The alarm bells started to ring in his mind almost immediately. De Guingand thought there would be an angry reaction from Bradley (he was right; there would); Monty's words might put Eisenhower in a difficult position vis-à-vis the US public and Marshall back in Washington (again he was right); and that it might mean that there would be no future employment of American troops under British, i.e. Montgomery's command. Naturally this was what Monty wanted fervently; to remain in charge of the two US armies in the north.

'I sensed that a difficult stage in Anglo–American relations had been reached [de Guingand didn't know the half of it] . . . so I flew down and spent a night with Bedell Smith at Eisenhower's Headquarters in Rheims.' Thereafter, de Guingand had a long chat with Ike and 'we discussed the problem in all its aspects. I told him I thought the matter could be set right and asked him to let me see what could be done to help.'

Next morning he flew to Monty's HQ and told him of the 'dangerous situation which was arising'. According to de Guingand, Monty reacted like a man at once. 'Give me the writing pad,' he commanded. Thereupon he drafted 'a generous signal' to Ike, saying he would do anything to help. That evening he drove to Brussels and met Alan Moorehead, and explained the problem. 'I at once explained the dangers of the present trend of press comment.' They seemed to buy his desire that the correspondents should restrain their praise of Montgomery and criticism of Eisenhower. Years later de Guingand wrote: 'From that day I think I can say that the danger subsided.' De Guingand, the loyal subordinate who received little reward for his loyalty after the war from Monty, was wrong. The ripples caused by the conference and Monty's leadership of US troops in the Ardennes would go on for months, years to come.

What happened next was predictable. It was almost as if the anti-Montgomery faction at Bradley's headquarters was just waiting for the 'little field marshal' to open his big mouth and say something stupid or clearly anti-American: something that would attack the prestige of the US Army – and naturally General Bradley's as well.

In due course Bradley threw a fit of bad temper, the like never seen before by his staff – or so he said. Immediately he read the somewhat garbled account of what Monty had said, he snorted (he was) 'all-out, right-down-to-the-toes mad'.

Over the phone, he told Ike: 'After what happened, I cannot serve under Montgomery', if Ike were to put Montgomery in permanent overall command. If Ike, his old friend, was to do that, he would request an immediate transfer back to the United States.

Poor Eisenhower. He knew that this threat was pure blackmail. The pressure grew ever more intense when the new 'Hero of Bastogne', Patton, supported Bradley, declaring he would resign too if Montgomery took over. In other words, if Eisenhower retained Montgomery in his present command, in charge of two US armies, the 1st and 9th, he'd lose his most senior US leader plus his subordinate who was currently making the headlines back in the States. That might well mean career suicide for Eisenhower. It would end his hopes of ever running for President of the United States. Who would vote for an American who put a Britisher in over the heads of American generals when those generals led far more men than the British? He might even incur Roosevelt's wrath if he supported Monty. He knew through the grapevine that FDR wasn't in the war to ensure the survival of the British Empire. In the final analysis, there would be a conflict of interest between Britain and America on that particular issue in due course. The President and his subordinates, such as General MacArthur and Admiral King, both intensely anglophobic, were ensuring that the British were being kept out of the Pacific as much as possible. The reason was clear. FDR didn't want the British to have too much of a say there after Japan's defeat with regard to her former colonies. It seems that Eisenhower now started to pay more attention to the advice of his chief-of-staff, Bedell Smith. He *definitely* wouldn't be in Europe for the rest of his career. He'd better start 'thinking American', if he wanted his future to develop in the manner that the Republican Party was envisaging for him.

Now Bradley began to develop a public image. So far he had always made poor copy for the war correspondents. Now he would seemingly never venture out of his HQ without being attended by at least fifteen newspapermen. Up to now the general whom Ernie Pyle, the best known of the US war correspondents, had tried to turn into the 'GI General', had been hopeless at public relations. He looked dull. He was dull. He never involved himself in affairs with women, as Eisenhower and Patton had (Patton thought himself 'a great swordsman' and on his last leave to the UK in 1945 he took with him nine condoms and boasted he had used eight of them). He had never made flamboyant boasts or outrageous claims as Monty did.

Now Bradley was making quite wild statements and making sure that the correspondents became aware of them. This again was a headache for Eisenhower. That second week of January 1945, after Monty's outrageous briefing, the Supreme Commander must have been more aware than ever that he could no longer govern the coalition in the fairly unbiased manner that he had done so far. He had to begin taking sides, even if one of the members of the Allied coalition was hurt. Naturally he had to opt for his own people and the party who could be hurt would, of course, be Montgomery who had caused all the trouble in the first place.

On 8 January 1945 the two arch-anglophobes, Ingersoll and Hansen, spent most of the night in Luxembourg working out an unauthorised statement to be issued to the press on the following day. Bradley, it was said, didn't like the idea at first. He told Ingersoll, the former editor and newspaperman: 'I can't do it. The Army is my life, Ingersoll. A direct order [by SHAEF not to give a press conference] is a direct order and I can't break it.' Finally, after Ingersoll urged him that his reputation and the honour of the US Army was at stake, he gave in. 'Tell Chet [Hansen] to get the press up here tomorrow morning – *without informing Paris*' [author's italics].

News of Bradley's reaction flew across the Channel, including the statement in his forgotten briefing on the 9th that Monty's command of the US 1st and 9th Armies was temporary. They would revert to Bradley's command as soon as the two armies joined up and split the Bulge. Bradley also pointed out in that statement to the press that, as Ingersoll put it in 1946:

Montgomery could *not* have won the battle of the Ardennes because (a) he played no part in it until the basic strategy of the defense had been worked out, and (b) even then, he commanded only the northern half of a battle which had been decided, as all the world knew, at Bastogne.

The result was, as a triumphant Ingersoll wrote:

It did the job. The release caught the Montgomery press in London off balance and instead of rolling with the punch, for once they tipped their hand. They screamed with rage and called Bradley names. He was accused of having 'insulted Montgomery'.

To continue with the boxing metaphor, it did seem that the Bradley statement hit Churchill below the belt. But the PM contained his surprise quickly enough. He saw immediately the dangers lying ahead for his special relationship. He phoned Eisenhower and, according to Ingersoll, told the latter that 'all this bother came from a small group of Montgomery's friends'. Churchill said further that Montgomery was 'an embarrassment to the British Government'. Thereafter Churchill spoke to the House of Commons, effusively lauding the 'American fighting man' who had vastly outnumbered the handful of British soldiers who had fought in the Bulge.

Eisenhower did his bit, too, though he must have realised that he could no longer appease Bradley. The latter wanted no less than the command of the whole of the US 12th Army group. He awarded Bradley the Bronze Star, usually given to combat soldiers. He recommended to Marshall that Bradley should be given his fourth general's star. Marshall refused, however; the Chief-of-Staff wasn't too pleased with Bradley's performance during the battle.

This affront Bradley blamed on Eisenhower. Bradley felt that Ike was just another enemy, as was Patton, who had won all the glory at Bastogne. It seemed Bradley could be pleased only with the greatest difficulty.

As Ingersoll summed it all up just after the war:

On the rocky road of Anglo–American military relations, the Ardennes was a milestone. Until the Ardennes, Bradley and his officers had made an honest attempt to deal fairly and frankly with the British . . . After the Ardennes no one was frank any more. Bradley – and Patton, Hodges and Simpson under Bradley's direction – proceeded to make and carry out their plans without the assistance of the official channels, on a new basis openly discussed only among themselves.

In order to do this they had to conceal their plans from the British and almost literally to outwit Eisenhower's Supreme Headquarters, half of which was British . . . They completely succeeded in both objectives and won the war.

Envoi

.

I sent him [Eisenhower] a Christmas card, a much warmer greeting
than I sent to anyone else, and the result has been silence.
If I've lost the friendship of that great and good man,
it would be very distressing to me.
FM B L Montgomery, Christmas 1959

He [Montgomery] got so damn personal to make sure that the
Americans and me, in particular, had no credit, had nothing to do
with the war that I eventually just stopped communicating with him.
I was just not interested in keeping up communication
with a man that just can't tell the truth.
Eisenhower to author Cornelius Ryan just before his death

On the evening of 5 May 1945 Montgomery signalled Brooke from his HQ in northern Germany:' British Empire part in the German War in Western Europe is over or almost so. 'All forces in the north of Germany, some two million in all had surrendered *personally* to Monty. It was the climax of a forty-year career as a British officer and, in a way, a vindication of what he stood for and believed in. Later he signalled Brooke once more from Luneburg, where Britain's Hanoverian kings had commenced the long path to the British throne a thousand years before: 'I was persuaded to drink some champagne at dinner tonight.'

Rightly so. The little field marshal deserved it. For the last five months, under Bradley's baleful influence, Ike had relegated Monty's British Army (apart from the March crossing of the Rhine) to what amounted to the flank guard to Bradley's 12th Army Group. Monty had not been able to achieve that long dreamed of 'pencil-like thrust' of forty divisions to Berlin, the heart of the Reich.

But in these first days of May 1945 he had stolen a march on the Yanks whose noses he had rubbed cruelly in the dirt. He turned a local surrender before Hamburg into a mass one, and was putting so much pressure on the Germans that Hitler's vaunted '1,000 Year Reich', which lasted exactly twelve years and five months, was about to do the same. It would take Eisenhower's HQ at Rheims two days to achieve that aim after Monty had sent the German surrender delegation to sign the peace. But that was no concern of his.

But comparing the pictures of the surrender, at Monty's HQ and the later ones at the boys' schools at Rheims, it is clear who was the real conqueror of the Germans. In the American pictures at Rheims, Bedell Smith, Tedder and Kay Summersby are holding up the fountain pens with which the surrender was signed. It is a typical happy PR shot of the kind commonplace at the end of a successful US political election. That of the Montgomery surrender is much more sombre and soldierly, conveying the sense of loss and dramatic seriousness of the end of the shooting war.

Monty, smartly dressed for once, facing the defeated, hangdog German delegation in a darkened tent, with the victor personally signing with a penny wooden pen of the kind you would find in any British rural post office back home. This was obviously no PR exercise.

But that had been in May. The ripples of the Ardennes episode and Monty's speech continued to spread wider and wider. By the end of that summer both Churchill and Roosevelt had gone. They were replaced by Attlee and Truman. All the two of them had in common was that they were small and had been officers in France in the First World War. For different reasons there was no 'special relationship' between the two new leaders.

Back in 1940 Churchill had asked America to 'give us the tools and we will finish the job'. Unfortunately, despite Roosevelt's promise to ignore the dollar sign, America had not given anything without requiring payment. Within two years, by 1943, Britain's £1,924 million investments in Canada were sold off to pay for raw materials bought in the US. To make sure that the Americans got their money, Roosevelt dispatched the cruiser *Louisville* to Simonstown, South Africa to pick up £42 million in gold, Britain's last negotiable asset. America demanded that Britain transfer all her scientific and technological secrets to the United States, everything from penicillin, to atomic development to the new radar fuses used by the artillery. Leases on the islands of Newfoundland, Trinidad, Jamaica, etc. were demanded in order to set up US bases there.

Broke as she was, Britain still hoped that the Americans would bale her out financially in the post-war world. She was wrong. As the great economist Keynes wrote of the situation that year: 'The Americans were interested in the future, not in the past. Old soldiers [i.e. the British allies] showing their medals were not a persuasive advocate.' In the end the Americans would provide a loan that would help to fund the new socialist 'Welfare State', including the National Health Service, anathema to many Americans. But they did so at twice the interest rate that the British Government had refused to pay the year before.

Although FDR was dead, many of the people who were in power in the US now, politically, militarily, economically, had had close dealings with the British during the war. They hadn't become anglophobes during this period (even the Kennedys had married into an aristocratic British family). But they had come to suspect British motives, especially in the area of foreign policy. Further they had lived through the decline of British power and influence in the last two years of the war. They realised all too well that Britain was on the way to becoming a third-rate power just as she had become the junior partner in Churchill's vaunted 'special relationship'. The anti-Americanism of many of the new socialist rulers of the British Isles didn't help much. The future lay in America's hands, perhaps with the Soviet Union her partner, as some thought – for a while.

In the military in Washington, the power was concentrated in people such as Bradley, even Eisenhower, and lesser generals who had served with and *under* Montgomery during WWII. These US generals were unlikely to favour Britain's cause after the insults and snubs levelled at them during the Battle of the Bulge and especially that condescending speech of 7 January 1945. In 1950, when South Korea was attacked by the communist North, Britain rallied to the US cause, but only as one of the sixteen members of the UN force sent to that country. Today, all that seems to be remembered of Britain's part in that post-war coalition is the determined efforts of Mr Attlee to prevent Truman using the atom bomb on the communist enemy.

When Churchill came to power again, he attempted to revive the 'special relationship', primarily in the form of NATO and its role in the Cold War. It didn't work. There was little substance to it. Monty, who was posted to NATO in France, found himself as deputy to a series of American commanders, one of whom, General Ridgway, once a corps commander in NW Europe under his leadership, was not exactly a great fan of the 'Marshal'.

When, as Churchill's successor, Anthony Eden tried to defend British interests in 1956 at Suez, Ike, now President of the United States, soon put an end to 'Eden's nonsense'. Later Eisenhower maintained that it had been his 'major foreign policy mistake' in not supporting Britain in their attempt to stop the demagogic antics of the Egyptian dictator, Colonel Nasser. Ike might have been right. Thereafter, the USA would have to take over Britain's role in the Middle East with consequences which have lasted to this day and the Second Gulf War of 2003.

Whatever the truth of that matter is, it was clear that, as *The Times* obituary of Eden had it in 1977: 'He was the last Prime Minister to believe Britain was a great power and the first to confront a crisis which proved she was not.'*

As for Montgomery, that 'intensely compacted hank of steel wire', as George Bernard Shaw had once called him, the soldier who had caused all the trouble back in 44/45, he went on to outlive them all – Churchill, Eisenhower, Patton and the rest. Only Bradley, the great survivor, managed to outflank the 'Field Marshal', living on another twelve years after Monty died.

Montgomery 'soldiered on' until he could do so no longer. During the war he had lost all his possessions in the German bombing. He had applied to King George VI for a 'grace and favour home', but the poor,

---

*In 1957, his health destroyed by the Suez crisis, Eden took a recuperative cruise on RMS *Rangitata*. His cabin steward then was a man who would one day occupy the same position that Eden had in Churchill's government – Deputy Prime Minister. His name? John Prescott. One could interpret that as an elequent statement of Britain's decline since Suez, I suppose.

weak, stuttering monarch, who during that conflict had always been so eager to visit Monty's various HQs, refused. So Montgomery had to make money through his books (in the beginning he had refused to follow 'Ike', 'Brad' and 'Georgie' (Patton) into print in order to produce some cash) in order to pay for the home he had to buy*

Naturally his books caused as much controversy as his statements had during the war. In the United States they aroused a great deal of ire. But as the 1950s gave way to the 60s, American anger at the man who had caused so much trouble during the Battle of the Bulge, the US's major battle in Europe, subsided and Monty became something of a 'Grand Old Man' whenever he travelled to the States. Not with American historians however. There is nothing like the wrath of an academic, fighting battles from inside his book-lined strongpoint. For the academic warrior, Montgomery cannot be forgiven. Whatever he did during those two weeks or so when he was the secret commander of more American troops than any US general, it was wrong. As for the British Army, it appears never to have played even a minor role during the Battle of the Bulge.

Monty being Monty never took a blind bit of notice of what the academics, American or otherwise, said. After all, they were mere scribblers, despite their degrees and their titles. They'd never been at the sharp end. He had – several times. Hadn't he once been left for dead on the battlefield in the 'Old War'?

As he grew older, ill and fell into his dotage, Monty seemed to concern himself with the men he had sent to their deaths. One visitor recalled how, when he came to see a sick Monty in his bed, the little field marshal was strangely agitated. 'What is troubling you, Field Marshal'? he asked.

Monty replied: 'I couldn't sleep last night – I had great difficulty. I can't have very long to go now. I've got to meet God – and explain all those men I killed at Alamein.'

He was right. In the early hours of 24 March 1976, the day after he had crossed the Rhine twenty-one years before and set out in his final attempt to achieve greatness, Montgomery's heart gave out. The news was flashed across the world: MONTY IS DEAD.

On the afternoon of Thursday 1 April 1976 Montgomery was laid to rest. He was buried in a simple pine coffin in a village churchyard. But his grave was surrounded by wreaths, eighty of them, from all over the world. Tributes came in, too, from the great and the good as well as from more humble folk. One wreath came from no less a person than 'Brad'. Now he was the last survivor of that wartime coalition in Europe who knew where the skeletons were buried. In a tribute which accompanied the wreath, Five Star General Bradley declared generously: 'With the

---

*Brooke was treated even more shabbily. In the end he was forced to sell his precious books on birds, prints, etc. in order to make enough money to live on.

passing of Field Marshal Montgomery the world has lost a giant and I have lost a comrade in arms.' It was fulsome praise from an American rival who said: 'Dear Monty liked to tweak our "Yankee noses", as he himself called it, but he was a fine wartime leader.'

Indeed, Montgomery had often done enough in that year 44/45, and, in particular, during the fighting in the Ardennes. Now there'd be other 'special relationships' between the 'limeys' and the 'Yanks', but in the future there'd be no more Montys to 'tweak' those 'Yankee noses'. Montgomery's day was over. Britain would never see his like again.

Bibliography

Ambrose, Stephen E, *Eisenhower: Volume 1: Soldier, General of the Army, President Elect, 1890–1952*, New York: Simon & Schuster, 1983.
____ *Eisenhower*, New York: Simon & Schuster, 1983.
____ *The Supreme Commander. The War Years of General Dwight D Eisenhower*, London: Cassell, 1968.
Baxter, Colin F, *Field Marshal Bernard Law Montgomery, 1887–1976: A Selected Bibliography*, Westport CT: Greenwood Press, 1999.
____ *The War in North Africa, 1940–1943*, Westport CT: Greenwood Press, 1996.
Blaxland, Gregory, *Destination Dunkirk. The Story of Gort's Army*, London: William Kimber, 1973.
____ *The Plain Cook and the Great Showman. The First and Eighth Armies in North Africa*, London: William Kimber, 1977.
Blumenson, Martin, *Mark Clark. The Last of the Great World War II Commanders*, New York: Congdon & Weed, 1984.
Bradley, Omar, *A Soldier's Story*, New York: Henry Holt, 1951.
Bradley, Omar and Blair, Clay, *A General's Life. An Autobiography*, New York: Simon & Schuster, 1983.
Buchanan, A Russell, *The United States and World War II*, 1964.
Burns, James, *Roosevelt. The Soldier of Freedom*, New York: Harcourt Brace, 1970
Chalfont, Alun, *Montgomery of Alamein*, London: Weidenfeld & Nicolson, 1976.
Collins, J Lawton, *Lightning Joe. An Autobiography*, Baton Rouge LA: Louisiana State University Press, 1979.
Colville, John Rupert, *The Fringes of Power. Downing Street Diaries, 1939–1955*, London: Hodder & Stoughton, 1985.
d'Este, Carlo, *Fatal Decision. Anzio and the Battle for Rome*, New York: Dutton, 1991.
Edmonds, Robin, *The Big Three: Churchill, Roosevelt and Stalin in Peace and War*, London: Hamish Hamilton, 1990.
Frye, Alton, *Nazi Germany and the American Hemisphere, 1933–1941*, Washington: Center of Military History, 1967.

Greenfield, Kent, *American Strategy in World War II. A Reconsideration*, Washington: Center of Military History, 1963.

Gregory, Ross, *America 1941: A Nation at the Crossroads*, 1989.

Hayes, Grace P, *The History of the Joint Chiefs of Staff in World War II*, 1982.

Hearden, Patrick, *Roosevelt Confronts Hitler: America's Entry into World War II*, 1987.

Karl, Barry, *The Uneasy State: the US 1915–1945*, 1984.

Kimball, Warren F, *The Juggler. Franklin Roosevelt as Wartime Statesman*, American Almanac, 1991.

Lamb, Richard, *Churchill as War Leader: Right or Wrong?*, London: Bloomsbury, 1991.

_____ *Montgomery in Europe 1943–45: Success or Failure?*, New York: Franklin Watts, 1984.

Larrabee, Eric, *Commander in Chief: Franklin Delano Roosevelt, his Lieutenants, and their War*, New York: Harper & Row, 1987.

Louis, William, *Imperialism at Bay: The US and the Decolonization of the British Empire, 1941–45*, New York: Oxford University Press, 1978.

McNish, R, *Iron Division: The History of the 3rd Division*, London: Ian Allen, 1978.

Mather, Carol, *Aftermath of War: Everyone Must Go Home*, London: Brassey's, 1992.

Offner, Arnold, *The Origins of the Second World War. American Foreign Policy and World Politics, 1917–1941*, 1975.

Smith, Graham, *When Jim Crow Met John Bull: Black American Soldiers in World War II Britain*, London: Tauris, 1987.

Tedder, Arthur W, *With Prejudice: The War Memoirs of Marshal of the Royal Air Force Lord Tedder*, London: Cassell, 1966.

Thompson, R W, *The Battle for the Rhineland*, London: Hutchinson, 1958.

_____ *Churchill and the Montgomery Myth*, New York: Evans, 1968.

_____ *Montgomery, the Field Marshal: The Campaigns in Northwest Europe, 1944–45*, New York: Scribner, 1970.

Thorne, Christopher, *Allies of a Kind: The United States, Britain and the War Against Japan, 1941–1945*, Bloomington IN: Indiana University Press, 1978.

Viorst, Milton, *Hostile Allies: FDR and Charles de Gaulle*, 1965.

Weigley, Russell, *Eisenhower's Lieutenants: the Campaigns of France and Germany, 1944–1945*, Bloomington IN: Indiana University Press, 1981.

Whiting, Charles, *The Battle of the Bulge: Britain's Untold Story*, Stroud: Sutton, 1999.

_____ *Bounce the Rhine*, New York: Stein & Day, 1985.

_____ *Bradley*, New York: Ballantine, 1971.

_____ *A Bridge at Arnhem*, London: White Lion, 1974.

_____ *Finale at Flensburg. The Story of Field Marshal Montgomery's Battle for the Baltic*, London: Leo Cooper, 1974.

____ *Kasserine: First Blood*, New York: Stein & Day, 1984.

____ *The Last Assault: The Battle of the Bulge Reassessed*, London: Leo Cooper, 1994.

____ *The Last Battle: Montgomery's Campaign April–May 1945*, Marlborough: Crowood, 1989.

____ *Patton*, New York: Ballantine, 1970.

Wilson, Theodore A, *The First Summit: Roosevelt and Churchill at Placentia Bay, 1941*, Lawrence KS, University of Kansas Press, 1969.

Index